517185

THE NEW WOMAN OF COLOR

THE NEW WOMAN OF COLOR

The Collected Writings
of Fannie Barrier Williams,
1893–1918

EDITED WITH AN INTRODUCTION BY
MARY JO DEEGAN

Northern Illinois University Press

DeKalb

© 2002 by Northern Illinois University Press

Published by the Northern Illinois University Press, DeKalb, Illinois 60115

Manufactured in the United States using acid-free paper

All Rights Reserved

Design by Julia Fauci

Library of Congress Cataloging-in-Publication Data

Williams, Fannie Barrier.

The new woman of color: the collected writings of Fannie Barrier Williams, 1893–1918 /

edited with an introduction by Mary Jo Deegan.

   p.   cm.

Includes bibliographical references and index.

ISBN   0-87580-293-1 (alk. paper)

1. African Americans—History—1877–1964. 2. African Americans—Social conditions.

3. African American women—Social conditions. 4. African Americans—Societies, etc.

5. United States—Race relations. 6. Williams, Fannie Barrier—Political and social views.

7. Williams, Fannie Barrier. 8. African American women political activist—Biography.

9. African American women social reformers—Biography. I. Deegan, Mary Jo,

1946– II. Title.

E185.6.W7 2002

973′.0496073—dc21   2001051333

To Cecilia E. Dawkins and Chester L. Veal

For Their Friendship and Chicago Memories

Contents

Editor's Preface

Fannie Barrier Williams first came to my attention in 1975 when I found her article on the institutional structure in Chicago's Black Belt (see selection no. 19). When I asked other scholars about her, she was described as either unknown or a minor figure at Hull-House. The recent explosion in scholarship on African American women, however, dramatically changes our knowledge about this group, including Williams. She can now be recognized as a significant community leader, intellectual, sociologist, and ally of Jane Addams. Williams was a new woman who worked in African American social settlements, and a notable voice from Chicago. It is a great pleasure to introduce her to a wider audience.

In preparing this selection of her writings, I rarely update her language and only correct minor inconsistencies in punctuation and typographical errors.

My thanks to Karen L. Jania of the Bentley Historical Library at the University of Michigan for answering questions about S. Laing Williams; to an anonymous reviewer of an earlier draft of this book; to Martin Johnson of Northern Illinois University Press; and to Michael R. Hill, my stalwart colleague and life-partner.

ACKNOWLEDGMENTS FOR ILLUSTRATIONS

Fannie Barrier Williams, 1894
P. 637 in *The World's Congress of Representative Women,* Vol. 2, edited by Mary Wright Sewell. Chicago: Rand, McNally and Co, 1894. Archival photography by Michael R. Hill.

Fannie Barrier Williams, ca. 1902
P. 196 in *Progress of A Race: The Remarkable Advancement of the American Negro,* edited by J.W. Gibson and W.H. Crogman, 1902. Harrisburg, Pa.: Minter Co., 1902. Archival photography by Michael R. Hill.

Fannie Barrier Williams, ca. 1922
P. 87 in *The Story of the Illinois Federation of Women's Clubs.* Chicago: Privately printed, 1922. Archival photography by Michael R. Hill.

S. Laing Williams, ca. 1900
P. 69 in *A New Negro for a New Century,* edited by Booker T. Washington. Chicago: American Publishing House, 1900. Archival photography by Michael R. Hill.

Jane Addams and Mary McDowell, ca. 1916
University of Illinois at Chicago, University Library, Department of Special Collections, Jane Addams Memorial Collection. (JAMC neg.64)

Ida B. Wells-Barnett, ca. 1920
Ida B. Wells Papers, Special Collections Research Center, the University of Chicago Library. Box 10, folder 1, item 10.

Elizabeth Lindsay Davis, ca. 1902
P. 225 in *Progress of A Race: The Remarkable Advancement of the American Negro,* edited by J.W. Gibson and W.H. Crogman. Harrisburg, Pa.: Minter Co., 1902. Archival photography by Michael R. Hill.

Celia Parker Woolley, n.d.
P. 66 in *The Story of the Illinois Federation of Women's Clubs.* Chicago: Privately printed, 1922. Archival photography by Michael R. Hill.

Booker T. Washington, 1899
Frontispiece. *The Future of the American Negro.* New York: Small, Maynard & Co., 1899. Archival photography by Michael R. Hill.

W.E.B. DuBois, 1918
Library of Congress, Photographic Reproductions, Washington, D.C.; 518336, LCW5262-16767, photography by C.M. Battey.

Plainly I would have been far happier as a woman if my life up to the age of eighteen years had not been so free, spontaneous and unhampered by race prejudice. I have still many white friends and the old home and school associations are still sweet and delightful and always renewed with pleasure, yet I have never quite recovered from the shock and pain of my first bitter realization that to be a colored woman is to be discredited, mistrusted, and often meanly hated. My faith in the verities of religion, in justice, in love and many sacredly taught sentiments has greatly decreased since I have learned how little even these stand for when you are a colored woman.

—Williams 1904b, 92

The power of organized womanhood is one of the most interesting studies of modern sociology.

—Williams 1894a, 701

Liberty to be all that we can be, without artificial hindrances, is a thing no less precious to us than to women generally.

—Williams 1894a, 709

She must view the promised land of a better and juster age than ours and not aspire to enter it.

—Williams 1904i, 547

The Negro woman's club of to-day represents the new Negro with new powers of self-help, with new capacities, and with an intelligent insight into her own condition. It represents new interests, new anxieties and new hopes. It means better schools, better homes and better family alignments, better opportunities for young colored men and women to earn a living, and purer social relationships.

—Williams 1912/1902a, 203

FANNIE BARRIER WILLIAMS AND HER LIFE AS A NEW WOMAN OF COLOR IN CHICAGO, 1893–1918

Mary Jo Deegan

Fannie Barrier Williams dedicated her life to realizing a dream for all Americans: the right to the pursuit of happiness in one indivisible nation based on truth and justice.[1] As a new woman of color, she eloquently argued on 18 May 1893 before a group composed primarily of white women:

> The colored women, as well as all women, will realize that the inalienable right to life, liberty, and the pursuit of happiness is a maxim that will become more blessed in its significance when the hand of woman shall take it from its sepulture in books and make it the gospel of every-day life and the unerring guide in the relations of all men, women, and children (Williams 1894a, 711).

Such a vision may seem naïve and passé in our more cynical age, but Williams believed in and defended this future that could flourish without creating even more injustice and divisiveness in the process. Many people have fought for this dream, like her friend the American Nobelist Jane Addams and the African American Nobelist Martin Luther King, Jr. Others have despaired of its realization during the many decades that have elapsed since her era. Once again hearing her voice from Chicago may help reinvigorate her dream and bring it to a new millennium.

Unlike other notable African American women of her era who were born in the South during slavery, like Anna Julia Cooper (1892) or Ida B. Wells-Barnett (1970), Williams was born in freedom in the North and raised in a stable family that encouraged her formal education. She represented a northern experience and worldview more similar to the background of the great sociologist W.E.B. DuBois (1903b) than to that of her African American contemporaries from the south.

As an educated African American woman who traveled widely—born in New York in 1855 and having taught in the South during Reconstruction in the 1870s, Williams had a broad range of human experiences and trials to test her courage and form her strongly held opinions before she came to Chicago in 1887. Her spirited essays reflect an observant mind, a zest for life, and a familiarity with leading movers and shakers, both black and white. Williams was an insightful, feisty, articulate sociologist: an intelligent author and orator. She was also a physically beautiful woman, witty, intelligent, and charismatic. As the wife of a lawyer, she lived among the upper class of black Chicago; this, however, did not indicate great wealth as much as a high social position and sophisticated access to knowledge.

In 1904, Williams added her voice to a controversial debate on industrial education, along with the other "Greatest thinkers of the Black Race" including William Lloyd Garrison (1904), the white neo-abolitionist; Kelly Miller (1904), the black sociologist; Booker T. Washington (1904), the founder of the Tuskegee Institute; T. Thomas Fortune (1904), the militant newspaper editor; and DuBois (1904), the eminent sociologist and civil rights activist. Her inclusion within this stellar male group—with whom she is rarely identified today—indicates her significance as an African American intellectual during that era.

Her eminent, intellectual female friends included Celia Parker Woolley (1887, 1889, 1892, 1894, 1903, 1904), head of the Frederick Douglass Center (FDC) and a Unitarian minister; Jane Addams (1910), sociologist and head of the social settlement Hull-House; Mary McDowell (Deegan 1988a), sociologist and head of the University of Chicago Social Settlement; Susan B. Anthony, suffragist; and Elizabeth Lindsay Davis (1922), noted black clubwoman and founder of Chicago's Phyllis Wheatley Club for Homeless Girls.[2] Ida B. Wells-Barnett (1970), sociologist and civil rights advocate, was also a friend of Williams in the 1890s, but their friendship ended around 1907 (see discussion later in this introduction).

The recent, long overdue, interest in the lives and thoughts of African American women places Williams at the heart of a tumultuous era, one fraught with racial discrimination and injustice as well as the powerful resistance to such unfairness and the optimistic energy to fight it (see *Black Women in America* 1993; Hendricks 1993; Knupfer 1996; Lemert 1998; McMurray 1998; Neverton-Morton 1989). Her writings, orations, and leadership helped shape that era as revealed in this anthology.

In this introduction to her work, I analyze her biographical location and relevant interests (Schutz 1970) as well as the significant people who shaped her life as an intellectual in a northern city that dominated the early development of sociology. Williams's work at Chicago's monumental World's Columbian Exposition of 1893 brought her contributions to a national arena through her highly successful and controversial speeches at the Woman's Congress and at the Parliament of Religions. No sooner had this whirlwind ended, than she was caught up unexpectedly in a cause célèbre as a black woman proposed for membership in the Chicago Woman's Club (CWC). For fourteen agonizing months, starting in November 1894, a citywide and then a national controversy waged over her entry into the group (see "Fannie Barrier Williams" 1894; Williams 1902a, 216–18; and her account in "Club Movement Among Colored Women"). Although she was finally accepted as a member, she was one of the few black women to enter this club for many years.

Williams participated in the CWC until she left Chicago in 1926, but her primary energy and expertise in clubwork was as a leader in African American women's clubs. Her proficiency as a social commentator also expanded into work with social settlements, a major institutional anchor for women in sociology, and through popular influential essays on African American life and culture.

Williams was controversial when she was alive and she remains controversial today. Sometimes criticized as an elitist (e.g., McFeely 1991, 367), as an accommodationist (Lamping 1982; Spear 1967), or as a dilettante (Lamping 1982), her writings contradict these interpretations and stand as a witness to her erudition, leadership, growth, and complexity. She is an important African American voice from the urban North—Chicago—who actively articulated her interracial dream from 1887 until 1918. Her insights and analyses remain in the forefront of contemporary issues and debates.

BIOGRAPHY

EARLY BIOGRAPHY, 1855–1870   Fortunately, Williams wrote a spirited autobiography for the popular journal the *Independent,* published on 14 July 1904. She composed it in response to a series the magazine had published on 17 March 1904 that presented the views of "A Southern Colored Woman" (1904), "A Southern White Woman" (1904), and "A Northern White Woman" (1904), in which the African American woman was assumed to reside only in the South. Williams's life as a freeborn black woman from the North who had worked as an adult in the South and then returned to the North represented a strongly contrasting perspective to the lives of these other, more typical, women. Her experience, her voice from Chicago, was underrepresented both then and now. Although this lively piece introduced Williams to the general public, it was understandably short on precise details. This is her only autobiography, and no archival collection of her papers exists,[3] a situation typical for most African Americans in Chicago, especially women.[4]

Fannie Barrier was born in Brockport, New York, on 12 February 1855 to Harriet Prince and Anthony J. Barrier, the youngest child in a family with two daughters and a son. Her father was a barber, coal merchant, homeowner, and leader in the local Baptist church (Smith 1992, 1251). Her early life was filled with egalitarian, biracial interactions and did not prepare her for the color line she encountered in the South as a school teacher. Her subsequent life in Chicago, moreover, added a perspective that enabled her to see and articulate the regional and historical differences dividing women's experiences in the United States.

Williams's fascinating autobiography is included here and needs little repetition. It is important to emphasize that she was descended from at least three generations of free African Americans; was reared in Brockport, New York; was light skinned and aware of her multiple, racial/ethnic heritages; was used to pleasant early social relations with whites; and was educated at local public schools. Like many other educated young women from the northeast, Williams was well read in the transcendentalists, including Ralph Waldo Emerson and the radical pacifist Henry David Thoreau.[5] Although her family was Baptist, she became a Unitarian and was highly critical of Christianity, like another eminent woman Margaret Fuller (Deegan and Rynbrandt 2000; Woolley 1894). She graduated from the State Normal School at Brockport in 1870, having taken the academic and classical courses that certified her as a school teacher.

Upon graduation, in that early cohort of educated women, Williams made an unusual choice for an African American woman when she joined other northeastern "school marms" to train the young, newly emancipated children of the South. Her unique role in comparison to that of the white women who went south arose from the fact that she was not going to "help the helpless" but to represent her own community and to find herself in their shared fate. Later, Williams wrote respectfully about these white female teachers who lived in the South during this time of tumult and who were often mocked and misunderstood in their attempt to reach out to the poor and disadvantaged (see her comments in "Club Movement among Colored Women"). In addition, she wanted to experience the—to her— mysterious and dangerous South and thereby bring to a close her sheltered, bourgeois existence. The Civil War had ended only in 1865, and she wished to see firsthand the rapidly changing situation in the violent states that had enslaved millions.

FURTHER EDUCATION AND TEACHING, 1870–1887   Williams taught for a number of years in the South, not only because she wanted a challenge, but also because she wanted to be part of a grand historical change. In the South she encountered all the difficulties and indignities of life in the Reconstruction era that one would expect for an independent, previously sheltered, African American woman.

Williams traveled throughout the South by train, then the major form of transportation and one that became increasingly segregated as Reconstruction failed to attain racial justice. On one occasion she claimed her French ancestry to remain seated in a white Jim Crow car, but the wit and survival skills she used in this instance to respond to an unjust system are denounced by some biographers as a sign that Williams "sometimes" exhibited a pattern of passing as French (e.g., Logan 1982, 656; Smith 1992, 1253). Although this fleeting event consisted of only five French words, it is criticized even in short biographies (e.g., Fishel 1971, 620; McFeely 1991, 366) and interpreted as a sign that she regularly passed as white. Such a harsh interpretation of Williams, who did *not* pass as white in her everyday life and who fought for African American rights, ideas, and history throughout her life, blames the victim of discrimination instead of the oppressor.

At some point, Williams taught school in Washington, D.C., where she met other educated and articulate members of the black elite, probably including Anna Julia Cooper. During this time, she also studied at Boston's New England Conservatory of Music and then at the School of Fine Arts in Washington, D.C. In the latter school she worked under several portrait artists and established her reputation as a painter. Here in the nation's capital, she met her future husband, Samuel Laing Williams.

S. Laing Williams and Fannie Barrier Williams, 1887–1921

S. Laing Williams,[6] like Fannie Barrier, was an ambitious, educated, and astute leader. Born in Savannah, Georgia, in 1858 during the slavery era, information on the life of this remarkable man is even sketchier than it is for his wife. At nine years of age he moved to La Peer, Michigan, where he attended local schools and graduated from La Peer High School with honors. In spite of his early restrictive background in the South, he went on to graduate in 1881 from the University of Michigan, where he was the first (or among the first!) African Americans to earn a degree from the Department of Literature, Science, and the Arts.[7] He briefly taught school in Alabama, where perhaps he met Booker T. Washington, who ultimately became a close friend of his. The Alabama job was followed by an appointment to the Pension Office in Washington, D.C. Williams then studied law and graduated from the Columbian Law School (later called George Washington Law School) with a B.L. in June 1884 and an M.L. in June 1885. He moved to Chicago to practice law—either in 1885 according to J.W. Gibson and W.H. Crogman (1902, 573) or in 1887 after his marriage (e.g., Jackson 1986, 772; Riggs 1993, 557).

Fannie was thirty-two years of age when they married in 1887, and by that time she clearly had a mind of her own and was no longer the sheltered woman who had left New York to find adventure. S. Laing and Fannie Barrier Williams relocated to Chicago shortly after their wedding. They lived there for many decades where they became important figures in the small circle of African American leaders, the "Elite 400" (Knupfer 1995, 58) in the "then-wild west."[8]

S. Laing created this entrée shortly after their arrival when he organized the Prudence Crandall Club, a literary society named after a white woman from New England who trained free African Americans in a secret school (described in Williams's writings on the club movement). As a graduate in the arts from the University of Michigan, he had a long commitment to this aspect of African American culture. The literary group was limited to twenty-five couples, all of whom rose to prominence in Chicago's black community. The club flourished for several decades (Spear 1967, 66–67), and the Williamses were at the center of this powerful group.

In 1889, S. Laing Williams became a law partner with Ferdinand L. Barnett, the lawyer and newspaper editor who married Ida B. Wells in 1895. S. Laing "affiliated himself with the law firm of Barnett & Williams for 15 years" ("Brilliant Jurist Gets Final Call to High Bar" 1921). In 1904 he left the practice after being appointed a judge.[9]

Williams and Barnett were friends before Ida B. Wells came to Chicago, and S. Laing probably also knew the first Mrs. Ferdinand Barnett, Mollie Araham (?), when they were students together at the University of Michigan. Around 1890, he had even filled out an alumni questionnaire from the University of Michigan with information about her, noting that she earned a Ph.B. in the class of 1880, married Barnett in November 1883, bore two children, and died on 25 January 1890 ("Necrology," S. Laing Williams [University of Michigan, Bentley Library], hereafter referred to as "Necrology"). Probably the two couples were friends, and surely acquaintances, before her death.

When Ida B. Wells married Barnett in 1895, she entered this already established relationship. These two new couples were friends from approximately 1895 to 1907. In 1903, for example, they worked with other Chicagoans, black and white, to invite DuBois to Chicago to discuss his monumental new book, *The Souls of Black Folk* (DuBois 1903a; Wells-Barnett 1970, 279–80). Although the men appeared to have an extended relationship, their wives did not (see McMurry 1998). Before telling the story of the ill-fated friendship of the two women, however, several other people need to be introduced and the biography of S. Laing Williams must be completed.

From an early but unspecified date, S. Laing and Booker T. Washington—the powerful, controlling, former slave who founded the Tuskegee Institute and ultimately influenced the school of race relations developed at the University of Chicago (Drake 1983)—were close, personal friends. They both grew up in Georgia during slavery and shared a common background and high ambitions for achievement. A sign of their mutual respect was seen in 1895 when Washington invited S. Laing to deliver the commencement address at Tuskegee Institute (Spear 1967, 67). After 1900, S. Laing was Washington's closest Chicago ally and arranged the latter's schedule during Chicago visits. They frequently corresponded and a published record of their alliance now exists (see Washington 1972–1989, passim).

S. Laing performed some unsavory "spying" on African Americans in Chicago who might be planning anti-Washington activities (see Williams's correspondence in Washington 1972–1989). Rayford Logan (1982, 657) documents that Williams also ghostwrote a book for Washington, *Frederick Douglass* (Washington [Williams] 1907). Spear (1967, 67), using extensive footnotes, also confirmed that Williams was hired by Washington in 1904 to do this task.

Fannie Barrier Williams, 1894

Fannie Barrier Williams, ca. 1902

Fannie Barrier Williams, ca. 1922

S. Laing Williams, ca. 1900

Jane Addams and Mary McDowell, ca. 1916

Ida B. Wells-Barnett, ca. 1920

Elizabeth Lindsay Davis, 1900

Celia Parker Woolley, n.d.

Booker T. Washington, 1900

W.E.B. DuBois, ca. 1918

Washington (1907, 7) claimed sole authorship of this work, merely noting in the preface that he relied heavily on *both* Williamses to share their memories of Douglass and their editorial skills in refining the final copy:

> S. Laing Williams of Chicago, Ill., and his wife Fannie Barrier Williams, have been of incalculable service in the preparation of this volume. Mr. Williams enjoyed a long and intimate acquaintance with Mr. Douglass, and I have been privileged to draw heavily upon this fund of information. He and Mrs. Williams have reviewed this manuscript since its preparation and have given it their cordial approval.

Although neither Logan nor Spear speculates that Fannie Barrier helped in the process, Washington acknowledges her help in a manner equal to S. Laing's and she was a professional writer while her husband was not. This may indicate that she shared in the ghostwriting.

In 1906, Williams also published an account of his travels with Douglass during the fall of 1893 after the World's Columbian Exposition ended. They visited Iowa, Nebraska, and Missouri, where Douglass gave rousing lectures on his life and his opposition to lynching. This is one of S. Laing's major acknowledged publications.

Many scholars consider these (and other) actions of Williams on behalf of Washington to be a sign of Williams's sycophantic desire to curry Washington's support of his appointment to the position of federal assistant attorney in Chicago (e.g., Logan 1982, 657). In fact, Washington did help Williams gain a position as an assistant district attorney for northern Illinois between 1908 and 1912. In 1905, however, apparently some of Washington's opponents, including John G. Jones and Edward Morris, both African American lawyers, "used their influence to block a federal appointment for Washington's friend, S. Laing Williams" (Spear 1967, 63). In 1908, nevertheless, S. Laing became a federal assistant attorney in Chicago, a post he held sporadically until 1912.[10] In the latter year, President Woodrow Wilson removed several federal appointees, including Williams.

Most scholars agree that S. Laing Williams is difficult to assess or categorize, and as a result the scholarship on him is also sometimes hard to follow. Although he clearly supported Washington, he often took a militant stance on race relations. Thus he held the position of vice president of the Chicago branch of the National Association for the Advancement of Colored People (NAACP), a group opposed by Washington, and was generally an astute activist (see Spear 1967, 66–67). Williams even had an office in the local branch's headquarters in 1914, but the group could not afford his fees and they discontinued his services (Reed 1997, 31). While Spear praised Williams's abilities, Christopher Reed (1997, 31) dismissed him as a "struggling attorney without exceptional leadership skills." Yet another source for evaluating his work is Clarence Darrow, the famous litigator and radical supporter of labor and free speech, who was a lifelong friend of Williams.

Such an ambiguous view of Williams might represent scholarly efforts to dichotomize the ideas of African Americans following the division and animosity between the two leaders, Washington and DuBois. I consider the complex body of work and ideas that Williams produced to be a result of the different pattern of race relations that prevailed in Chicago. Although the dichotomization of race relations networks and concepts characterized people in many other cities, especially New York, such was not the case in Chicago.[11] Fannie Barrier exhibited the same independence of ideas and organizational work combined with loyalty to Washington as did Williams, but the scholarly respect shown for S. Laing rarely extends to her. She suffers from far more biting criticism.

In 1920, S. Laing was injured in an automobile accident and this event precipitated his retirement. He died on 21 December 1921, and a service for him was held at the Abraham Lincoln Centre, where Darrow delivered the eulogy ("Brilliant Jurist" 1921). One obituary, in the white *Chicago Daily News,* stated that he was "one of the best known negro [sic] lawyers in the United States" and "regarded by members of his race as one of its most brilliant orators" ("Necrology"). His classmates from the University of Michigan recalled that "[w]e remember his genial and dignified personality, his literary tastes and studious habits. The only colored man in the class, he was a general favorite" ("Necrology"). After his passing, Fannie became noticeably less active in the rich world of friends and activities revolving around women's work in sociology that had previously filled her life.

Fannie Barrier Williams's Life in Chicago

The Prudence Crandall Club immediately placed Williams in the center of the social status system in black Chicago, a position she retained throughout her life and career there. Little is known about this vital group, but it clearly included within its circle what would later be recognized as the "old settlers" as well as another group that St. Clair Drake and Horace Cayton (1945, see 32–51) called the "refined." They were the powerhouse in the "black metropolis," an African American community that had high hopes for its own identity while at the same time playing a defensive role in a Jim Crow society that scorned and abused blacks. Donald L. Miller (1996, 501–2) numbers the Barnetts and Dr. Daniel Hale Williams, the physician who founded the interracial Provident Hospital, among this group.

In 1891, Williams made her first major public contribution to the African American community when she worked with Daniel Hale Williams to found the Training School for Nurses, including African American nurses, at Provident Hospital. This institution employed an interracial staff of doctors and nurses, in which the nurses assumed a vital role in creating a professional occupation for women, especially African American women, who were often barred from such professions. Williams labored long and hard to obtain funding for the school and to legitimize nurses' training for African American women (see Aptheker 1982, 104–6, on the importance of African American nurses prior to 1900). The capitalist meatpacker Philip Armour probably provided funds for this nursing school and his support was the origin of Williams's friendship with and loyalty to him.

WILLIAMS AND THE COLUMBIAN EXPOSITION, 1893   The first words of Fannie Barrier Williams to attain national importance were spoken at the World's Columbian Exposition of 1893, where she described the intellectual progress of African American women. Some scholars (e.g., Lemert 1998, 201) consider her speech there the most important of the two hundred or more delivered at the exposition's Woman's Congress. Williams addressed this group along with a panel of African American women, Cooper (1894) and Fannie Jackson Coppin (1894), as her discussants. Williams also served as Honorary American President of the Woman's Congress the next day, on 19 May, and chaired an interracial panel that included a paper by Sarah Jane Early (1894) on "The Organized Efforts of Colored Women in the South to Improve Their Condition," discussed by Hallie Q. Brown. In addition, Williams spoke at the World's Parliament of Religions, another grand event at this World's Fair. All religions were represented there, and their religious leaders attended, talked, argued, and met face to face, often for the first time. This interdenominational event changed the way many of the attendees responded to a range of religious groups, and some of those who attended forged lifelong ties with other religious leaders. Williams again delivered a succinct and penetrating speech.

Although Williams obtained prestigious opportunities because of her role in the planning of the women's building and women's work at the fair, her participation at the fair was also historically important for what it revealed about the state of race relations. First, it documented an unfortunate racist response from some leading white women who opposed the participation of African American women at the fair. Second, their attitude then provoked significant protests by African American women. Third, Williams initially by-passed the white women and was able to participate through an appeal to a U.S. Congressman, because Congress had authorized the fair and appropriated funds for it.

Congress—because it followed the popular Victorian "Doctrine of the Separate Spheres" (Deegan 1988a, 198–99)—defined women as part of a distinct group that need not be funded. According to this view, middle-class married women's labor outside the home was expected to be conducted as unpaid, volunteer work. The structure for women's work at the fair, moreover, was controlled primarily by wealthy, white married women closely tied to traditional female values exercised in the home. These women made up the Board of Lady Managers, which was composed of 117 representatives selected from wealthy women across the country (Weimann 1981, 42). The unmarried women from Hull-House, however, did not fit this pattern or expectation. They spoke at the world's fair as experts, but were not involved in the administrative structure that planned the women's exhibits and building. The complicated world of women at the fair must be understood in order to comprehend the racial conflict that ensued and how Williams partially avoided being involved in it.

In November 1890, a white woman named Mary Logan requested that the work of black women be separately identified and placed in a distinct category to document the progress made since the end of the Civil War. Apparently there were African American "lady managers" at this time (Weimann 1981, 104), including Imogene Howard of New York state (*Noted Negro Women* 1893, 289–94), and there were items created by, but not identified as created by, blacks that were planned for exhibition. Lettie Trent, representing African American women, argued that this was not assertive enough: she wanted an African American committee led by an African American woman and empowered to collect specifically identified black items for a distinct exhibit. Her request triggered a response that resulted in white women—first Mary Logan and then Mary Cantrill (Weimann 1981, 104–5)—being appointed to represent the interests of black women. This decision made matters worse and a series of meetings of African American women followed. Jeanne Madeline Weimann (1981, see pp. 105–16 and 73–101) extensively documents the growing fiasco and its connection both to an earlier scandal in which a white woman was not financially recompensed and to another incident involving a group of competing claimants to authority over women's work at the fair.[12]

Williams appeared at this stage of the conflict—December 1891, when she contacted a Chicago congressional representative with the suggestion that two black women be appointed to positions as "clerks in the Installation Department to solicit exhibits of black work." Williams then took her request to Bertha Honoré Palmer, the head of the Lady Managers (Weimann 1981, 117), and the plan was adopted—to the outrage of some African American women who wanted a black Lady Manager to be employed by and appointed to the executive board, with a committee of three to help her (Weimann 1981, 117).

Before hiring Williams, Palmer had tried to employ Hallie Q. Brown,[13] an African American educator and author (Fisher 1993), to fill one of these positions, but Brown had her own work to complete and thought the position was defined too narrowly. Palmer than asked a Mrs. Curtis, who also declined. Williams was the third woman asked, and she accepted a paid position in an office run by the fair commissioners. Williams discovered and gathered black exhibits for six to seven months, until the office budget was cut and she lost her position. Williams wanted to continue this paid work under the women's committee, but it was unfunded. A short, somewhat acrimonious, correspondence ensued, but no paid position was forthcoming. Palmer wanted Williams to continue in an unpaid position [like the overwhelming majority of volunteer positions held by white women (Weimann

1981, 120–21)], but Williams found this unacceptable. Ultimately, Williams presented a paper and led a session at the Woman's Congress, thereby suggesting that they reconciled their differences. A total of twenty-two African American women participated as speakers at a number of conferences (Massa 1974), but Williams gained the most notoriety.

The eloquent abolitionist and former slave Frederick Douglass figures in this World's Fair event in several ways, for he was the U.S. ambassador to Haiti with his own permanent place at the Haitian Pavilion. His friend Ida B. Wells passed out thousands of copies of her pamphlet—"The Reasons Why the Colored American Is Not in the World's Columbian Exposition" (1893)—from a desk at the pavilion (McFeely 1991, 369). This pamphlet was a protest against the barriers to full participation and representation of blacks in the exhibits, as well as a scathing documentation of lynching and injustice. Douglass wrote a preface to the pamphlet (Douglass 1893), legitimating Wells through his public support. When he later eloquently spoke at the congress, Wells boycotted his speech as too little, too late. She later regretted her stance because she had missed the powerful oration that moved his listeners to tears (Wells-Barnett 1970, 118–19).

Douglass was also a friend of Williams and her husband, and they hosted a successful reception for him in April of 1893. As McFeely (1991, 366) noted: "The Williamses were as delighted with their distinguished guest as he was with their hospitality, and they provided a bright black buffer against some exceedingly silly white darkness that lay ahead." S. Laing Williams (1906) traveled with Douglass later that fall, the septuagenarian having been energized from his experiences in Chicago.

WILLIAMS AND WOMEN'S CLUBS, 1893–1926 In addition to Williams's work in 1893 at the World's Columbian Exposition and the World's Parliament of Religions, she and Mary Church Terrell (1940) helped to establish the National League of Colored Women in that same year. They joined forces again in 1896 to help found the National Association of Colored Women (NACW). Williams knew personally many of the early leaders in African American women's clubs and this knowledge informed her later descriptions of the women and their clubs' accomplishments.

As noted earlier, in November 1894 Williams was nominated to become a member of the powerful CWC by its president, Ellen Henrotin, who had also played a major role at the World's Columbian Exposition. Williams's close friend Celia Parker Woolley (1894), a former president of the CWC who spoke at the Parliament of Religions, cosponsored Williams as well. Although Henrotin, Woolley, and Williams expected the nomination to be routinely accepted, they had seriously underestimated the racist attitude of other white women in Chicago. When the conflict became apparent, Henrotin declared: "There is no doubt Mrs. Williams will become a member of [the Chicago] Woman's Club" ("Fannie Barrier Williams" 1894). Despite such determination, Williams became the focus of a protracted battle to keep her out of the women's club. In time these three courageous women won the skirmish, but they lost the war against racism: Williams was one of only a few African American woman to join the club for many years. Williams, however, seemed to be able to sway the stony hearts of the white women after all, for on 2 February 1901, the *Colored American* ("The Color-Line Exit" 1901) reported:

> The Chicago Woman's Club at their meeting last week voted 175 to 63 in favor of allowing colored women to become members of the national federation of clubs. In spite of the numerous letters sent them from various Southern clubs the majority was overwhelming. While this does not mean the [automatic] acceptance of membership of the colored clubs, it means a great deal, as this club is the nuclei [*sic*] around which all the other clubs gather.

Indeed, this vote did not change the federation, but it seems Williams had an impact on the Chicago club. The Ida B. Wells Club of Chicago also formally thanked the CWC for this support.

By 1897, Williams had made a significant impact in the national arena of black and white women. Her frequent essays, the most well-known ones included here,[14] firmly built her reputation in a wide variety of circles: in African American women's clubs, in social settlements, and among women in new occupations. In addition, she became an expert on the "new Negro" of Washington's era (Washington 1900),[15] the "new woman," (Smith-Rosenberg 1985, 245–96), the "new Negro woman," (Giddings 1984, part II), and art. Here I use Williams's (see 1902a, 203; 1904i, 546) writings on the new woman or new Negro and combine this term with her (Williams 1904a) preferred name for Americans of African descent, "colored," in the title of this book. Williams was a new woman of color, and she promoted the ideas and work of other new women of color.

One example of her national leadership in African American women's clubs comes from the first biannual convention of the NACW in 1897. At this meeting, Williams accepted a leading role for the next convention to be held in Chicago in 1899 (Wesley 1984, 43). She organized "the Woman's Conference" and was elected its president to provide entertainment for this major event. Numerous papers were presented under the guidance of the convention president, Mary Church Terrell. African American women from across the country gathered here, as well as Booker T. Washington. Williams's many white friends, including Mary McDowell, the sociologist from the University of Chicago Social Settlement and a former Hull-House resident, and Ellen Henrotin, who had sponsored Williams in the CWC, delivered speeches, too (Wesley 1984, 45–46). Wells-Barnett (1970, 258–60), who was not part of the planning committee for the convention hastily arranged for a luncheon at Hull-House that was hosted by Addams. The *Chicago Times Herald* and DuBois characterized the event as politically significant because it crossed the color line

(Wesley 1984, 48). Williams, then president of the Illinois Federation of Colored Women's Clubs, also spoke at the interracial Unitarian All Souls Church on the topic of the importance of education and club work (Wesley 1984, 46). As a result of her speeches and club work, Williams was invited to undertake a lecture tour through the South, at a time when it was increasingly governed by Jim Crow laws, and this she reported on in her autobiographical account.

Williams as Journalist and Sociologist

Williams became a leading intellectual black voice through her writings in newspapers. Her work as a journalist probably began when she was hired by Josephine St. Pierre Ruffin, her Boston friend, club woman, and editor of *Woman's Era*. This was the first newspaper for and by African American women, and Williams became a correspondent for them in 1895 during its founding year.

In 1905 and 1906, Williams published several articles in the influential African American national newspaper the *New York Age*, but how she arranged for this work is unknown. Williams also had an occasional column in the white *Chicago Record Herald* around 1906 and 1907. This journalistic writing was necessary because professional outlets for her social, cultural, and intellectual critiques, i.e., sociology and social science journals, were not open to African American women.

Williams is specifically located in a major intellectual tradition and discipline: sociology and the particular work of female sociologists who made Chicago its epicenter. I consider Williams a central figure in a small yet vital group of African American women who were "founding sisters" (Deegan 1991) during the classical era of sociology from 1890 to 1920, when it first emerged as a distinct discipline within the academy and wider society. The University of Chicago became the worldwide academic foundation for the discipline (Faris 1967), and Hull-House became its worldwide applied foundation (Deegan 1988a). Patricia Lengermann and Jill Niebrugge-Brantley (1998) call the female sociologists in Chicago the "women of the Chicago school," and Williams was part of this intellectual and politically engaged circle.

THE GOLDEN ERA OF WOMEN IN SOCIOLOGY: WOMEN'S WORK AND IDEAS WITHIN THEIR SEPARATE SPHERE   Sociology was attractive to women in the nineteenth century because of their concern with "the woman question." Women played formative roles in the development of the social sciences between 1870 and 1890 (Leach 1989) within a division of labor that was compatible with the aforementioned Doctrine of the Separate Spheres. This gender-segregated ideology allowed for the growth of a separate woman's network in sociology and was led by women who emphasized the study of home, women, children, and family.

Because women were assumed to have higher "emotional and cultural sensitivity" than men, the women were deemed ideal professionals to improve society and make it more humane. This doctrine also permeated and organized Williams's ideas.

The network of white male sociologists tended to be abstract, formal, and academic (Deegan 1978, 1981, 1987, 1988a, 1988b). The women worked outside the academy in social settlements, women's organizations, and women's colleges. In Chicago, the women's network was centered at Hull-House, but it also flourished elsewhere in social settlements around the city, nation, and world. Williams followed this gendered pattern during her extensive work in Chicago's social settlements and became one of the leading experts on African American social settlements throughout the United States. Williams acknowledged Hull-House and Addams as leaders in this social movement.

Because of the discipline's initial openness to women and the belief in a special "sphere" for women's work in sociology, women flocked to the academy for training between 1892 and 1920. During this "golden era of women in sociology" (Deegan 1987, 1991, 1996a, 1997), a fruitful, applied sociology emerged with an elaborate theory of society: feminist pragmatism. This American theory unites liberal values and belief in a rational public with a cooperative, nurturing, and liberating model of the self, the other, and the community. Feminist pragmatism emphasizes education and democracy as significant mechanisms to organize and improve society.[16] It emerged in Chicago because sociologists there observed the rapid urbanization, immigration, industrialization, migration, and social change that took place before their eyes. The Great Migration of African Americans from the South to the North was part of this massive movement of people in search of more freedom and prosperity.

Williams was also a feminist pragmatist, although any speeches she gave in 1893 with this focus happened before the flowering of pragmatism at the University of Chicago (Deegan 1999; Feffer 1993). Despite this historical "gap" in epistemology, Williams's speeches shared the Chicago women's fundamental emphasis on democracy and education.[17] She delivered, in fact, one of the most stirring speeches on the right to liberty, democracy, education, and justice at the previously mentioned World's Columbian Exposition in 1893. This speech is a manifesto for women of color and for the white women who were their allies to join hands for a future built on the faltering ideals of a great land. It is little wonder that its powerful language and call to justice yielded controversy and debate. The speech expressly states the optimism and epistemology underlying feminist pragmatism. It is also the most important early statement of the relations between race and gender expressed within this circle of theorists and activists. It is a major declaration in what I call the "Hull-House school of race relations" (Deegan 2000a).

Williams worked with a number of feminist pragmatists in Chicago: Jane Addams, Mary McDowell, and Celia Parker Woolley. She and these three women were active in the Chicago branches of the NAACP and the National Urban League (NUL) as well. They defied the norm for many African Americans, who chose between either the DuBois or the Washington faction associated with these two civil rights organizations (see Reed 1997). Chicagoans, black and white, are characterized by their refusal to dichotomize their loyalties and this emerged, at least in part, from their stance as pragmatists (see Campbell 1992; Deegan 1988b, 1999; Mead 1999; West 1989).

The female sociologists were all active in the women's club movement, and Addams and Woolley, like Williams, were members of the CWC. Addams and her Hull-House colleague Sophonisba Breckinridge were honorary members of the NACW (Salem 1990, 225). Addams was also the first honorary member of Alpha Kappa Alpha (AKA), the African American sorority (Giddings 1988, 64).

In addition, the women were all involved in Chicago social settlements: Addams headed Hull-House; McDowell directed the University of Chicago Social Settlement (UCSS); and Woolley led the Frederick Douglass Center (FDC). Williams was active in all three settlements, especially the FDC, but few details of her day-to-day participation remain. One indication of her involvement at the UCSS is her speech on "What Colored Women are Doing for History" in 1900 (see *University of Chicago Settlement* 1901, 13; see also Williams 1904c). Williams and Woolley were both Unitarians and active in All Souls Church. Jenkin Lloyd Jones (1904, 1905) led this progressive, national center that supported female ministers like Woolley (see Deegan and Rynbrandt 2000). Not surprisingly, Addams (1918) was a close friend of Jones, and she joined Williams and Woolley in the work of the Abraham Lincoln Centre that Jones led. All three of them, moreover, backed the work of the Unitarian minister Caroline Bartlett Crane (Deegan and Rynbrandt 2000). Chicago social settlements embodied the ideas and practices of women in sociology, and Williams was a vibrant part of this activity and intellectual life.

Williams lauded Hull-House publicly and the gentle spirit of Jane Addams "as the finest, the most typical, and most complete example of socialized kindness to be found in the world" (Williams 1904, 128–29). Addams similarly served as the model for Baptist women at their convention in 1915 (Giddings 1988, 175), reflecting the ideas shared by Williams and this group of African American women.[18] On this and other occasions, Williams noted her familiarity with the numerous social settlements in Chicago and supported their efforts toward a working democracy both for white immigrants (who were defined as being of different races at that time) and for African Americans traveling in the Great Migration from the rural south to the urban north (Deegan 2000a).

Throughout her writings, Williams argued for the importance of democratic ideals for African Americans, and this fueled her dream of a liberated America. As an educator, she was committed to the power of teaching and learning to eradicate illiteracy, employment barriers, and racial discrimination. Williams formed a deep bond with other women who were educators, black and white, and particularly praised African American women for their leadership in education in the black community. She was dedicated to social justice for women and for blacks, and she supported women's suffrage before women obtained the vote. Her social thought must be placed within a larger context of applied sociology based in Chicago and written by women employing feminist pragmatism and the praxis emerging from it.

Early women in sociology, such as Williams, developed ideas and practices that differed radically from those of their male counterparts. Two generations of women entered sociology during the golden era. The women of the first generation, born generally between 1855 and 1870, were "pioneers" who established a place for "women's sociological work" in a society with distinct spheres for each sex. The second generation of women, born between 1870 and 1890, were professionals who obtained male credentials in the academy but who sometimes chose and sometimes were forced to operate in the distinct women's world within sociology (Deegan 1987, 1988b).

The pioneers in the golden era, like Williams, battled for women's rights to higher education, suffrage, and fair wages for paid labor outside the home. They used social science to document women's restricted lives and opportunities and employed social settlements to build a community base for changing the society and enabling their neighbors' voices to be heard. The professionals combined the role established by the pioneers with formal training in the academy. This second generation was often mentored by the pioneers and by sympathetic male sociologists, often at the University of Chicago, an institution central to the development of the profession (Faris 1967; Kurtz 1984; Deegan 1988a, 1999). Progressive men such as John Dewey, George H. Mead, and W.I. Thomas encouraged the second generation as students. After graduation these women were rarely accepted as equal faculty members in the male academy, however, and they struggled on the margins of sociology departments (Deegan 1978, 1995). This established an early pattern of encouragement for women students to perform at their peak, while discriminating against women graduates as professional colleagues.

Powerful "founding sisters" virtually disappeared from male academies in sociology departments after 1920. Male sociologists erased their ties to these founding sisters and began a new era: the dark era of patriarchal ascendancy (Deegan 1991, 1995, 1996a). Williams's recognition within sociology suffered from this gendered invisibility that was deepened by her racial location within the discipline.

The Veil of Sociology, 1890–1920

While sociology was being established in the 1890s, racism flourished within America. From the 1880s until at least the late 1950s, the United States was sundered by legally separate worlds for black and white people. "Jim Crow" practices, especially powerful in the South, were reflected in segregated institutions in education, housing, transportation, restaurants, and medicine (Morris 1984; Stanfield 1985). DuBois referred to this external, structural pattern of racism as "the color line." It generated an entire lifeworld (Schutz 1962, 1967) surrounding black people that DuBois called "the Veil." Life within the Veil divided the self into a double consciousness with a sense of "twoness" corresponding to the divisions emergent from the color line (DuBois 1903a). This American apartheid was incorporated in patterns of face-to-face interaction leading to the genesis of the self (Mead 1934). Williams had plunged into the South and faced its Jim Crow practices when she taught and traveled there after 1870. Armed by this horrific experience, she fought Jim Crow's establishment in Chicago from 1887 until she left the city in 1926.

Williams clearly read the books of DuBois, even participating in a discussion led by him in 1903, but she did not always agree with his ideas. Her attitude was partially based on her friendship and alliance with Washington, who opposed the work of DuBois, but it also emerged from her own views on racial integration and the nature of multiracial identity. Although DuBois (and most white Americans) considered any descendant of an African a "Negro," Williams viewed her ancestry as more complex. For our discussion, Williams's combination of the ideas of both DuBois and Washington places her within a network of African American sociologists who were aligned with both Hull-House and its view of white women's work in sociology (see Deegan 1988b, 2000a).

African American sociologists suffered specific, even greater divisions within their "selves" than other African Americans (Mead 1934). As sociologists, they were empowered to speak about racism through their formal knowledge of race relations and the social construction of inequality. Simultaneously, they lived within multiple layers of discrimination as African Americans and sociologists in a white-defined, hegemonic profession (Ladner 1973; Deegan 1995) and lifeworld (Schutz 1962). The professional self (Deegan and Hill 1991) of African American sociologists generated a particular reality and experience that rarely informed the everyday practice and theoretical knowledge of "white sociology" (Ladner 1973). I call this liberating, yet oppressive (Deegan 2000b), practice of American sociologists "the Veil of sociology," referring to the different power, marginality, and legitimacy of white and black sociologists within this structure of knowledge and higher education.

African American sociologists created a network of scholars who worked within the Veil in the larger society and in sociology. African

American men found employment within activist social agencies or the black academy (Blackwell and Janowitz 1973; Stanfield 1985, 1993), but few African American women worked in these academies or held high position in social agencies or civil rights organizations. The women, like Williams, experienced a "gendered Veil" in sociology, limiting their access to the public sphere as both women and as African Americans.

THE GENDERED VEIL OF SOCIOLOGY   African American women in sociology experienced restricted access to professional opportunities and networks compared to white men, African American men, and white women. African American women survived and triumphed over the deep structures of discriminations, nonetheless, drawn to the powerful opportunities created by the sociological imagination and voice. This resulted in a "golden era for African American women in sociology" with its unique network, opportunities, intellectual work, and professional praxis. Four of the most significant women in the African American network were Williams, Wells-Barnett, Terrell, and Cooper (Lemert 1998).[19] Their work was characterized by a sociological theory and practice[20] oriented toward the standpoint of the oppressed, especially African Americans and African American women. Their analysis considered the interaction between race and power, and between gender and power. It was an analysis structured by history, ideology, material resources, manners, and emotion—an active cooperative model with an emphasis on fighting for civil and cultural rights from the viewpoint of feminist pragmatism. These characteristics reflect a variety of sociological tasks: teaching, writing, and community organizing emergent from a sociological perspective.[21]

These four female sociologists all wrote and taught the sociological theory and praxis of race relations, and they were active in black women's clubs, social welfare organizations, civil rights groups, and social settlements. Cooper, Williams, and Wells-Barnett have been identified as sociologists by other sociologists (for Cooper see Lemert 1998; for all the women, Lengermann and Niebrugge-Brantley 1998; for Wells-Barnett see Broschart 1991; Lengermann and Niebrugge-Brantley 1998), and I am identifying all of them as sociologists (see Deegan 1988a for a fuller discussion of such criteria). All the women wrote socioautobiographies reflecting their experiences as black women in America. This sociological style of writing is similar to the reflections of DuBois (e.g., 1903, 1940) on his life and training and to that of Addams (1910, 1930) and Gilman (1892, 1935) on the struggle for women's rights and expanded opportunities during this era.

All four women wrote on race relations and on gender using a structural and politicized analysis. Their use of feminist pragmatism is striking and aligns them with the white female sociological network. Simultaneously, their use of a race relations format echoed the epistemology of the African American men in sociology who worked behind the Veil. They often knew these men through joint work in civil rights organizations, as well. This group of African American women was highly educated; they were articulate community leaders and authors.

A striking indication of a Gendered Veil in sociology is that most white founding sisters in the United States were members of the American Sociological Society, but none of the black founding sisters were. Similarly, two African American men—Monroe Work (*Publications of the American Sociological Society,* 6, 1912, 101) and George Edmund Haynes (Ibid., 12, 1918, 256)—were members. African American women began to earn doctorates in sociology decades after white women and black men (see Deegan 2000a). Cooper, Terrell, and Washington, however, were all active in the Southern Sociological Congress (see McCulloch 1913, 680).[22]

Williams, Cooper (1858–1964), Terrell (1863–1954), and Wells-Barnett (1862–1931), part of the pioneer generation of female sociologists, were all born before 1870, as were the white women pioneers. The meaning of the Civil War, however, dramatically differed for the two groups. Both Wells-Barnett and Cooper were born into slavery. In contrast, Terrell and Williams were born into free African American families that expected higher education and a middle-class life for their daughters. The crucial, defining moment for all African Americans was the end of legal slavery in 1865.[23] For the white pioneers, usually descended from abolitionists, political activism and the fight for social justice profoundly shaped their understanding of themselves and society.[24]

These African American women were prominent in their local communities and the national world of African Americans. They organized African American women through club work, and joined African Americans in civil rights struggles. They were prolific writers—especially Wells-Barnett and Williams— and powerful orators. They allied themselves with white women in sociology in a pattern distinct from the general hostility and barriers between their groups (see Deegan 1988b). These African American and white women both fit Paula Giddings (1984, 153–70) discussion of "radical interracialists," although Giddings limited her category to black women.[25]

All these women married, and Terrell, Cooper, and Wells-Barnett were also mothers. They blended their activities at home with high-profile work in race relations, thereby combining both family and social claims (Addams 1910). Their lives as activists and wives—and usually mothers—differed radically from the lives of the white women in the profession, usually never-married women living with other women who shared their values and career interests (Deegan 1996a, 1996b). In fact, Wells-Barnett was shocked and outraged to think that some white women believed she had to choose between family and social claims: she wanted and did both. Terrell, Wells-Barnett, and Williams had egalitarian marriages and shared commitments with their spouses long before such patterns became common in the white community.

Although these women lived behind the Gendered Veil of sociology, their lives were characterized by vivacity, strength, and resistance to oppression.

They forged alliances and fought battles with each other behind the Veil, and their relationships are often complex. Wells-Barnett is particularly important here because she, like Williams, lived in Chicago, worked in social settlements, and was an active African American women's club member.

NEW WOMEN OF COLOR FROM CHICAGO: IDA B. WELLS-BARNETT AND FANNIE BARRIER WILLIAMS As noted earlier, S. Laing Williams and Ferdinand Barnett were law partners for approximately fifteen years—between 1889 and 1904. The men and their wives were associated to some degree after Ida B. Wells came to Chicago for the Columbian Exposition in 1893, and they all shared a crucial friendship with Frederick Douglass. Wells-Barnett and Fannie Barrier Williams were both active in the early years of the FDC, from 1904 until approximately 1907,[26] but Wells-Barnett (1970, 279–88) had a falling-out with the white head of the settlement—one of Fannie's closest friends, Celia Parker Woolley—whom Wells-Barnett considered a racist.

After several years of friendship, problems between Woolley and Wells-Barnett began to surface after Woolley did not promote Wells-Barnett for the presidency of the Frederick Douglass Women's Club. Woolley suggested initially that the candidate be selected by the members without her favoring only one individual, but Wells-Barnett believed this was a misdirection to cover Woolley's active opposition to her candidacy. Wells-Barnett (1970, 287–88) recalled that Woolley wrote after their breach "how much she missed me and asked me to come back," but Wells-Barnett had made a complete break with Woolley, the FDC, and its women's club.

Sometime around this period, Wells-Barnett and Williams also parted, ostensibly because Williams supported Booker T. Washington, a relationship discussed later in this essay. Leslie H. Fishel (1971, 621) argued that Williams had turned to Washington by 1900, but this date—that I consider incorrect—does not explain the women's joint work from 1903 to 1907. There were several other points of contention between the two women, in addition to their views on Washington. For example, when Wells-Barnett resigned her position as corresponding secretary of the Afro-American Council in 1902, Williams then filled the office (Logan 1982, 656). Linda O. McMurray (1998, 250) suggests that Williams and Wells-Barnett both wanted to be "big fish" in the little pond of Chicago's black elite. If they were rivals, Williams was the more successful "contestant" in the competitive world of African American elite women. McMurray (1998, 250) also quotes from a 17 October 1902 article in *The Broad-Ax* that stated the women "hate each other like two she-rattlesnakes." Dorothy Salem (1990, 169) even suggests that Wells-Barnett partially opposed the Chicago Urban League because Williams supported it!

Despite these difference, the two women worked together years after 1902. Both Wells-Barnett and Williams maintained lifelong ties to other feminist pragmatists, such as Addams, and were active in Chicago's

African American elite, so there were probably numerous occasions when their paths crossed. And both women remained friends of Josephine St. Pierre Ruffin. Wells-Barnett (1970), moreover, never singled out Williams for criticism in her autobiography, although Williams is absent from the text. In contrast, Wells-Barnett (1904, 1970) was not restrained in her criticism of Washington.

NEW WOMEN OF COLOR FROM THE NORTH AND SOUTH: FANNIE BARRIER WILLIAMS, ANNA JULIA COOPER, AND MARY CHURCH TERRELL   The only documented meeting I have found between Williams and Cooper was their shared podium at the 1893 Columbian Exhibition. This was a major event for African American women, but still only one event. They may have known each other within the small circle of Washington's African American elite, through the National League of Colored Women—of which they were both members, or through the NACW. As college graduates and intellectuals, Williams and Cooper were part of an elite group of women during their era.

Cooper's most important writing, *A Voice From the South* (1892), explores the lives and restrictions of women oppressed by a slave heritage, by the failures of the Reconstruction period, and by a Jim Crow society. Cooper spoke for the majority of African American women, who endured lives in which there was no voice to represent them and suffered from the oppression of capitalism, feudal relations, sexism, and racism. Williams's voice from Chicago was very different. She articulated a dream of America, a democratic vision that called for national unity and justice. She chose to approach urban America, represented by Chicago, and tried to understand the role of women as both leaders and as embodied females with a unique culture. Williams celebrated marriage and a new equality in that relationship. She drew on education to help her dream come alive. Cooper and Williams expressed two distinct voices and visions. They are not dichotomous, but they are distinct. Hazel Carby (1986) fruitfully compared the work of Wells-Barnett and Cooper. The voices of both Cooper and Williams, and more, are needed to help understand the lives of African Americans, men and women, Americans, and the eras they experienced.

Williams and Terrell were allies in the founding of both the NLCW and the NACW, as noted. Their husbands were both lawyers, allies of Washington, egalitarian partners, and more conservative than their wives. Williams and Terrell both became society leaders in their black communities and lived in Washington, D.C., at some point in their lives. They were college graduates, authors, orators, and allies of white female sociologists based at Hull-House. Terrell (1940) does not single out Williams as a close friend in her autobiography, but they clearly shared many common interests and supported each other on significant occasions.

Terrell, unlike Williams, lived to witness the civil rights struggles of the 1950s and 1960s and to take part in them. During these years, Terrell assumed a leadership role once again, making her legacy as a community activist clearer to scholars than is that of Williams. Wilma Peebles-Wilkins and E. Aracelis Francis (1990) compared the work of Wells-Barnett and Terrell (see also Salem 1990, 149), and such analysis needs to be extended to Williams.

FANNIE BARRIER WILLIAMS AND BOOKER T. WASHINGTON

Williams's relationship to Washington is a complex one that has been misunderstood by several of her most important biographers (with the exception of Jackson 1986). Williams has been interpreted harshly by several scholars (e.g., Riggs 1993) and termed a "Bookerite" by Fox (1970, 159). Allan H. Spear (1967, 70), an especially important critic, depicted her as someone originally in favor of black rights, who later became an opponent of them due to her opportunistic ties to Washington:

> Perhaps Fannie Barrier Williams never completely lost her faith in equal rights and equal opportunity, but by 1900 she had become a leading exponent of the doctrine of self-help and racial solidarity, actively writing and speaking in behalf of Booker T. Washington. . . . It is, of course, possible that Mrs. Williams simply changed her mind. Yet it can hardly be coincidental that her most active work for the Tuskegee cause came at the very time her husband was seeking a federal job.

Jessie Carney Smith (1992, 1253) similarly states that "[h]er views were tempered by 1900, when she began to drift to the conciliatory and practical views of Booker T. Washington." Smith (1992, 1254) argues that Williams *either* changed her opinions *or* was politically expedient. This harsh view of Williams as a person who "perhaps" sold her soul to aid her husband's appointment as a federal judge is found in Salem (1993, 557), Fishel (1971, 621), and Spear (1973, 828), as well.

Her contemporary, Julius Taylor, editor of Chicago's *The Broad-Ax,* shared the dichotomized view of Washington versus DuBois. In a puerile commentary in 1904, Taylor referred to Williams as "Mrs. Fannie Barrier Booker T. Washington Williams [Who] Slops Over on the Negro Question" (Taylor cited in Knupfer 1998, 11). After assaulting her character and a speech she delivered, he continued:

> Perhaps we may be mistaken, but we are of the opinion that Mrs. Williams needed a new fall dress and some other finery and that Booker Washington was willing to give her several hundred dollars of the money he begs from the public to enable her to obtain the new traps (Ibid., 12).

S. Laing, who was then president of the Hyde Park Colored Republican Club, attacked such "disgraceful acts" of editors who supported political enemies of the black community (cited in Knupfer 1998, 12). After all, not only was Fannie Barrier Williams subjected to these schoolyard tactics, but S. Laing was depicted as implicitly accepting monetary favors from Washington for his wife's shallow behavior.

Although Williams was possibly venal, it appears she was not as corrupt as these scholars generally depict her. I assume that Williams helped her husband achieve his life's ambition, but such actions by a wife are usually considered loyal. In addition, her husband, who even reported on the actions of Washington's foes, is treated more sympathetically than she is (e.g., Spear 1967, 66–69). The frequently biting criticism of her life and accomplishments may explain the paucity of serious scholarship on her ideas and work.

In contrast to this scholarly condemnation, I find her relationship to Washington complex, given her husband's long friendship with him. She struggled to support *both* Washington's position and a variety of more militant positions for a number of years. This balancing act includes the years after 1900, contrary to the "Bookerite" depiction accorded her after 1900 in Fishel (1971, 621), Smith (1992, 1253–54), and Spear (1967, 70). Her 1904 article on "Industrial Education"—the topic that was the crux of the intellectual differences between Washington and DuBois—favored both men's positions. She argued eloquently that both the worker and the scholarly leader needed to act hand in hand rather than in opposition to each other. The uncompromising attitude of some militants and some accommodationists divided African Americans into one of two competing, incompatible groups. Since Williams contributed a chapter to a book allegedly edited by Washington and published in 1900,[27] this apparently became an irreversible sign that she was a "Bookerite." The ideas represented in her writings in this anthology, however, do not support such an interpretation. Those scholars and activists—like Williams, who tried to avoid oversimplification of ideas and practices in expressing themselves are caught in this polarized debate, nonetheless.

The concept of "cooperative allies," a characteristic race relations pattern in Chicago (Drake and Cayton 1945; Reed 1997) and among feminist pragmatists, is interpreted by advocates of a polarized stance as "vacillating," merely because these radical interracialists refused to accept such a narrow, dichotomized position. A more fruitful comparison to Williams's ideas and practices can be made by studying the work of Jane Addams and Martin Luther King, Jr., as mentioned earlier. The other half of this problematic debate concerns Williams and DuBois.

FANNIE BARRIER WILLIAMS AND W.E.B. DUBOIS Williams and DuBois shared several vital interests. Briefly, Williams read his *Souls of Black Folk* (1903a) and discussed it with him in 1903, as noted above. She favored higher education, encouraged the talented tenth as leaders, championed the fine arts, and was a persuasive orator and community leader. Both Williams and DuBois (Deegan 1988b) supported the work of female sociologists at Hull-House and the work of the NAACP in Chicago. Both were born and raised in the East and experienced relatively happy and stable childhoods as the children of free African Americans. Both traveled to the South as late adolescents and became school teachers there. Both were appalled by the color line and the Veil they experienced during Reconstruction, and this became a life-altering experience.

Two divisive issues separated them: first, in 1904 Williams did not support using the name "Negro," although she did use it later, a word that DuBois (1903) championed; and second, Williams sometimes supported the work of Washington, whom DuBois bitterly opposed. For DuBois, any African American who supported Washington had crossed a line that made him an enemy. DuBois did not, in my opinion, draw this line for his white allies at Hull-House, although some contemporary scholars suggest that he did (see Deegan 1988b).

SUMMARIZING WILLIAMS'S RELATIONS BEHIND THE VEIL OF SOCIOLOGY Williams was active in a number of circles within sociology. As a friend and staunch ally of many female sociologists, both black and white, she helped generate a golden era for women in the discipline. A highly educated artist and leader, Williams offered a rationale for what she called the African American "better-class" by advancing a claim for legitimacy for hard-working but despised African Americans and by supporting "the talented tenth" (DuBois 1903b). She defended higher education, the life of the mind, intellectual thought, and a search for leadership and excellence. In this way, she promoted the arguments of DuBois, and was herself a representative of the talented tenth. Her active community leadership included attending conferences and, having critiqued their work earlier, recommending high art to her African American audience.

In addition to participating in these sociological networks, Williams supported and discussed the work of Richard R. Wright, Jr., a Chicago sociologist and a central figure in Chicago's Trinity Mission (Deegan 2000a; and McMurray 1991). Her analysis of this short-lived institution that combined the goals of a Christian mission with those of a social settlement is one of the most important writings on Wright's work in Chicago.

Simultaneously, Booker T. Washington—one of her husband's best friends—advocated vocational and manual education for the masses of poor, and often illiterate, southern African Americans.[28] Williams, who had taught this same group of people, was sympathetic to the massive problems facing blacks in the South. She understood the common problems of making and defending a family, building a home, and fighting Jim Crow laws. She may have been influenced by the feminist pragmatists' position in support of vocational education, too. Their sophisticated argument was not an accommodation to a low social status but a radical restructuring of labor so that working with one's hands was valued as highly as working with one's mind (see Feffer 1993). In this context, Williams strengthened the population of African Americans living behind the color line in poverty. Simultaneously, she balanced her husband's ambitions and friendship, and often challenged the bias that tried to force her to chose between Washington and DuBois. Her attempt to independently consider the issues in this debate characterized her work and that of the white and black Chicagoans working for African American civil rights in Chicago (see Reed 1997).

SUMMARIZING THE RELATIONSHIPS WITHIN THE GENDERED VEIL OF SOCIOLOGY Williams was a central figure in sociology, especially within the African American women's network. She had an uneven, tumultuous relationship with Wells-Barnett, probably knew Cooper, and worked with Terrell on behalf of African American women's clubs. Both Williams and Terrell married men who worked with Washington to gain favors within the legal system, and both men were lawyers and judges. Wells-Barnett also married a lawyer who worked primarily in a private practice, probably limiting his legal opportunities in the public sphere because of his opposition to Washington. The circle of African American female sociologists behind the Gendered Veil is largely unknown. When greater scholarship is available, Williams's position will be important to explore.

Although Williams's alliances need considerably more research and analysis, she was sometimes allies with and sometimes opposed to an important group of black and white feminist pragmatists. Williams's life as a sociological colleague remains sketchy, but she was clearly the center of numerous ties, alliances, influences, ideas, and debates within the Gendered Veil. She held a central position within the golden era for women in sociology—both white and black—and within the male and female network behind the Veil of sociology. A major reason for this influence emerges from her social thought, which I examine more fully below.

Williams's Writings

THE SPEECH THAT MOVED THE WOMAN'S CONGRESS The Woman's Congress of 1893 was a mighty event drawing tens—if not hundreds—of thousands of visitors. Many feminist pragmatists in addition to Williams spoke there: Jane Addams, Julia Lathrop, Florence Kelley, Celia Parker Woolley, Anna Garlin Spencer, Marion Talbot, Caroline Bartlett Crane, and others (Deegan 1991; Deegan and Rynbrandt 2000; Rynbrandt 1999). It is impossible to know how many of these sessions Williams attended, but likely she heard some of the speeches given by her friends and allies.

As already mentioned, Williams gave her major address when she was the leading speaker in a panel on black women that was held at the Woman's Congress on 18 August 1893. Williams's powerful speech called for democracy and American ideals to be put into action, beginning immediately—at the Woman's Congress of the Columbian Exposition. Understandably, this eloquent and passionate speech, "The Intellectual Progress and Present Status of the Colored Women of the United States since the Emancipation Proclamation," is frequently reprinted. Its contents justify such recognition, but its intellectual themes also serve to anchor her other writings. It is the first clear statement of the voice and vision of Williams, a feminist pragmatist from Chicago who was a new woman of color.

Many white women were shocked by the radical idea that Williams presented: that African American women were leaders, dignified and worthy of equal status with white women of similar accomplishments. She also stated clearly that African American women were, moreover, victimized by white men who abused them sexually, morally, and spiritually.

Despite the then-shocking nature of her speech, Williams stressed the lives of "respectable" women like herself, and in this regard she has a class bias. Although Williams sometimes used elitist words like "the best people," her arguments for educated, intellectual, and responsible leaders carry a positive aspect that supports a more militant, community-empowered vision. Williams argues poignantly for Americans to stand up for their beliefs in equality, justice, democracy, and respect for law. Her traditional, liberal argument had a powerful appeal to the conscience of white women in America. The broad-based support for the goals of her speech made Williams a popular lecturer throughout the United States, although Southern white women who invited her to speak often fell short of their intention to rise above racial hatred.

This speech was immediately discussed by the panelists Cooper and Coppin. They basically supported Williams, while at the same time emphasizing women of all social classes. Williams stressed middle-class women and the morally worthy African American woman of all classes. (Her emphasis on morality addressed journalistic slurs on African American women.) Cooper (1892) focused on the special expertise and interest of African American women of the South (Cooper 1894, 712). Fannie Jackson Coppin (1894), a graduate of Oberlin College as was Cooper (Lemert 1998), continued the discussion of the ideas presented by Williams and stressed the feminist pragmatist's familiar call for more education. Frederick Douglass (1894) closed this session with praise for the three women's erudite and expressive public voice: a landmark that he had never expected to see. "It is the new thing under the sun," he noted, "a new heaven is dawning upon us, and a new earth is ours" (Douglass 1894, 717). He was, of course, too optimistic about the significance of this breakthrough.

On the next day, Williams introduced the session in which Sarah Jane Early (1894a) addressed "The Organized Efforts of the Colored Women of the South to Improve Their Condition." Early discussed the religious work performed by southern African American women, complimenting Cooper's previous discussion and anticipating the soon-to-be organized NACW, in which Williams played a major role. This paper was discussed by Hallie Q. Brown (1894), the woman who had refused the position at the Columbian Exhibition later accepted by Williams.[29] Early (1894b, 1120) also addressed the Parliament of Religions, where she spoke on "The Relation of the Home and Christian Temperance" as part of the African Methodist Episcopal Congress. Williams, a Unitarian, was much more critical of Christianity than Early was. (See discussion of this speech in the general analysis of Williams's writings on African Americans.)

AFRICAN AMERICAN WOMEN   Williams frequently analyzed African American women, sometimes adopting a voice as their representative, sometimes as an expert, sometimes as a journalist with an essay to sell, and sometimes as a sister of other African American women. These various roles reflect a range of styles, audiences, and intentions.

Although Williams tried to join biracial clubs and remained active in the CWC, her deepest loyalties and commitments were with the club movement of African American women. In two major essays, one in 1900 and another in 1902 (the latter a more reflexive and improved draft and partially republished here as item 3 of part II),[30] Williams discussed a variety of facets of this work, including its history, chronological development, leaders, relations with white women's clubs, and impact on African American life and women.

Once again, Williams's autobiography appeared in her writings when she documented her experiences in the CWC. She also discussed another interracial controversy that involved the refusal of the predominantly white National Federation of Women's Clubs (NFWC) to recognize Williams's friend Josephine St. Pierre Ruffin—editor of the *Woman's Era*—as a representative of a club for women of color. This complicated racist incident was muddled by conflicting versions of what happened, and Williams clearly documented the order of events and responses in her important essay.

A shorter and more critical analysis of this topic (with the same title) was published in *The Voice of the Negro* in 1904 (republished here as item 4 of part II). Here Williams faced a smaller, predominantly black, audience in which she felt more comfortable criticizing some of the internal politics of "The Club Movement among the Colored Women," especially in the NACW. As an organizer of this group, Williams personally knew most of the leaders and wrote from an informed position. Her analysis provides a contrast to Wells-Barnett's views (1970, 258–61) on these same political issues, for Wells-Barnett wrote as one who ultimately left the group while Williams wrote as an insider who remained.

Williams had high hopes and expectations for the participation of African American women in both domestic and public life, and in business. She did not argue, however, that African traditions survived during slavery and then carried over into the modern age. Instead, she portrayed African American women as women with the world and all its possibilities

open before them precisely because they did *not* have a tradition that restricted them.

This does not mean that Williams was simplistically optimistic and/or
accommodationist in response to the discrimination facing African American women. On the contrary, Williams provided a thorough statement of
the limited occupational structure open to the everyday woman of African
descent. In "The Problem of Employment for Negro Women," she analyzed their restricted opportunities and the ways in which they could respond with dignity and ingenuity to the domestic labor available, while
also suggesting how to ameliorate this occupational disaster. Cogently stat-
ing her view, she accurately anticipated that many people would misunder-
stand her intent:

> I do not wish to be understood as advocating the restriction of colored girls
> to house service, even when that service is elevated to the rank of a profes-
> sion. My only plea is that we shall protect and respect our girls who honestly
> and intelligently enter this service, either from preference or necessity.
>
> It seems to me that we lose a great opportunity if we fail to take hold of
> this problem in a thoroughly broad and philosophic way and work out its
> solution.

Williams was not advocating Washington's position: acceptance of a restrictive, low status. She rather argued on behalf of a survival technique
and an intellectual and philosophical approach to broaden the options for
women who were restricted in their choices. With sophisticated theoretical
reasoning, she called on Henry Thoreau's self-discipline as a model for human growth and dignity during times of injustice.

Her article on "The Woman's Part in a Man's Business" strongly reiter-
ated that African American women are the most interesting women in
America because the world stands before them. Women and men in this
community, for example, did not suffer from the burden of patriarchy justified by most western ethnic groups. Both sexes in the African American
community were emancipated together and started from the same historical
and social location: "It is because of this equality of condition and training
that colored women are destined to share more intimately in the management of Negro business enterprises, than is true of any other class of
women." Williams may have been writing of her own marriage and her contributions to her husband's career in this well-articulated and fervent piece.

Many scholars, as noted earlier, argue that Williams was an elitist, and
some would say that her concern with "better people" in her early writings
reflects such a bias. But there is less justification for these assertions in
Williams's later writings. Her discussion of "The Colored Girl" reveals her
sensitivity to young women who work in unskilled positions, often at the
mercy of employers, especially those who are white men. She aptly summarized these positions for women at the bottom of the social scale.

The colored girl may have character, beauty and charms ineffable, but she is not in vogue. The muses of song, poetry and art do not woo and exalt her. She is not permitted or supposed to typify the higher ideals that make life something higher, sweeter and more spiritual than a mere existence. Man's instinctive homage at the shrine of womankind draws a line of color, which places her forever outside its mystic circle.

The white manhood of America sustains no kindly or respectful feeling for the colored girl; great nature has made her what she is, and the laws of men have made for her a class below the level of other women. The women of other races bask in the clear sunlight of man's chivalry, admiration, and even worship, while the colored woman abides in the shadow of his contempt, mistrust or indifference.

In "Colored Women of Chicago," written in 1914, Williams supports an underpaid and underemployed *class:*

> the women who work with their hands in the humbler walks of life, as cooks, housecleaners, laundresses, caretakers, and domestics. One of the most interesting sights in our public streets in the early morning hours is the large army of colored women going in all directions to do their day's work. These women deserve great credit for their eager willingness to aid their husbands in helping to provide a living for themselves and their families.

As in earlier writings, Williams consistently advocated the work of clubwomen and their organizations. She particularly mentioned that in Chicago the "most important undertaking among colored women is the establishment of the Phyllis Wheatley Home." Williams was a member of its board, organized and led by Elisabeth Lindsay Davis, another lifelong friend of Williams. In 1914, Chicago women won the municipal franchise, and Williams saw this as a victory for the growing civil rights of both women and African Americans. She anticipated that this would "lift colored women to new importance as citizens." Women's experience in clubs and social settlements, moreover, would help them combat racism and sexism.

AFRICAN AMERICAN LIFE AND CULTURE   Williams's 1893 speech on "Religious Duty to the Negro" at the *Parliament of Religions* was even more militant and uncompromising than her address to the Woman's Congress. She calls to account the complicity of white Christians in the practice of slavery and their attempts to make slaves docile and accepting of injustice. She praises, however, the deep spirituality of the Africans, thereby noting the effect of African culture on this aspect of daily and institutional life. "Religious duty" is a strength established by the African American women who had a wider role here than any other group. African American women demonstrated this powerful community voice through their participation and leadership in the *World's Congress of Religion,* at which Williams,

Early, and seven other African American women spoke (Massa 1974). Williams tartly ended her speech there with a call for more religious—and less church—action.

Williams defended the need for industrial education in an important national debate, noted earlier. In this debate, Williams criticized both "academic biases" that opposed manual labor—referring implicitly to the position of DuBois—and "advocates of Industrial Education who insist that nothing else will solve the race problem"—referring explicitly to Washington's position. Industrial education is not the opposite of liberal education, she argued, but includes history, sociology, chemistry, and other forms of knowledge (Williams 1904a, 492). Women need such education as much as the men, who were the usual focus of discussion.

Williams noted the special problems inherent in the education of African Americans: illiteracy and restricted opportunities. Given her familiarity with teaching in the South, she was well positioned for this analysis. Teaching the despairing masses, she argued, did not negate the training of professionals, artists, and leaders. "The doors of the universities are always open to the few who have the gifts and tastes for scholarship" (Williams 1904a, 495), for as DuBois (1903b) noted these are "the talented tenth." Williams once again supported both the poor and the elite and argued for a democratic community built on education for all. Again she echoed the positions of feminist pragmatists on vocational education. But this particular issue is so identified in the African American community with Washington that comparisons with the positions of other intellectuals and community leaders on this issue are often lacking.

Williams also wrote a number of insightful articles on everyday life and culture. Here she analyzed the brutal impact of racial discrimination on African Americans and often provided at least a brief note of criticism toward her community. These trenchant and hard-hitting writings were dismissively and inaccurately summarized by Marilyn Lamping (1982, 433) as follows: "While a large part of her writing is concerned with advocacy for blacks, particularly women, as a well-educated, genteel woman writing at the turn of the century, W.[illiams] also wrote articles reviewing books, discussing art, advocating travel, and exploring domestic matters." Lamping suggests that these latter essays were not about women or blacks or racial justice, but reflected "ladylike," shallow, and conservative views. Her interpretation is incorrect.

These same topics are covered in a series of articles in *The Voice of the Negro,* reprinted in this volume. In "Do We Need Another Name?" Williams poses the provocative question of how to respond to the numerous efforts to create a respectful and dignified name for blacks. She cites DuBois as favoring the word "Negro" and Dr. A. R. Abbott[31] as favoring the word "Afro-American." Williams, however, favors "colored," which is less specific but more inclusive. "Colored" was also the word chosen by Mary Church Terrell (1940) in her autobiography, *A Colored Woman in a White*

World (1940); by the members of the National Association of Colored Women; and by the founders of the National Association for the Advancement of Colored People, so Williams was not alone in her preference for this nomenclature. Her choice of the word is reflected in the title of this book.

"Public opinion" is critiqued by Williams in many of her writings. It stands for a generalized belief that the everyday person holds to be true or just, even when it is wrong and unjust. Public opinion emerges from a general social process subject to change in response to rational debate and progressive actions. It is the subject of her essay "The Negro and Public Opinion," but the concept appears in her speech at the Colombian Exhibition and in her discussions of domestic labor, art, and the leadership of Susan B. Anthony.

Similarly, "The Smaller Economies" deals with both domestic labor and its professionalization in home economics. The topic was of interest to many women in this era—especially feminist pragmatists, who supported "civic housekeeping" (Rynbrandt 1999) in order to combine traditional female values with a job in the marketplace. It was the topic of a large meeting of women held in Chicago in 1904, at which time Henrotin was again president of the CWC. A committee was appointed to help plan this conference on "Woman in the Industrial, Social, Professional and Home Life," and on 30 April 1904, it reported on its fruitful work (Frank and Jerome 1916, 235–36). Williams enthusiastically commented in "An Extension of the Conference Spirit" that this interracial conference was a resounding success, including the presentation of her own paper on "The Problem of Employment for Negro Women."

In "Vacation Values," Williams stressed the importance of travel for African Americans, whose ability to do so was restricted by Jim Crow laws on transportation. Although undertaking a journey was difficult, the very fact of doing so created conditions that dramatically increased the benefits of travel. Vacations can be a way to experience more liberating environments, learn new ideas, and forge new friendships: "It may be a World Congress in London, England, a Chautauqua in Iowa, or a National Assembly of Educators in New Jersey" (Williams 1905, 864) that opens the mind to greater freedom. Meeting new people is enjoyable, and it expands personal horizons and interracial interactions.

In the "Refining Influence of Art," Williams discusses the CWC's program (first established at Hull-House) creating lending libraries of art. This innovation was adopted later by the Art Institute of Chicago and then nationally by public libraries. Williams advocated selecting art that celebrated the everyday life of blacks and recommended the work of Jean Francois Millet,[32] who studied the poor in France. Having formally studied at the School of Fine Arts in Washington, D.C., Williams was speaking as an authority with advanced training and not as a woman who dabbled in genteel interests. Although Williams advocated the display of high art (which some consider an elitist position), that is precisely what art experts advocate.

SOCIAL SETTLEMENTS   As a guiding figure and voice for African American and biracial social settlements in Chicago and around the nation, Williams's invaluable documentation of these organizations provides the best information now available on this broad network. She was involved, furthermore, with social settlements in the predominantly white ethnic neighborhoods around Hull-House and the University of Chicago Social Settlement. She also worked tirelessly for the interracial FDC and more sporadically for the Abraham Lincoln Centre. At the latter settlement, her interests were associated with those of her husband and with her church membership at the Unitarian All Souls Church, which founded the Abraham Lincoln Centre. Williams promoted the FDC in a series of articles, as well as in a moving eulogy to Celia Parker Woolley, the head of the FDC and her lifelong personal friend.

THE FREDERICK DOUGLASS CENTRE   The Frederick Douglass Centre became a focus for Williams's ideas and work—from its planning in 1903—until 1918, when Woolley died. In 1918 it became part of the Wendell Phillips Social Settlement (WPSS), and the FDC building was established as the headquarters of the National Urban League in Chicago. The WPSS, in turn, closed down about 1925. Williams also devoted her energy and time to the Phyllis Wheatley Center headed by her friend Elizabeth Lindsay Davis (see items 18 and 19 in part IV), but Williams wrote most frequently about the FDC and played a central and continuous role there. At one point, Williams (1904c, 505) used the sobriquet, "the black Hull House," for the FDC to underline its importance and to show that it was modeled after "the finest, the most typical, and most complete example of socialized kindness to be found in the world" (Williams 1904c, 503). This epistemological claim is one of many links between Williams and the feminist pragmatism of Addams and other Hull-House sociologists.

Williams also discussed the FDC in a short response to a yellow journalist's hysterical interpretation of black and white women drinking tea together. Williams tried to explain how the goals of a social settlement differ from the intent of civil rights groups like the Afro-American Council or the Niagara Conference. She subtitled her article, "A Question of Social Betterment and Not Social Equality," to emphasize the distinctions between the neighborly, social basis of settlement work and the more formal, political, and legal goals of civil rights groups. Her article analyzed the social meaning of Jim Crow in Chicago and the resistance to it through the nonviolent act of black and white women drinking tea. Unfortunately, some contemporary scholars interpreted this article as an indication that Williams opposed social protest groups, which she did not. "The Frederick Douglass Centre" was again the topic in two more articles for the Southern Workman in 1906, reprinted here.

CHICAGO'S AFRICAN AMERICAN SOCIAL SETTLEMENTS AND INSTITUTIONS   Although Williams usually wrote about Chicago social settlements, she authored a significant theoretical article on "The Need of Social Settlement Work for the City Negro." A version of this speech was followed by a lengthy, unsigned, national overview of black social settlements published in the 1905 *Proceedings of the Hampton Negro Conference*. Written either by Williams, a committee, or some other person, it is not included here because of the ambiguity of its authorship. A shorter version retained its theoretical section and was reprinted in the *Southern Workman*, where it reached a national audience, and this version is included here.

In another major article, Williams discussed the institutional structure generating "Social Bonds in the 'Black Belt' of Chicago." Explaining the priority of the church as a community institution, she also noted the significance of secret societies and the influence of social settlements. She again discussed the FDC and the Trinity Mission, founded by the Chicago sociologist Richard R. Wright, Jr. Her institutional analysis of the south-side black community is a high point in the Hull-House school of race relations (Deegan 2000b).

THE EXCELLENT BECOMES THE PERMANENT: WILLIAMS'S EU-LOGIES FOR WHITE FRIENDS Eulogies were often a formal art form during the Victorian and Progressive eras, perfected by the eloquence of Jane Addams (1932) as a funeral orator who celebrated the departed's social contributions to the community. Williams participated in this social tradition when she honored three white friends after their deaths: Philip Armour, for his employment of black workers in the meatpacking industry and his support of Chicago's Provident Hospital; Celia Parker Woolley, for her lifelong commitment to social justice and civil rights; and Susan B. Anthony, for her commitment to blacks and women.[33] Such funeral orations were a common pattern among social reformers

All these eulogies document important interracial cooperation that has either been understudied or forgotten. Several books, for example, analyze the failure of meatpackers to hire black workers (the most important is Herbst (1932), but only Williams noted the significance of Armour in resisting such discrimination. Armour also founded the Armour Institute that supported the professionalization of women's work in the home and in domestic life. Williams and other feminist pragmatists were profoundly interested in this process (see her essays on the "Colored Women of Chicago" and the "Conference Spirit"). In addition, Armour was financially generous to the interracial training program at Provident Hospital, mentioned above.

Williams "paid touching tribute in behalf of the colored people" (Williams 1907, 203) in her eulogy for Susan B. Anthony, delivered at the annual meeting of the National American Woman Suffrage Association (NAWSA) in 1907. Harper reprinted only a portion of this speech in her 1922 compilation of *The History of Woman Suffrage*. Perhaps a fuller record of this eulogy will be found as scholarship on Williams increases.

Ida B. Wells-Barnett (1970, 225–31, 279–88) considered Woolley and Anthony to be, if not racist, at best lacking in commitment to blacks. Williams, however, was able to show a very distinct facet of their dedication to blacks, especially to black women.[34] Woolley, moreover, was honored and respected by other African American Chicagoans, for example, Elizabeth Lindsay Davis (1918; 1922, 66–67), and Dr. George C. Hall (1918) from the Chicago branch of the NAACP. Woolley and Williams enjoyed a deep friendship spanning the 1893 World's Fair, the CWC nomination, and the Frederick Douglass Centre, along with its women's club. Only Woolley's death severed their tie.

Her Later Years, 1921–1944

After S. Laing Williams died in 1921, the public roles and activities of Fannie Barrier Williams decreased. By this time she was seventy-six years old, and the aging and mourning processes can at least partially account for her decline. In addition, she probably missed her friends, who were also aging, retiring, or dying. In 1920, women generally celebrated the achievement of suffrage, but Williams's white colleagues at Hull-House and the University of Chicago became the subject of red-baiting and social ostracism during most of this decade (A. Davis 1973; Deegan 1988a, 1991). The centrality of these women to sociology through social settlement work declined, too, and the golden era for African American women in sociology was simultaneously eclipsed.

Williams still had one major accomplishment ahead of her. In 1924, she was appointed to the Chicago Public Library Board, becoming the first woman and the first African American to hold this position. In 1926, she resigned from the board and returned to Brockport, New York, to reside with her sister. They lived together until Williams died on 4 March 1944 at the age of eighty-nine. She was laid to rest in the Barrier family plot.

CONCLUSION

Fannie Barrier Williams was a leader, an orator, an intellectual, and a sociologist. Her experiences as an African American who viewed life in the North, the Midwest, and the South, and in urban and smalltown America, provide an astonishingly wide perspective on the Unites States and the African American community. Grounded in Chicago with its rapid social change, structural dislocations, labor agitation, and exhilarating energy, Williams created an impressive set of writings on the vital issues of her day that bear the impress of her life in that city from 1887 to 1926. These writings continue to shed light on controversial issues—for example, is it more effective to work separately as a group of African Americans or to cooperate with whites in the move toward integration? Is it better to cherish biracial or multiracial identities or to prefer African American identity for any descendant of the African diaspora? Is it better to work for social change through a popular "correct" position or to try for intellectual and political independence? Is it better to recognize class and leadership differences or stress unity? Williams was clearly a person of multiple racial and regional heritages trying to articulate a new vision for the "new Negro" and the "new woman." While addressing a multidimensional audience of all classes, races, and genders, she found a powerful voice and added a new direction to our understanding of these issues and topics. She was a feminist pragmatist who worked with a number of social settlements, especially with Hull-House and the Frederick Douglass Centre. Although Williams was neither a saint nor a perfect woman, she was an important voice from Chicago: a voice worth knowing and reading.

Williams juggled the Victorian demands for moral women, in the face of scurrilous racist attacks against "immoral" African American women, the predominant cult of true womanhood, and the Doctrine of Separate Spheres. When Williams defended married African American women in a Victorian, upper-middle-class society, she sometimes sounded elitist, but these women—although they were leaders in their beleaguered communities—had few allies. Williams's middle-class emphasis also emerged from her position as part of the talented tenth. She often crossed class lines, however, and supported women who engaged in manual labor for low wages while they struggled against gigantic barriers to economic independence.

Williams was part of a long tradition of "neo-abolitionist" Chicagoans, who continued the work of Lincoln in a new age. She and many of her like-minded friends—Addams, Jones, Woolley, and McDowell—not only built branches of national civil rights organizations but often supported both the NAACP—advocated by DuBois—and the NUL—advocated by Washington's allies. As Williams and her husband shared in this vital work, they—and other Chicagoans both black and white—avoided the dichotomous choice of supporting either vocational education or higher education, embodied in the leadership of Washington or DuBois. This Chicago view of race relations is a rich tradition unexplored by most scholars of American race relations, and Williams gives a voice to this view.

African American women like Williams played a vital role in sociology through their lives of resistance, their writings on women and race relations, their organization of women's clubs, and their accomplishments in blending family and social claims. Although their work has been obscured by the Gendered Veil in sociology, African American women made substantial contributions to the discipline, to their families and communities, and to the wider society. The golden era of African American women in sociology was created by these pioneers, who generated a noble tradition that remains virtually unexplored. Chicago was the center of this worldwide movement, and the women of Hull-House were the stars in the network of applied sociologists. Williams's crucial role in this effort was to link the networks of white women, African American women, and African

American men. The women of this group were strongly influenced by the white men who were active in the Chicago school of sociology, an enterprise that these women had also helped establish (Deegan 1988a; 1991; 1996a; 1997; Lengermann and Niebrugge-Brantley 1998). This group of female sociologists has been neglected in the annals of sociology and misunderstood by scholars in women's studies, black studies, history, and American studies. It is unsurprising that Williams shared their scholarly fate. Although Williams could be conservative when discussing the role and life of the elite African American wife, particularly in the 1890s, she was a challenging intellectual, often shaped by the gendered, racial, and class lines surrounding her. It is not her flaws that fascinate me: it is her frequent transcendence of her own limits that is exciting. This volume is a step toward presenting her voice from Chicago to a contemporary, national audience.

Williams inspires us with her courage and eloquence. Her plea before an assembly of predominantly white women at the World's Columbian Exhibition in 1893 remains a haunting unanswered call to justice:

> When you learn that womanhood everywhere among us is blossoming out into greater fullness of everything that is sweet, beautiful, and good in woman; when you learn that the bitterness of our experience as citizen-women has not hardened our finer feelings of love and pity for our enemies; when you learn that fierce opposition to the widening spheres of our employment has not abated the aspirations of our women to enter successfully into all the professions and arts open only to intelligence, and that everywhere in the wake of enlightened womanhood our women are seen and felt for the good they diffuse, this Congress will at once see the fullness of our fellowship and help us to avert the arrows of prejudice that pierce the soul because of the color of our bodies (item 2, p. 95).

NOTES

1. Williams's dream preceded that of Martin Luther King, Jr., but there are many similarities in their arguments and views. I refer here particularly to King's (1986, 218–20) stirring "I Have a Dream" speech delivered at the March on Washington on 28 August 1963.

2. The first name was spelled "Phyllis" on the letterhead of the group, although the correct spelling is "Phillis" (see Shields 1993).

3. I hope that more of her papers and correspondence will be found as she becomes better known. No archival deposits for Fannie Barrier Williams are noted in the archival program RLIN or the *Manuscript Collections Indexed in the National Union Catalogue*. Two of her letters are included in the published papers of Booker T. Washington, and S. Laing Williams briefly mentions her in his published correspondence to Washington. See the *Booker*

T. Washington Papers, 14 vols., ed. by Louis Harlan (1972–1989).

4. Anne Knupfer (1996) also found this to be the case in her study of African American women's clubs in Chicago (Knupfer did not explore Williams in any depth). My examination of the Ida B. Wells-Barnett papers in the Special Collections Research Center of the Regenstein Library at the University of Chicago revealed no papers of Williams. Furthermore, her relationship to Wells-Barnett is rarely discussed in the literature on Wells-Barnett. Linda O. McMurry (1998) briefly considers Williams and portrays her negatively. The very small collection on Elizabeth Lindsay Davis and the Phyliss Wheatley organizations in the Department of Special Collections at the library of the University of Illinois at Chicago contains no papers on Williams. No archive exists for the Frederick Douglass Centre, although some early letters—primarily from the 1890s—between Woolley and Jenkin Lloyd Jones are in the Jones papers in the special collections at the Regenstein Library; no references to Williams are found there, however. Several biographical entries on Fannie Barrier Williams exist, and I use them extensively here. Generally they rely on her autobiography, but make the erroneous assumption that she became a strict follower of Washington after 1900.

No archival collection for S. Laing Williams exists either. For his correspondence with Booker T. Washington see note 3 above. Several useful items are found in his "Necrology" file at the University of Michigan.

5. For more background readings on the movement see *The Transcendentalists,* edited by Perry Miller (1950). Cornel West (1989) traces Emerson's work, including his ideas on African Americans, and its connection to the pragmatist movement. West's analysis could extend fruitfully to Williams's writings.

6. He is called "Laing" in some publications and "S. Laing" in others. The latter name is used here.

7. Williams's obituary in the *Chicago Defender* stated that he was the first African American to graduate from the University of Michigan. This honor goes to Gabriel Hargo, however, who graduated from the Law Department there in 1870. My thanks to Karen L. Jania of the Bentley Library, the University of Michigan, for supplying this information.

8. Chicagoans knew that the frontier had moved west long before 1887, but many people from the East saw Chicago as wild and untamed at that time. Marion Talbot's (1936) friends, for example, feared for her life when she left Boston in 1892 to take a job at the newly opened University of Chicago. The World's Columbian Exposition in 1893 was instrumental in making Chicago an important, recognized urban center.

9. Spear (1967, 66) claims that the partnership of Williams and Barnett lasted only "for a short time," and that Barnett had become "a bitter ideological foe" (p. 68) by 1904.

10. S. Laing Williams was appointed in 1908 and was "discharged a year later, but Washington arranged for his re-appointment" (Spear 1967, 68), which lasted until 1912.

11. Ida B. Wells-Barnett held distinct opinions, too. She was a strong

opponent of Washington and she did not trust DuBois.

12. Eliza Ann Starr—artist, educator, and aunt of the cofounder of Hull-House, Ellen Gates Starr—led a group called the "Queen Isabella Society" that lobbied unsuccessfully against the Doctrine of the Separate Spheres. The society wanted the role of women to be equal to that for men at the fair and asked that this idea guide the Lady Managers (see Adams 1994, Cushwa-Leighton Library, College Archives, Saint Mary's College, Notre Dame, Indiana).

13. Brown (1892) wrote a letter of protest lamenting the lack of a separate African American representative at the fair. Her own participation at the event (Brown 1894) indicates a later response by the white female organizers. Wells-Barnett published Brown's letter in 1893 in a pamphlet she distributed at the fair.

14. I include all the major and nonredundant nonfiction writings I could locate, including book chapters and newspapers articles, here. I have not cited her one fictional piece, "After Many Days: A Christmas Story" (1902b). This short story has many didactic features, but exhibits a different intent and style from her nonfiction writings. I examined all issues of the *Southern Workman* (1899–1922) and the *Voice of the Negro* (1904–1907), as well as portions of the *Colored American* that were available to me on microfilm.

15. This phrase appears in the title *A New Negro for a New Century*. The publisher, J.E. MacBrady, apparently chose the title. The author of this work, however, is difficult to determine. It was published first in 1900 as written by Washington, and it became popularized as a book by him. In fact, Washington wrote only one extensive section and it seems that MacBrady, who compiled the readings, wanted to profit from Washington's name. After Washington protested this use of his name, a new edition listed Washington, Norman Barton Wood, and Fannie Barrier Williams as coauthors. I use Washington as the author here because it became known as Washington's book. This "fact" influenced later scholars to mark 1900 as the point at which Williams became a supporter of Washington and was thus no longer a radical.

Alain Locke (see 1925) defined this concept very differently in the 1920s when it characterized the literary and intellectual movement called the Harlem Renaissance (see also Andrews 1994).

16. This definition combines my earlier terms "critical pragmatism" and "cultural feminism." "Critical pragmatism" applies knowledge to everyday problems based on radical interpretations of liberal and progressive values. "Cultural feminism" assumes the superiority of traditionally defined feminine values over traditional masculine values (Deegan 1988a, 25 (quotes), 225–308).

Feminist pragmatism is linked to the "Chicago school of sociology," the "Chicago school of symbolic interactionism," and the "Chicago school of race relations." The proliferation of "Chicago schools" and the gendered nature of these labels is simplified by the more encompassing concept "feminist pragmatism." The latter term is useful to scholars across disciplines for making distinctions between cultural, radical, Marxist, and/or liberal feminism. For example, Charlene Haddock Seigfried (1991, 1996) observes that feminist pragmatism stresses the union of realism and idealism, symbols and behavior, public and private life, and the mind and the body.

17. I cannot go into the fascinating issue of intellectual precedence here, but I offer a few speculations about how the emergence of feminist pragmatism occurred. Perhaps Williams read Harvard pragmatists who were active in the 1880s. She did read Addams and the rudiments of this approach were established by 1893, so this might have been an influence, or perhaps the speeches of Williams influenced Addams. Another possible influence is that of the Transcendentalists (West 1989), who may have influenced both Williams and other pragmatists in similar ways.

18. Williams does not mention the Baptist women in her discussions of African American women's club work, an apt criticism raised by Salem (1990).

19. Other women in this group were Janie Porter Barrett (1865–1948); Lugenia Burns Hope (1871–1947); and Margaret Murray Washington (ca. 1865–1925). While Williams probably knew all of these women, the three mentioned here directly impacted her writings.

20. These characteristics blend the ideas of Collins (1990); Lengermann and Niebrugge-Brantley (1998); and Deegan (1988a, 1991, 1996a, 1996b, 1997).

21. Dirk Käsler (see Deegan 1988a, 9) established a set of criteria for determining who is and is not a sociologist. Fulfilling only one of these criteria is sufficient to be considered a sociologist.

22. My thanks to Connie Frey for providing this information.

23. The legal elimination of slavery occurred in 1863 with the Emancipation Proclamation, but many slaves remained in bondage until freed by Union soldiers at the end of the Civil War in 1865.

24. A notable exception to this abolitionist heritage was the family of Sophonisba Breckinridge: her grandfather was the vice president of the Confederacy. See James C. Klotter (1981) for a thorough discussion of this large and politically powerful family.

25. Giddings (1984, 171) wrote: "The White advocates of interracial cooperation did not have 'integration' in mind, or even 'separate but equal.'" Her characterization of white women does not apply to Addams, Woolley, and McDowell.

26. Wells-Barnett's (1970) autobiography is often vague, so 1907 is a conservative guess. Wells-Barnett wrote that a term of the first presidency had been completed; this may have been two or three years. She also wrote, however, that the FDC declined after she left it. Since Woolley died in 1918, perhaps Wells-Barnett was active for a period longer than 1904 to 1907.

27. See explanation in note 15.

28. For an often moving account of daily life in the South and the problems of illiteracy, see Charles S. Johnson (1934).

29. A number of protests, including Brown's, over the treatment of white women were published in African American newspapers and can now be found on www.binghamton.edu/~womhist.

30. Although Williams includes pictures of these women in both chapters, most of the images are widely available now. See for example, *Black Women In America,* 2 vols. (1993).

31. Abbott is described in Washington (1900, 143) as a prominent physician who was "One of the Eight Colored Surgeons Commissioned as Surgeon in the United States Army by President Lincoln."

32. Jean Francois Millet (1814–1875), famous for his paintings of peasants, is represented by numerous pastels and other works in the collections of the Museum of Fine Arts, Boston. Williams studied art at this institution.

33. Jenkin Lloyd Jones, Williams's minister and a close friend of Woolley, also delivered a eulogy on this occasion (see Harper 1922, 203–4).

34. Terrell (1940) also shared Williams's respect for Anthony, which indicates potential network ties among these three women.

THE NEW WOMAN OF COLOR

Part One

· AUTOBIOGRAPHY ·

ONE

A NORTHERN NEGRO'S AUTOBIOGRAPHY

(The three articles that we printed in *The Independent* last March[1] [1904] called forth more replies than any articles we have recently published. We were obliged to reject all of them, however, except the following, which discusses a phase of the negro problem not touched upon by the three anonymous women, and often generally overlooked by the American people. This article therefore supplements the others, and the four taken together picture the negro problem from the feminine standpoint in the most genuine and realistic manner shown in any articles we have seen in print.

—EDITOR [of *The Independent*])

In *The Independent* of March 17th last, I read, with a great deal of interest, three contributions to the so-called race problem, to be found in the experiences of a Southern colored woman, a Southern white woman and a Northern white woman.

I am a Northern colored woman, a mulatto in complexion, and was born since the war[2] in a village town of Western New York. My parents and grandparents were free people. My mother was born in New York State and my father in Pennsylvania. They both attended the common schools and were fairly educated. They had a taste for good books and the refinements of life, were public spirited and regarded as good citizens. My father moved to this Western New York village when he was quite a boy and was a resident of the town for over fifty years; he was married to my mother in this town and three children were born to them; he created for himself a good business and was able to take good care of his family. My parents were strictly religious people and were members of one of the largest white churches in the village. My father, during his membership in this church, held successively almost every important office open to a layman, having been clerk, trustee, treasurer and deacon, which office he held at the time of his death, in 1890. He was for years teacher of an adult Bible class composed of some of the best men and women of the village, and my mother is still a teacher of a large Bible class of women in the same Sunday school. Ours was the only colored family in the church, in fact, the only one in the town for many years, and certainly there could not have

"A Northern Negro's Autobiography," *Independent* 57 (14 July 1904): 91–96.

been a relationship more cordial, respectful and intimate than that of our family and the white people of this community. We three children were sent to school as soon as we were old enough, and remained there until we were graduated. During our school days our associates, schoolmates and companions were all white boys and girls. These relationships were natural, spontaneous and free from all restraint. We went freely to each other's houses, to parties, socials, and joined on equal terms in all school entertainments with perfect comradeship. We suffered from no discriminations on account of color or "previous condition," and lived in blissful ignorance of the fact that we were practicing the unpardonable sin of "social equality." Indeed, until I became a young woman and went South to teach I had never been reminded that I belonged to an "inferior race."

After I was graduated from school my first ambition was to teach. I could easily have obtained a position there at my own home, but I wanted to go out into the world and do something large or out of the ordinary. I had known of quite a number of fine young white women who had gone South to teach the freedmen, and, following my race instinct, I resolved to do the same. I soon obtained a situation in one of the ex-slave States. It was here and for the first time that I began life as a colored person, in all that that term implies. No one but a colored woman, reared and educated as I was, can ever know what it means to be brought face to face with conditions that fairly overwhelm you with the ugly reminder that a certain penalty must be suffered by those who, not being able to select their own parentage, must be born of a dark complexion. What a shattering of cherished ideals! Everything that I learned and experienced in my innocent social relationships in New York State had to be unlearned and readjusted to these lowered standards and changed conditions. The Bible that I had been taught, the preaching I had heard, the philosophy and ethics and the rules of conduct that I had been so sure of, were all to be discounted. All truth seemed here only half truths. I found that, instead of there being a unity of life common to all intelligent, respectable and ambitious people, down South life was divided into white and black lines, and that in every direction my ambitions and aspirations were to have no beginnings and no chance for development. But, in spite of all this, I tried to adapt myself to these hateful conditions. I had some talent for painting, and in order to obtain further instruction I importuned a white art teacher to admit me into one of her classes, to which she finally consented, but on the second day of my appearance in the class I chanced to look up suddenly and was amazed to find that I was completely surrounded by screens, and when I resented the apparent insult, it was made the condition of my remaining in the class. I had missed the training that would have made this continued humiliation possible; so at a great sacrifice I went to a New England city [Boston], but even here, in the very cradle of liberty, white Southerners were there before me, and to save their feelings I was told by the principal of the school, a man who was descended from a long line of abolition ancestors, that it would imperil the interests of the school if I remained, as all of his Southern pupils would leave, and again I had to submit to the tyranny of a dark complexion. But it is scarcely possible to enumerate the many ways in which an ambitious colored young woman is prevented from being all that she might be in the higher directions of life in this country. Plainly I would have been far happier as a woman if my life up to the age of eighteen years had not been so free, spontaneous and unhampered by race prejudice. I have still many white friends and the old home and school associations are still sweet and delightful and always renewed with pleasure, yet I have never quite recovered from the shock and pain of my first bitter realization that to be a colored woman is to be discredited, mistrusted and often meanly hated. My faith in the verities of religion, in justice, in love, and in many sacredly taught sentiments has greatly decreased since I have learned how little even these stand for when you are a colored woman.

After teaching a few years in the South, I went back to my home in New York State to be married. After the buffetings, discouragements and discourtesies that I had been compelled to endure, it was almost as in a dream that I saw again my schoolmates gather around me, making my home beautiful with flowers, managing every detail of preparation for my wedding, showering me with gifts, and joining in the ceremony with tears and blessings. My own family and my husband were the only persons to lend color to the occasion. Minister, attendants, friends, flowers and hearts were of the purest white. If this be social equality, it certainly was not of my own seeking and I must say that no one seemed harmed by it. It seemed all a simple part of the natural life we lived where people are loved and respected for their worth, in spite of their darker complexions.

After my marriage my husband and I moved to one of the larger cities of the North, where we have continued to live. In this larger field of life and action I found myself, like many another woman, becoming interested in many things that come within the range of a woman's active sympathy and influence.

My interest in various reform work, irrespective of color, led me frequently to join hand in hand with white women on a common basis of fellowship and helpfulness extended to all who needed our sympathy and interest. I experienced very few evidences of race prejudice and perhaps had more than my share of kindness and recognition. However, this kindness to me as an individual did not satisfy me or blind me to the many inequalities suffered by young colored women seeking employment and other advantages of metropolitan life. I soon discovered that it was much easier for progressive white women to be considerate and even companionable to one colored woman whom they chanced to know and like than to be just and generous to colored young women as a race, who needed their sympathy and influence in securing employment and recognition according to their tastes and ability. To this end I began to use my influence and associations to further the cause of these helpless young colored women, in an effort to save them to themselves and society, by finding, for those who must work, suitable employment. How surprisingly difficult was my task may be seen in the following instances selected from many of like nature:

I was encouraged to call upon a certain bank president, well known for his broad, humane principles and high-mindedness. I told him what I wanted, and how I thought he could give me some practical assistance, and enlarged upon the difficulties that stand in the way of ambitious and capable young colored women. He was inclined to think, and frankly told me, that he thought I was a little over-stating the case, and added, with rather a triumphant air, so sure he was that I could not make good my statements as to ability, fitness, etc., "We need a competent stenographer right here in the bank now; if you will send to me the kind of a young colored woman you describe, that is thoroughly equipped, I think I can convince you that you are wrong." I ventured to tell him that the young woman I had in mind did not show much color. He at once interrupted me by saying, "Oh, that will not cut any figure; you send the young woman here." I did so and allowed a long time to elapse before going to see him again. When I did call, at the young woman's request, the gentleman said, with deep humiliation, "I am ashamed to confess, Mrs. —— [Williams], that you were right and I was wrong. I felt it my duty to say to the directors that this young woman had a slight trace of Negro blood. That settled it. They promptly said, 'We don't want her, that's all.'" He gave the names of some of the directors and I recognized one of them as a man of long prayers and a heavy contributor to the Foreign Mission Fund; another's name was a household word on account of his financial interest in Home Missions and Church extension work. I went back to the young woman and could but weep with her because I knew that she was almost in despair over the necessity of speedily finding something to do. The only consolation I could offer was that the president declared she was the most skillful and thoroughly competent young woman who had ever applied for the position.

I tried another large establishment and had a pleasant talk with the manager, who unwittingly committed himself to an overwhelming desire "to help the colored people." He said that his parents were staunch abolitionists and connected with the underground railway, and that he distinctly remembered that as a child he was not allowed to eat sugar that had been cultivated by the labor of the poor slave or to wear cotton manufactured by slave labor, and his face glowed as he told me how he loved his "black mammie," and so on *ad nauseam*. I began to feel quite elated at the correctness of my judgment in seeking him out of so many. I then said: "I see that you employ a large number of young women as clerks and stenographers. I have in mind some very competent young colored women who are almost on the verge of despair for lack of suitable employment. Would you be willing to try one of them should you have a vacancy?" The grayness of age swept over his countenance as he solemnly said: "Oh, I wish you had not asked me that question. My clerks would leave and such an innovation would cause a general upheaval in my business." "But," I said, "your clerks surely do not run your business!" "No," he said, "you could not understand." Knowing that he was very religious, my almost forgotten Bible training came to mind. I quoted Scripture as to "God being no respecter of persons," and reminded him that these young women were in moral danger through enforced idleness, and quoted the anathema of offending one of "these little ones" whom Christ loved. But he did not seem to fear at all condemnation from that high tribunal. His only reply was, "Oh, that is different," and I turned away, sadly thinking, "Is it different?"

This still remains a sad chapter in my experience, even though I have been successful in finding a few good positions for young colored women, not one of whom has ever lost her position through any fault of hers. On the contrary, they have become the prize workers wherever they have been employed. One of them became her employer's private secretary, and he told me with much enthusiasm that her place could scarcely be filled, she had become so efficient and showed such an intelligent grasp upon the requirements of the position. My plea has always been simply to give these girls a chance and let them stand or fall by any test that is not merely a color test.

I want to speak of one other instance. It sometimes happens that after I have succeeded in getting these girls placed and their competency has been proved, they are subjected to the most unexpected humiliations. A young woman of very refined and dignified appearance and with only a slight trace of African blood had held her position for some time in an office where she had been bookkeeper, stenographer and clerk, respectively, and was very highly thought of both by her employer and her fellow clerks. She was sitting at her desk one day when a man entered and asked for her employer. She told him to be seated, that Mr. ——— would be back in a moment. The man walked around the office, then came back to her and said: "I came from a section of the country where we make your people know their places. Don't you think you are out of yours?" She merely looked up and said, "I think I know my place." He strolled about for a moment, then came back to her and said: "I am a Southern man, I am, and I would like to know what kind of a man this is that employs a 'nigger' to sit at a desk and write." She replied: "You will find Mr. ——— a perfect gentleman." The proprietor came in, in a moment, and ushered the man into his private office. The Southern gentleman came out of the office very precipitately. It evidently only took him a few seconds to verify the clerk's words that "her employer was a perfect gentleman."

It may be plainly seen that public efforts of this kind and a talent for public speaking and writing would naturally bring to me a recognition and association independent of any self-seeking on my own account. It, therefore, seemed altogether natural that some of my white friends should ask me to make application for membership in a prominent woman's club on the ground of mutual helpfulness and mutual interest in many things. I allowed my name to be presented to the club without the slightest dream that it would cause any opposition or even discussion. This progressive club has a membership of over eight hundred women, and its personality fairly represents the wealth, intelligence and culture of the women of the city. When the members of this great club came to know the color of its new applicant there was a startled cry that seemed to have no bounds. Up to this time no one knew that there was any anti-Negro sentiment in the club. Its purposes were so humane and philanthropic and its grade of individual membership so high and inclusive of almost every nationality that my indorsers thought that my application would only be subject to the club's test of eligibility, which was declared to be "Character, intelligence and the reciprocal advantage to the club and the individual, without regard to race, color, religion or politics." For nearly fourteen months my application was fought by a determined minority. Other clubs throughout the country took up the matter, and the awful example was held up in such a way as to frighten many would-be friends. The whole anti-slavery question was fought over again in the same spirit and with the same arguments, but the common sense of the members finally prevailed over their prejudices. When the final vote was taken I was elected to membership by a decisive majority.

Before my admission into the club some of the members came to me and frankly told me that they would leave the club, much as they valued their membership, if I persisted in coming in. Their only reason was that they did not think the time had yet come for that sort of equality. Since my application was not of my own seeking I refused to recognize their unreasonable prejudices as something that ought to be fostered and perpetuated; besides, I felt that I owed something to the friends who had shown me such unswerving loyalty through all those long and trying months, when every phase of my public and private life was scrutinized and commented upon in a vain effort to find something in proof of my ineligibility. That I should possess any finer feeling that must suffer under this merciless persecution and unwelcome notoriety seemed not to be thought of by those who professed to believe that my presence in a club of eight hundred women would be at a cost of their fair self-respect. I cannot say that I have experienced the same kind of humiliations as recited in the pathetic story of a Southern colored woman in *The Independent* of March 17th [1904], but I can but believe that the prejudice that blights and hinders is quite as decided in the North as it is in the South, but does not manifest itself so openly and brutally.

Fortunately, since my marriage I have had but little experience south of Mason and Dixon's line. Some time ago I was induced by several clubs in different States and cities of the South to make a kind of lecture tour through that section. I knew, of course, of the miserable separations, "Jim Crow" cars, and other offensive restrictions and resolved to make the best of them. But the "Jim Crow" cars were almost intolerable to me. I was fortunate enough to escape them in every instance. There is such a cosmopolitan population in some of the Southwestern States, made up of

Spanish, Mexican and French nationalities, that the conductors are very often deceived; besides, they know that an insult can scarcely go further than to ask the wrong person if he or she be colored. I made it a rule always to take my seat in the first-class car, to which I felt I was entitled by virtue of my first-class ticket. However, adapting one's self to these false conditions does not contribute to one's peace of mind, self-respect, or honesty. I remember that at a certain place, I was too late to procure my ticket at the station, and the conductor told me that I would have to go out at the next station and buy my ticket, and then, despite my English book, which I was very ostentatiously reading, he stepped back and quickly asked me, "Madame, are you colored?" I as quickly replied, *"Je suis française."* *"Française?"* he repeated. I said, *"Oui."* He then called to the brakeman and said, "Take this lady's money and go out at the next station and buy her ticket for her," which he kindly did, and I as kindly replied as he handed me the ticket, *"Merci."* Fortunately their knowledge of French ended before mine did or there might have been some embarrassments as to my further unfamiliarity with my mother tongue. However, I quieted my conscience by recalling that there was quite a strain of French blood in my ancestry, and too that their barbarous laws did not allow a lady to be both comfortable and honest. It is needless to say that I traveled undisturbed in the cars to which my ticket entitled me after this success, but I carried an abiding heartache for the refined and helpless colored women who must live continuously under these repressive and unjust laws. The hateful interpretation of these laws is to make no distinction between the educated and refined and the ignorant and depraved Negro.

Again, the South seems to be full of paradoxes. In one city of the far South I was asked to address a club of very aristocratic white women, which I did with considerable satisfaction to myself because it gave me an opportunity to call the attention of these white women to the many cultured and educated colored women living right there in their midst, whom they did not know, and to suggest that they find some common ground of fellowship and helpfulness that must result in the general uplift of all women. These women gave me a respectful and appreciative hearing, and the majority of them graciously remained and received an introduction to me after the address. A curious feature of the meeting was that, although it had been announced in all the papers as a public meeting, not a colored person was present except myself, which shows how almost insurmountable a color line[3] can be.

In another city I had a very different experience, which betrayed my unconscious fear of the treachery of Southern prejudice, though following so closely upon the pleasant experience above related. I noticed, while on my way to the church where I was advertised to speak to a colored audience, that we were being followed by a half a dozen of what seemed to me the typical Southern "crackers," red shirt and all. I was not thinking of moonshiners, but of Ku-Klux clans [*sic*], midnight lynching parties, etc. My fears were further increased when they suddenly stopped and separated, so that my friends and I were obliged to pass between the lines of three so made. My friends tried to reassure me, but I fancied with trembling tones, and my menacing escort then closed up ranks and again followed on. Finally they beckoned to the only gentleman with us and asked him what I was going to talk about. He told them the subject and hastened to console me. When we got to the church and just before I rose to speak, these six men all filed in and sat down near the platform, accompanied by another individual even more fierce in appearance than they were, whom I afterward learned was the deputy sheriff of the town. My feelings are better imagined than described, but I found myself struggling to hold the attention only of this menacing portion of my audience. They remained to the close of the lecture and as they went out expressed appreciation of my "good sense," as they termed it.

This recital has no place in this article save to show the many contrasts a brief visit to the Southland is capable of revealing. It is only just to add that I have traveled in the first-class—that is, white—cars all through the South, through Texas, Georgia, and as far as Birmingham, Ala., but I have never received an insult or discourtesy from a Southern white man. While, fortunately, this has been my experience, still I believe that in some other localities in the South such an experience would seem almost incredible.

I want to refer briefly to the remarks of one of the writers in *The Independent* with reference to the character strength of colored women. I think it but just to say that we must look to American slavery as the source of every imperfection that mars the character of the colored American. It ought not to be necessary to remind a Southern woman that less than fifty years ago the ill-starred mothers of this ransomed race were not allowed to be modest, not allowed to follow the instincts of moral rectitude, and there was no living man to whom they could cry for protection against the men who not only owned them, body and soul, but also the souls of their husbands, their brothers, and, alas, their sons. Slavery made her the only woman in America for whom virtue was not an ornament and a necessity. But in spite of this dark and painful past, I believe that the sweeping assertions of this writer are grossly untrue and unjust at least to thousands of colored women in the North who were free from the debasing influence of slavery, as well as thousands of women in the South, who instinctively fought to preserve their own honor and that of their unfortunate offspring. I believe that the colored women are just as strong and just as weak as any other women with like education, training and environment.

It is a significant and shameful fact that I am constantly in receipt of letters from the still unprotected colored women of the South, begging me to find employment for their daughters according to their ability, as domestics or otherwise, to save them from going into the homes of the South as servants, as there is nothing to save them from dishonor and degradation. Many prominent white women and ministers will verify this statement.

The heartbroken cry of some of these helpless mothers bears no suggestion of the "flaunting pride of dishonor" so easily obtained, by simply allowing their daughters to enter the homes of the white women of the South. Their own mothers cannot protect them and white women will not, or do not. The moral feature of this problem has complications that it would seem better not to dwell on. From my own study of the question, the colored woman deserves greater credit for what she has done and is doing than blame for what she cannot so soon overcome.

As to the Negro problem,[4] the only thing one can be really sure of is that it has a beginning, and we know that it is progressing some way, but no one knows the end. Prejudice is here and everywhere, but it may not manifest itself so brutally as in the South. The chief interest in the North seems to be centered in business, and it is in business where race prejudice shows itself the strongest. The chief interest in the South is social supremacy; therefore prejudice manifests itself most strongly against even an imaginary approach to social contact. Here in the Northern States I find that a colored woman of character and intelligence will be recognized and respected, but the white woman who will recognize and associate with her in the same club or church would probably not tolerate her as a fellow clerk in an office or [shop].

The conclusion of the whole matter seems to be that whether I live in the North or the South, I cannot be counted for my full value, be that much or little. I dare not cease to hope and aspire and believe in human love and justice, but progress is painful and my faith is often strained to the breaking point.

Part Two

· AFRICAN AMERICAN WOMEN ·

Two

THE INTELLECTUAL PROGRESS OF THE COLORED WOMEN OF THE UNITED STATES SINCE THE EMANCIPATION PROCLAMATION

Less than thirty years ago the term progress as applied to colored women of African descent in the United States would have been an anomaly. The recognition of that term to-day as appropriate is a fact full of interesting significance. That the discussion of progressive womanhood in this great assemblage of the representative women of the world is considered incomplete without some account of the colored women's status is a most noteworthy evidence that we have not failed to impress ourselves on the higher side of American life.

Less is known of our women than of any other class of Americans.

No organization of far-reaching influence for their special advancement, no conventions of women to take note of their progress, and no special literature reciting the incidents, the events, and all things interesting and instructive concerning them are to be found among the agencies directing their career. There has been no special interest in their peculiar condition as native-born American women. Their power to affect the social life of America, either for good or for ill, has excited not even a speculative interest.

Though there is much that is sorrowful, much that is wonderfully heroic, and much that is romantic in a peculiar way in their history, none of it has as yet been told as evidence of what is possible for these women. How few of the happy, prosperous, and eager living Americans can appreciate what it all means to be suddenly changed from irresponsible bondage to the responsibility of freedom and citizenship!

The distress of it all can never be told, and the pain of it all can never be felt, except by the victims and by those saintly women of the white race who for thirty years have been consecrated to the uplifting of a whole race of women from a long-enforced degradation.

The American people have always been impatient of ignorance and poverty. They believe with Emerson[5] that "America is another word for opportunity," and for that reason success is a virtue and poverty and ignorance are inexcusable. This may account for the fact that our women have

The World's Congress of Representative Women, ed. Mary Wright Sewell (Chicago: Rand, McNally, 1894) 2: 696–711.

excited no general sympathy in the struggle to emancipate themselves from the demoralization of slavery. This new life of freedom, with its far-reaching responsibilities, had to be learned by these children of darkness mostly without a guide, a teacher, or a friend. In the mean vocabulary of slavery there was no definition of any of the virtues of life. The meaning of such precious terms as marriage, wife, family, and home could not be learned in a schoolhouse. The blue-back speller, the arithmetic, and the copy-book contain no magical cures for inherited inaptitudes for the moralities. Yet it must ever be counted as one of the most wonderful things in human history how promptly and eagerly these suddenly liberated women tried to lay hold upon all that there is in human excellence. There is a touching pathos in the eagerness of these millions of new homemakers to taste the blessedness of intelligent womanhood. The path of progress in the picture is enlarged so as to bring to view these trustful and zealous students of freedom and civilization striving to overtake and keep pace with women whose emancipation has been a slow and painful process for a thousand years. The longing to be something better than they were when freedom found them has been the most notable characteristic in the development of these women. This constant striving for equality has given an upward direction to all the activities of colored women.

Freedom at once widened their vision beyond the mean cabin life of their bondage. Their native gentleness, good cheer, and hopefulness made them susceptible to those teachings that make for intelligence and righteousness. Sullenness of disposition, hatefulness, and revenge against the master class because of two centuries of ill-treatment are not in the nature of our women.

But a better view of what our women are doing and what their present status is may be had by noticing some lines of progress that are easily verifiable.

First it should be noticed that separate facts and figures relative to colored women are not easily obtainable. Among the white women of the country, independence, progressive intelligence, and definite interests have done so much that nearly every fact and item illustrative of their progress and status is classified and easily accessible. Our women, on the contrary, have had no advantage of interests peculiar and distinct and separable from those of men that have yet excited public attention and kindly recognition.

In their religious life, however, our women show a progressiveness parallel in every important particular to that of white women in all Christian churches. It has always been a circumstance of the highest satisfaction to the missionary efforts of the Christian church that the colored people are so susceptible to a religion that marks the highest point of blessedness in human history.

Instead of finding witchcraft, sensual fetishes, and the coarse superstitions of savagery possessing our women, Christianity found them with

hearts singularly tender, sympathetic, and fit for the reception of its doctrines. Their superstitions were not deeply ingrained, but were of the
same sort and nature that characterize the devotees of the Christian faith
everywhere.

While there has been but little progress toward the growing rationalism
in the Christian creeds, there has been a marked advance toward a greater
refinement of conception, good taste, and the proprieties. It is our young
women coming out of the schools and academies that have been insisting
upon a more godly and cultivated ministry. It is the young women of a
new generation and new inspirations that are making tramps of the ministers who once dominated the colored church, and whose intelligence and
piety were mostly in their lungs. In this new and growing religious life the
colored people have laid hold of those sweeter influences of the King's
Daughters, of the Christian Endeavor and Helping Hand societies, which
are doing much to elevate the tone of worship and to magnify all that
there is blessed in religion.[6]

Another evidence of growing intelligence is a sense of religious discrimination among our women. Like the nineteenth century woman generally,
our women find congeniality in all the creeds, from the Catholic creed to
the no-creed of Emerson. There is a constant increase of this interesting variety in the religious life of our women.

Closely allied to this religious development is their progress in the work
of education in schools and colleges. For thirty years education has been
the magic word among the colored people of this country. That their greatest need was education in its broadest sense was understood by these people more strongly than it could be taught to them. It is the unvarying testi-
mony of every teacher in the South that the mental development of the
colored women as well as men has been little less than phenomenal. In
twenty-five years, and under conditions discouraging in the extreme, thousands of our women have been educated as teachers. They have adapted
themselves to the work of mentally lifting a whole race of people so eagerly and readily that they afford an apt illustration of the power of self-
help. Not only have these women become good teachers in less than
twenty-five years, but many of them are the prize teachers in the mixed
schools of nearly every Northern city.

These women have also so fired the hearts of the race for education that
colleges, normal schools, industrial schools, and universities have been
reared by a generous public to meet the requirements of these eager students of intelligent citizenship. As American women generally are fighting
against the nineteenth century narrowness that still keeps women out of the
higher institutions of learning, so our women are eagerly demanding the
best of education open to their race. They continually verify what President
[Jeremiah Eames] Rankin[7] of Howard University recently said, "Any theory
of educating the Afro-American that does not throw open the golden gates
of the highest culture will fail on the ethical and spiritual side."

It is thus seen that our women have the same spirit and mettle that characterize the best of American women. Everywhere they are following in the tracks of those women who are swiftest in the race for higher knowledge.

To-day they feel strong enough to ask for but one thing, and that is the same opportunity for the acquisition of all kinds of knowledge that may be accorded to other women. This granted, in the next generation these progressive women will be found successfully occupying every field where the highest intelligence alone is admissible. In less than another generation American literature, American art, and American music will be enriched by productions having new and peculiar features of interest and excellence.

The exceptional career of our women will yet stamp itself indelibly upon the thought of this country.

American literature needs for its greater variety and its deeper soundings that which will be written into it out of the hearts of these self-emancipating women.

The great problems of social reform that are now so engaging the highest intelligence of American women will soon need for their solution the reinforcement of that new intelligence which our women are developing. In short, our women are ambitious to be contributors to all the great moral and intellectual forces that make for the greater weal of our common country.

If this hope seems too extravagant to those of you who know these women only in their humbler capacities, I would remind you that all that we hope for and will certainly achieve in authorship and practical intelligence is more than prophesied by what has already been done, and more that can be done, by hundreds of Afro-American women whose talents are now being expended in the struggle against race resistance.

The power of organized womanhood is one of the most interesting studies of modern sociology. Formerly women knew so little of each other mentally, their common interests were so sentimental and gossipy, and their knowledge of all the larger affairs of human society was so meager that organization among them, in the modern sense, was impossible. Now their liberal intelligence, their contact in all the great interests of education, and their increasing influence for good in all the great reformatory movements of the age has created in them a greater respect for each other, and furnished the elements of organization for large and splendid purposes. The highest ascendancy of woman's development has been reached when they have become mentally strong enough to find bonds of association interwoven with sympathy, loyalty, and mutual trustfulness. To-day, union is the watchword of woman's onward march.

If it be a fact that this spirit of organization among women generally is the distinguishing mark of the nineteenth century woman, dare we ask if the colored women of the United States have made any progress in this respect?

For peculiar and painful reasons the great lessons of fraternity and altruism are hard for the colored women to learn. Emancipation found the colored Americans of the South with no sentiments of association. It will be admitted that race misfortune could scarcely go further when the terms fraternity, friendship, and unity had no meaning for its men and women.

If within thirty years they have begun to recognize the blessed significance of these vital terms of human society, confidence in their social development should be strengthened. In this important work of bringing the race together to know itself and to unite in work for a common destiny, the women have taken a leading part.

Benevolence is the essence of most of the colored women's organizations. The humane side of their natures has been cultivated to recognize the duties they owe to the sick, the indigent and the ill-fortuned. No church, school, or charitable institution for the special use of colored people has been allowed to languish or fail when the associated efforts of the women could save it.

It is highly significant and interesting to note that these women, whose hearts have been wrung by all kinds of sorrows, are abundantly manifesting those gracious qualities of heart that characterize woman of the best type. These kinder sentiments arising from mutual interests that are lifting our women into purer and tenderer relationship to each other, and are making the meager joys and larger griefs of our conditions known to each other, have been a large part of their education.

The hearts of Afro-American women are too warm and too large for race hatred. Long suffering has so chastened them that they are developing a special sense of sympathy for all who suffer and fail of justice. All the associated interests of church, temperance, and social reform in which American women are winning distinction can be wonderfully advanced when our women shall be welcomed as co-workers, and estimated solely by what they are worth to the moral elevation of all the people.

I regret the necessity of speaking to the question of the moral progress of our women, because the morality of our home life has been commented upon so disparagingly and meanly that we are placed in the unfortunate position of being defenders of our name.[8]

It is proper to state, with as much emphasis as possible, that all questions relative to the moral progress of the colored women of America are impertinent and unjustly suggestive when they relate to the thousands of colored women in the North who were free from the vicious influences of slavery. They are also meanly suggestive as regards thousands of our women in the South whose force of character enabled them to escape the slavery taints of immorality. The question of the moral progress of colored women in the United States has force and meaning in this discussion only so far as it tells the story of how the once-enslaved women have been struggling for twenty-five years to emancipate themselves from the demoralization of their enslavement.

While I duly appreciate the offensiveness of all references to American slavery, it is unavoidable to charge to that system every moral imperfection that mars the character of the colored American. The whole life and power of slavery depended upon an enforced degradation of everything human in the slaves. The slave code recognized only animal distinctions between the sexes, and ruthlessly ignored those ordinary separations that belong to the social state.

It is a great wonder that two centuries of such demoralization did not work a complete extinction of all the moral instincts. But the recuperative power of these women to regain their moral instincts and to establish a respectable relationship to American womanhood is among the earlier evidences of their moral ability to rise above their conditions. In spite of a cursed heredity that bound them to the lowest social level, in spite of everything that is unfortunate and unfavorable, these women have continually shown an increasing degree of teachableness as to the meaning of woman's relationship to man.

Out of this social purification and moral uplift have come a chivalric sentiment and regard from the young men of the race that give to the young women a new sense of protection. I do not wish to disturb the serenity of this conference by suggesting why this protection is needed and the kind of men against whom it is needed.

It is sufficient for us to know that the daughters of women who thirty years ago were not allowed to be modest, not allowed to follow the instincts of moral rectitude, who could cry for protection to no living man, have so elevated the moral tone of their social life that new and purer standards of personal worth have been created, and new ideals of womanhood, instinct with grace and delicacy, are everywhere recognized and emulated.

This moral regeneration of a whole race of women is no idle sentiment—it is a serious business; and everywhere there is witnessed a feverish anxiety to be free from the mean suspicions that have so long underestimated the character strength of our women.

These women are not satisfied with the unmistakable fact that moral progress has been made, but they are fervently impatient and stirred by a sense of outrage under the vile imputations of a diseased public opinion.

Loves that are free from the dross of coarseness, affections that are unsullied, and a proper sense of all the sanctities of human intercourse felt by thousands of these women all over the land plead for the recognition of their fitness to be judged, not by the standards of slavery, but by the higher standards of freedom and of twenty-five years of education, culture, and moral contact.

The moral aptitudes of our women are just as strong and just as weak as those of any other American women with like advantages of intelligence and environment.

It may now perhaps be fittingly asked: What mean all these evidences of mental, social, and moral progress of a class of American women of whom you know so little? Certainly you can not be indifferent to the growing needs and importance of women who are demonstrating their intelligence and capacity for the highest privileges of freedom.

The most important thing to be noted is the fact that the colored people of America have reached a distinctly new era in their career so quickly that the American mind has scarcely had time to recognize the fact, and adjust itself to the new requirements of the people in all things that pertain to citizenship.

Thirty years ago public opinion recognized no differences in the colored race. To our great misfortune public opinion has changed but slightly. History is full of examples of the great injustice resulting from the perversity of public opinion, and its tardiness in recognizing new conditions.

It seems to daze the understanding of the ordinary citizen that there are thousands of men and women everywhere among us who in twenty-five years have progressed as far away from the non-progressive peasants of the "black belt" of the South as the highest social life in New England is above the lowest levels of American civilization.

This general failure of the American people to know the new generation of colored people, and to recognize this important change in them, is the cause of more injustice to our women than can well be estimated. Further progress is everywhere seriously hindered by this ignoring of their improvement.

Our exclusion from the benefits of the fair play sentiment of the country is little less than a crime against the ambitions and aspirations of a whole race of women. The American people are but repeating the common folly of history in thus attempting to repress the yearnings of progressive humanity.

In the item of employment colored women bear a distressing burden of mean and unreasonable discrimination. A Southern teacher of thirty years experience in the South writes that "one million possibilities of good through black womanhood all depend upon an opportunity to make a living."

It is almost literally true that, except teaching in colored schools and menial work, colored women can find no employment in this free America. They are the only women in the country for whom real ability, virtue, and special talents count for nothing when they become applicants for respectable employment. Taught everywhere in ethics and social economy that merit always wins, colored women carefully prepare themselves for all kinds of occupation only to meet with stern refusal, rebuff, and disappointment. One of countless instances will show how the best as well as the meanest of American society are responsible for the special injustice to our women.

Not long ago I presented the case of a bright young woman to a well-known bank president of Chicago, who was in need of a thoroughly competent stenographer and type-writer. The president was fully satisfied with the young woman as exceptionally qualified for the position, and manifested much pleasure in commending her to the directors for appointment, and at the same time disclaimed that there could be any opposition on account of the slight tincture of African blood that identified her as a colored woman. Yet, when the matter was brought before the directors for action, these mighty men of money and business, these men whose prominence in all the great interests of the city would seem to lift them above all narrowness and foolishness, scented the African taint, and at once bravely came to the rescue of the bank and of society by dashing the hopes of this capable yet helpless young woman. No other question but that of color determined the action of these men, many of whom are probably foremost members of the humane society and heavy contributors to foreign missions and church extension work.

This question of employment for the trained talents of our women is a most serious one. Refusal of such employment because of color belies every maxim of justice and fair play. Such refusal takes the blessed meaning out of all the teachings of our civilization, and sadly confuses our conceptions of what is just, humane, and moral.

Can the people of this country afford to single out the women of a whole race of people as objects of their special contempt? Do these women not belong to a race that has never faltered in its support of the country's flag in every war since [Crispus] Attucks[9] fell in Boston's streets?

Are they not the daughters of men who have always been true as steel against treason to everything fundamental and splendid in the republic? In short, are these women not as thoroughly American in all the circumstances of citizenship as the best citizens of our country?

If it be so, are we not justified in a feeling of desperation against that peculiar form of Americanism that shows respect for our women as servants and contempt for them when they become women of culture? We have never been taught to understand why the unwritten law of chivalry, protection, and fair play that are everywhere the conservators of women's welfare must exclude every woman of a dark complexion.

We believe that the world always needs the influence of every good and capable woman, and this rule recognizes no exceptions based on complexion. In their complaint against hindrances to their employment colored women ask for no special favors.

They are even willing to bring to every position fifty per cent more of ability than is required of any other class of women. They plead for opportunities untrammeled by prejudice. They plead for the right of the individual to be judged, not by tradition and race estimate, but by the present evidences of individual worth. We believe this country is large enough and the opportunities for all kinds of success are great enough to afford our women a fair chance to earn a respectable living, and to win every prize within the reach of their capabilities.

Another, and perhaps more serious, hindrance to our women is that nightmare known as "social equality." The term equality is the most inspiring word in the vocabulary of citizenship. It expresses the leveling quality in all the splendid possibilities of American life. It is this idea of equality that has made room in this country for all kinds and conditions of men, and made personal merit the supreme requisite for all kinds of achievement.

When the colored people became citizens, and found it written deep in the organic law of the land that they too had the right to life, liberty and the pursuit of happiness, they were at once suspected of wishing to interpret this maxim of equality as meaning social equality.

Everywhere the public mind has been filled with constant alarm lest in some way our women shall approach the social sphere of the dominant race in this country. Men and women, wise and perfectly sane in all things else, become instantly unwise and foolish at the remotest suggestion of social contact with colored men and women. At every turn in our lives we meet this fear, and are humiliated by its aggressiveness and meanness. If we seek the sanctities of religion, the enlightenment of the university, the honors of politics, and the natural recreations of our common country, the social equality alarm is instantly given, and our aspirations are insulted. "Beware of social equality with the colored American" is thus written on all places, sacred or profane, in this blessed land of liberty. The most discouraging and demoralizing effect of this false sentiment concerning us is that it utterly ignores individual merit and discredits the sensibilities of intelligent womanhood. The sorrows and heartaches of a whole race of women seem to be matters of no concern to the people who so dread the social possibilities of these colored women.

On the other hand, our women have been wonderfully indifferent and unconcerned about the matter. The dread inspired by the growing intelligence of colored women has interested us almost to the point of amusement. It has given to colored women a new sense of importance to witness how easily their emancipation and steady advancement is disturbing all classes of American people. It may not be a discouraging circumstance that colored women can command some sort of attention, even though they be misunderstood. We believe in the law of reaction, and it is reasonably certain that the forces of intelligence and character being developed in our women will yet change mistrustfulness into confidence and contempt into sympathy and respect. It will soon appear to those who are not hopelessly monomaniacs on the subject that the colored people are in no way responsible for the social equality nonsense. We shall yet be credited with knowing better than our enemies that social equality can neither be enforced by law nor prevented by oppression. Though not philosophers, we long since learned that equality before the law, equality in the best sense of that term under our institutions, is totally different from social equality.

We know, without being exceptional students of history, that the social relationship of the two races will be adjusted equitably in spite of all fear and injustice, and that here is a social gravitation in human affairs that eventually overwhelms and crushes into nothingness all resistance based on prejudice and selfishness.

Our chief concern in this false social sentiment is that it attempts to hinder our further progress toward the higher spheres of womanhood. On account of it, young colored women of ambition and means are compelled in many instances to leave the country for training and education in the salons and studios of Europe. On many of the railroads of this country women of refinement and culture are driven like cattle into human cattle-cars lest the occupying of an individual seat paid for in a first-class car may result in social equality. This social quarantine on all means of travel in certain parts of the country is guarded and enforced more rigidly against us than the quarantine regulations against cholera.

Without further particularizing as to how this social question opposes our advancement, it may be stated that the contentions of colored women are in kind like those of other American women for greater freedom of development. Liberty to be all that we can be, without artificial hindrances, is a thing no less precious to us than to women generally.

We come before this assemblage of women feeling confident that our progress has been along high levels and rooted deeply in the essentials of intelligent humanity. We are so essentially American in speech, in instincts, in sentiments, and in destiny that the things that interest you equally interest us.

We believe that social evils are dangerously contagious. The fixed policy of persecution and injustice against a class of women who are weak and defenseless will be necessarily hurtful to the cause of all women. Colored women are becoming more and more a part of the social forces that must help to determine the questions that so concern women generally. In this Congress we ask to be known and recognized for what we are worth. If it be the high purpose of these deliberations to lessen the resistance to woman's progress, you can not fail to be interested in our struggles against the many oppositions that harass us.

Women who are tender enough in heart to be active in humane societies, to be foremost in all charitable activities, who are loving enough to unite Christian womanhood everywhere against the sin of intemperance, ought to be instantly concerned in the plea of colored women for justice and humane treatment. Women of the dominant race can not afford to be responsible for the wrongs we suffer, since those who do injustice can not escape a certain penalty.

But there is no wish to overstate the obstacles to colored women or to picture their status as hopeless. There is no disposition to take our place in this Congress as faultfinders or suppliants for mercy. As women of a common country, with common interests, and a destiny that will certainly bring us closer to each other, we come to this altar with our contribution of hopefulness as well as with our complaints.

When you learn that womanhood everywhere among us is blossoming out into greater fullness of everything that is sweet, beautiful, and good in woman; when you learn that the bitterness of our experience as citizen-women has not hardened our finer feelings of love and pity for our enemies; when you learn that fierce opposition to the widening spheres of our employment has not abated the aspirations of our women to enter successfully into all the professions and arts open only to intelligence, and that everywhere in the wake of enlightened womanhood our women are seen and felt for the good they diffuse, this Congress will at once see the fullness of our fellowship, and help us to avert the arrows of prejudice that pierce the soul because of the color of our bodies.

If the love of humanity more than the love of races and sex shall pulsate throughout all the grand results that shall issue to the world from this parliament of women, women of African descent in the United States will for the first time begin to feel the sweet release from the blighting thrall of prejudice.

The colored women, as well as all women, will realize that the inalienable right to life, liberty, and the pursuit of happiness is a maxim that will become more blessed in its significance when the hand of woman shall take it from its sepulture in books and make it the gospel of every-day life and the unerring guide in the relations of all men, women, and children.

THREE

CLUB MOVEMENT AMONG NEGRO WOMEN

THE NEGRO WOMAN in the United States has had a difficult task in her efforts to earn for herself a character in the social life of this country. By a sort of national common consent, she has had no place in the Republic of free and independent womanhood of America. Slavery left her in social darkness, and freedom has been slow in leading her into the daylight of the virtues, the refinements and the blessed influences that center in and radiate from the life of American free women. With individual exceptions, the colored woman, as the mother of a distinctive race in America, has been unknown. She has excited neither pity nor hope. The domestic routine of her household or cabin duties seemed to be her fixed status. She has been looked upon as a being without romance, incapable of exciting any of the sweet sentiments of femininity, any of the poetry of heart, or any of those delightful votaries that have glorified with song and chivalry the relationships of men and women.

SLAVERY IN AMERICA was debasing, but the debasement of the Negro woman was deeper than that of the Negro man. Slavery made her the only woman in all America for whom virtue was not an ornament and a necessity. What a terrible inheritance is this for the women of a race declared to be emancipated and equal sharers in the glories and responsibilities of the Republic!

DID THE GREAT WORK of "reconstruction" after the war of 1860 begin here at the root of all the Negro's ills? No, "reconstruction" was mainly political and not social. It was the work of practical statesmen, in which the sociologist had no part. Through all the clamor and confusion of those stirring times, the woman, scorned, subjective and silent, was covered with a hateful obscurity. She was simply unknown and unconsidered. It is true that the Negro race as a whole was not obscure. The enthusiasm and exaltation born of the triumphs of freedom and national

---

"Club Movement Among Colored Women," in *Progress of A Race: The Remarkable Advancement of the American Negro,* ed. J.W. Gibson and W.H. Grogman (1902; reprint, Naperville, Ill.: J.L. Nichols, 1912), 197–281.

unity, swept the Negro into a prominence that was simply phenomenal. The Negro unmanacled had been the dream of one half of the country during many years of strife, and when that dream became a fact, the Nation seemed to be fairly dazed by the very magnitude of its achievements. In those great days of national exaltation over the riddance of slavery and the saving of the Union, the terms freedom, equality and citizenship were clothed with a potency that seemed capable of working miracles. Making the colored people free and equal seemed equivalent to making them equal to every task that befits men of inherited enlightenment. While the Nation was being swept along by this kind of idealism, it was easy for colored men to be elected as governors of states, as state legislators, as congressmen, as United State senators, and to secure important appointments in the diplomatic and civil service of the government. Nothing so delighted the people of this great Nation as to witness this wonderful transformation scene "From the plantation to the halls of Congress." The Nation was so proud of itself that thousands of colored men worthily and unworthily occupied the front of the stage. These prominent Negroes filled the public eye.

Of course such common-place things as homemaking, family establishment, industrial and social independence, and the many social economies and refinements that make for race-character were not thought of. It seemed to be taken for granted that a people who could produce statesmen so quickly must have all those minor virtues and equipments that in other progressive races are the basis of human greatness.

THE NEGRO AS A SOCIAL FACTOR. It took the people of this country a long time to learn and understand that the Negro as a social factor, as a home-maker, as an equal participator in all the civil rights and privileges and responsibilities, as a contributor to the virtues and vices of the Nation, was more important than the Negro as a mere voter and office seeker. It took the colored people a long time to realize that to be a citizen of the United States was serious business, and that a seat in Congress was an insecure prominence unless supported by good women, noble mothers, family integrity, and pure homes. It was not until the Negro race began to have some consciousness of these primary things, that the women of the race became objects of interest and study.

It must not be understood that during all of this period of the colored man's political ascendancy and the colored woman's social obscurity that she was altogether unprogressive. In spite of some of the unspeakable demoralization of slavery, the womanhood of the race was marked by many of the virtues, mental and social, that are characteristic of the women of all races who are capable of a high state of development.

NOT A CHEAP SET OF WOMEN. One of the curious, but creditable, things for which the Negro race has been given but slight praise is that emancipation found thousands of colored women, both North and South, who could read and write, and who were guided and governed by womanly instincts and womanly principles. They were not a cheap set of women in the sense that their souls were dulled and uncultured. The fact is that the Negro woman in America has always been one of the most persistent of students. Though the laws and customs in the southern half of the country made it a crime to teach the Negro to read and write, and though race hatred and mob violence rendered it perilous for any colored person to seek an education, yet in the northern half thousands of colored women were educated.

There were thousands of colored women in the South who could not read and write, but they had an enlightenment of heart and mind that meant sometimes more than a knowledge of the three R's. The noble mother of Frederick Douglass was an interesting type of thousands of women who came out of slavery pure, strong, and capable of the best things of which the best of women are capable.

IN THE NORTHERN STATES   before the war hundreds of colored women secured their education in secret schools. The colored people living in the free states cried out for learning, and the colored young women were the ones most benefited. Such persecuted schools as the famous Canterbury Seminary, taught by Prudence Crandall in Canterbury, Connecticut, trained many of the young women who afterwards became pioneers in the larger and freer work of education of colored youth. Nearly every woman thus educated dedicated herself to the work of teaching. To these women the colored race is almost wholly indebted for the general intelligence that was found among the colored people of the North and that enabled them to be leaders in the early days of freedom. The colored women who laid the foundation of Negro intelligence in the Northern states form an interesting group. Among those deserving of more than a mere mention are Mrs. Fannie Jackson Coppin [1837–1913] of Philadelphia, Blanche V.H. Brooks, Frances Ellen Watkins Harper [1825–1911], Mrs. D.I. Hayden, Mrs. S.W. Early (1825–1907) of Tennessee, Mrs. Mary A. Shadd [Cary] 1823–1893], Maria Becraft, Mrs. Charlotte F. Grimke [1837–1914], Mrs. Henry H. [Sarah S.T.] Garnet [1836–1911], and Miss Fannie Richards [1841–1922] of Detroit, Michigan.[10] The work of no group of women in America is more easily traceable in the character and lives of good men and women than is that of these early colored educators. By common consent Mrs. Fannie Jackson Coppin ranks first in mental equipment, in natural gifts and achievements among colored teachers. She was among the first colored women of this country to receive a college education, having graduated from Oberlin. She was also the first colored woman who was permitted to teach in the training school of Oberlin. From Oberlin she went to Philadelphia, where for more than thirty years she was principal of the

Institution for Colored Youth, and was the most thoroughly controlling influence in molding the lives and character of the colored people of that great city. Mrs. Coppin would be regarded as eminent in any race where superior worth and dominant influence for good are recognized and properly rewarded.

MRS. FRANCES ELLEN WATKINS HARPER'S life and influence are a part of the permanent good for which the Negro stands in this country.

As teacher, lecturer, and writer of story and verse, she was in her earlier life more than a promise of the Dunbars,[11] the Campbells and the Chestnuts of a later generation.

Along with these women was Charlotte Forten Grimke, representing two family names well known in American history. Unlike Mrs. Coppin and Mrs. Harper, Mrs. Grimke was not a public woman in its strictest sense; hers was a gentle and unobtrusive spirit. She was one of the early teachers in the great missionary work of fitting a new race for high tasks. Her fine poetic and artistic taste, her exceptional gift as a writer brought her into a congenial fellowship with some of the most eminent literary men and women of our times. A more refined and unaffected character, a more thoroughly cultured woman can scarcely be found among those who helped to give character and grace to womanhood of the colored race in America.

THE HOWARDS, THE REASONS, THE RAY SISTERS[12] of New York and of a later generation can be safely classed among those who have helped to make the history, which marks the intellectual growth of the Negro race during the past twenty-five years.

WHITE WOMEN. It is but justice also to acknowledge that hundreds of educated, refined and thoroughly white-souled white women cheerfully left home and all the delights of life in the North and went South to ostracism and contempt with hearts and hands full of humane helpfulness. They penetrated and illumined regions of darkness untouched and unfelt by the amendments and statutes of liberty, in order to share in the work of redemption in which colored women were distinguishing themselves.

The progress of colored women as teachers and leaders in education may be fairly judged from the fact that about twenty-five thousand colored women are now engaged as teachers in the colored schools and colleges of the country. A large number of this generation of teachers have been trained in some of the best universities of the country and they teach everything required from the kindergarten to the university.[13]

THE CAPACITY OF THE NEGRO. The progress of colored women as teachers and students ought to be a conclusive answer to those who question the capacity of the Negro race for the highest development. It ought not to be surprising that the women who have so diligently prepared themselves by education and service should now be able to take hold of the great social problems which require for their solution the intelligence, courage, race pride, and the force of initiative such as have characterized the work of colored women as the educators of a race.

ORGANIZATION.   The organization of the colored women of the country into clubs, leagues and associations for the moral uplift of their race is a distinctive forward movement, and it is wonderfully significant of the long distance traveled in thirty years. The Negro woman's club of to-day represents the new Negro with new powers of self-help, with new capacities, and with an intelligent insight into her own condition. It represents new interests, new anxieties and new hopes. It means better schools, better homes and better family alignments, better opportunities for young colored men and women to earn a living, and purer social relationships. These are some of the things that have been made important and interesting to all of the people by the women's clubs.

THE CALL FOR CLUB WORK.   The causes for this new movement among colored women are not difficult to find. As before stated, the gradual decadence of the Negro as a political power in the South, has tended to force the race back upon itself, and to give to it the services of men whose superior intelligence found no outlet in politics. The studies and efforts of such men as DuBois, Washington and other Negro philosophers made the subjects in which women are chiefly concerned of commanding interest. Heretofore it seemed to be taken for granted that the schoolhouse would take care of itself, that the morals of the people, and home sanctities would grow out of the influence of the church alone, but women have discovered that all the agencies of civilization need to be safeguarded and supplemented by the organized intelligence of the people.

WOMEN DESERVE THE PRAISE.   While the colored men of the last decade have done much to give the race a consciousness of its own shortcomings, the colored women's club as a reformatory movement is wholly the creation of women. To them must be accredited the moral sense and the mental insight that enabled them to discover their own social disorders and imperfections and to suggest their remedies. In other words, they did not need to be told what was to be done or what to do. It was not the preacher who created in them an anxiety for a better home environment for themselves and their children. The conscience-call for kindergartens, day nurseries, reading rooms etc., was not man-made. The white women's clubs, as large, numerous, and generous as they sometimes are, sent no missionaries among their darker sisters to show them the way out of social darkness and despair. On the contrary the colored women began their club work in the same independent spirit with which they have taught themselves, and then began to teach others, even in the dark days before they became free. Without demonstration, or flourish of trumpets, the colored women began a more or less systematic study of social conditions.

FIRST CLUBS ORGANIZED.   Many clubs were organized for this purpose as early as in 1890. Between 1890 and 1895 many clubs were organized in the principal cities of the country, where the Negro population was large enough. Among the best known clubs of this period were The Ellen Watkins Harper Club of Jefferson City, Missouri, The Loyal Union of Brooklyn, The Ida B. Wells Club of Chicago, The Phyllis Wheatley Club of New Orleans, The Sojourner Truth [Club] of Providence, Rhode Island, The Woman's Era Club of Boston, and The Woman's League of Washington, D.C.[14]

An examination of the constitution and by-laws of these first organizations among colored women shows a degree of earnestness and freedom from affectation and pretense that is very refreshing, and speaks much for the strong character of the workers. Temperance, mothers' meetings, sewing school, rescue agencies, night schools, home sanitation and lectures on all subjects of social interest were some of the many things attempted and carried on by these clubs. These clubs made themselves felt for good in their respective communities. In some places these groups of women constituted the only organized force among the colored people for any purpose, and they are recognized as such in every instance where the organized voice of the colored people is needed.

THE BEST WOMEN INTERESTED.   The clubs during this period were in no way affiliated. They were purely a creation for local needs and had no other purpose than the betterment of their own communities. As a general rule those who, in the proper sense, may be called the best women in the communities where these clubs were organized became interested and joined in the work of helpfulness. It is perhaps the first instance of the women of culture, social standing and independence availing themselves of the opportunity to make use of their superior training.

The charge that the colored women of education and refinement had no sympathetic interest in their own race met a complete refutation in the zealous and unselfish service rendered the club movement by these very women.

CLUBS DESERVING SPECIAL MENTION.   Among the earlier clubs, special mention should be made of the Phyllis Wheatley Club of New Orleans, Louisiana, The Woman's League of Washington, D.C., and The

Woman's Era Club of Boston, Massachusetts. They have furnished the models for all the successful clubs that have followed them.

The Phyllis Wheatley Club is one of the best equipped clubs in the South, both as to the quality of its membership and the work accomplished. It has fostered and developed more interests that have affected helpfully the social life of the people, than any other club in the South. Among other successful undertakings, it has founded and sustained a training class for colored nurses, and largely assisted in the support of a colored orphans' home.

Its president, Mrs. Sylvanie Williams, is a fine example of the resourcefulness and noble influence that a cultivated woman can and will give to the uplift of her race.

THE WOMAN'S LEAGUE, WASHINGTON, D.C.   The Woman's League of Washington, D.C., has perhaps the largest membership of any club in the country. It has the advantage of being largely composed of the teachers of the district, and there is no lack of the right sort of intelligence and interest to make it one of the best agencies of social improvement to be found at the capital.

Mrs. Helen Cook[15] has been the president since its organization, and she has been assisted by such well-known women as Mrs. Anna J. Cooper, Mrs. J.H. Smythe, Miss Ella D. Barrier,[16] the efficient secretary, Mrs. Ida Bailey, Mrs. John R. Frances, Mrs. C.F. Grimke, Miss Victoria Thompkins, and many other ladies equally well known.[17]

The club has been in existence about twelve years, and during that time it has regularly conducted and carried on kindergartens, sewing schools, day nurseries, night schools, and penny saving banks right among the people who need this kind of service, as well as the example and sympathy of superior women.

As a woman of culture, refinement and financial independence, Mrs. John F. Cook has been, and is, a noted example and inspiration to women of her own social standing, in the serious work of social reform.

THE WOMAN'S ERA CLUB OF BOSTON, MASSACHUSETTS.   The Woman's Era Club of Boston, Massachusetts, is probably the best known club in the country. It was organized in February, 1893, and has about 200 members. It has a larger membership than any other club in the country, except perhaps the League of Washington. The personnel of its members represents a larger number of educated and refined women than probably any other club that could be mentioned.

The president, Mrs. Josephine St. Pierre Ruffin [1872–1924],[18] is of an unusually strong and interesting personality. She is also one of the best known club women in New England and is an influential member of many of the leading clubs in Massachusetts. Mrs. Ruffin's mental training, leisure, and aggressive nature amply qualify her for leadership. She has probably had more newspaper notice for her bold stand for the equal rights of women than any other colored woman in the country. The [Woman's] Era Club is the most influential organization of colored people in New England. It embraces in its purposes and plans many of the best features of club work.

The most distinctive work of the new club was the publication for several years of a monthly journal called *The Woman's Era*. This paper is the first publication ever successfully managed and published solely by colored women. Among its contributors were some of the brightest colored women of America. It had a wide circulation and did much to arouse the colored women of the country to the necessity of united effort.

THE DEVELOPMENT OF THE CLUB MOVEMENT. The next step in the development of the club movement among colored women was the formation of a National Association of colored women's clubs.

The Woman's League of Washington and the Woman's Era Club of Boston began the agitation for the affiliation of the clubs some time before its actual accomplishment, for which great credit is due them. In the spring of 1895,[19] the colored women of the country became justly excited over a scurrilous article appearing in a Missouri paper in which the colored women of the country were written down in the most libelous manner. The widespread feeling aroused by this cowardly attack resulted in the call for a National Conference issued by the Woman's Era Club of Boston, and was composed of delegates from all regularly organized colored women's clubs in the country. The Conference was held in Berkeley Hall, Boston, Massachusetts, from the 29th to the 31st of July inclusive. About one hundred women representing twenty-five clubs from ten different states composed the Conference.

Among them were such women as Mrs. J. St. P. Ruffin, Miss Maria Baldwin [1856–1922],[20] Mrs. [Florida Ruffin, 1861–1943] Ridley,[21] Mrs. Dickerson, Miss Imogene Howard, Mrs. Helen Cook of Washington, Mrs. Anna G. Cooper and Miss Ella D. Barrier who responded to the call.

The Conference attracted wide attention because it was the first of the kind ever held in this country, and because it was highly representative of the best intelligence of the women of the colored race.

The important work of the Conference was the organization of the National Association of Colored Women. The women quickly found that their power for good would be greatly increased by uniting their forces The first officers of the new Association, elected without contest or confusion, were as follows: President, Mrs. Booker T. [Margaret Murray] Washington [c. 1865–1925], Tuskegee, Alabama; Secretary, Mrs. U.A. Ridley, Brooklyn, Massachusetts; Treasurer, Mrs. Libbie C. Anthony, Jefferson

City, Missouri; Chairman Executive Committee, Mrs. Victoria E. Matthews [1861–1907].[22]

The organization of the National Association inspired new life in club work throughout the country. It gave an importance to the club work of colored women, and brought into public discussion social questions concerning the development of the race which had heretofore been neglected.

GROWTH OF THE ASSOCIATION. The power of the Association has grown from a few scattered and unaffiliated clubs throughout the country to an association of 400 clubs with a membership of from 50 to 200 each. It is estimated that from 150,000 to 200,000 women are being influenced for good more or less through the activity of these clubs, and hundreds of poor Negro homes have felt the cleansing and refining touch of the home department of these various clubs.

The National Association of Colored Women's Clubs has held four large National Conventions as follows:—Washington, D.C., in 1896; Nashville, Tennessee, in 1897; Chicago, Illinois, in 1899; and Buffalo in 1901.

The following women have served as presidents of the National Association: Mrs. Booker T. Washington, Mrs. Mary Church Terrell [1863–1954] for three terms, and Mrs. [Josephine] Silone Yates [1859–1912].[23]

THE INFLUENCE OF THE NATIONAL CONVENTIONS. The four national gatherings of the representatives of colored women's clubs have excited more public interest and newspaper comments and discussions of the social status of the colored race in this country than any conventions held by the colored people since the close of the war. The intelligent reports of committees on reformatory work attempted and accomplished have helped to bring into public notice the real needs of enlightenment among the masses of the race and have developed altogether new agencies for carrying out these reforms.

To the people who have known the Negro only as a menial it has been a delightful surprise to witness so many women accomplished and graceful in all the manners, capabilities and charms of personality that characterize the best women of the more favored races. The public has not yet ceased to wonder at these biennial exhibitions of the progress made by colored women throughout the country, and the opportunities offered to a large number of superior women who have not yet attached themselves to the work of the National Association. The only danger to the future usefulness of the National Association are the weaknesses that are common to most women's organizations, and the tendency to imitate men in their political organizations where strife for place and honor too often obscure the noble purposes and urgent needs of the work in hand, and also the purely womanly peculiarities of emphasizing the petty things that make for envy, jealousy and personal vanities. Unless the association can be sufficiently animated and inspired by the largeness of its opportunity and the dignity of its calling to save itself from the tendencies above enumerated, it will be in danger of losing the cooperation of the women who are capable of everything except bickerings and small personalities.

It must not be lost sight of that this great Association has helped to nationalize those vital interests that touch the whole social fabric of the colored race. Whether the National Association shall live or not, to carry out its pledges to itself and to the people, the interest that it has awakened in the great problems which concern the social uplift of the race must remain a part of the anxieties and responsibilities of the men and women who are striving in church and school and other agencies of reform to give a standard of character to the Negro race.

THE ATTITUDE OF WHITE WOMEN'S CLUBS.   The attitude of the white women's clubs toward the colored woman, as a club woman, has furnished one of the most interesting and stirring features in the history of the club movement. While many colored women in the Northern states have been welcomed as members to white women's clubs as individuals, the question of their admission in some instances has given rise to some of the fiercest controversies over the colored question that have been witnessed in this country for many years.

TWO INCIDENTS NOTED.   There have been two incidents in this connection that are illustrative of the extent of the interest aroused.

First. The admission of a colored woman into the Chicago Woman's Club.[24]

Second. The refusal of the National Federation of Women's Clubs at its biennial meeting in Milwaukee in 1900 to receive the credentials of Mrs. Josephine St. P. Ruffin representing the Woman's Era Club of Boston.

The first incident gave rise to a color controversy that lasted fourteen months. In the fall of 1894, Mrs. Ellen Henroten, late president of the National Federation, Mrs. Celia Parker Woolley, author and lecturer, and Mrs. Grace Bagley, a prominent club woman of Chicago, presented the name of Mrs. Fannie Barrier Williams of Chicago, with their endorsement, for membership in the Chicago Woman's Club. The name was presented in the same way that other women's names are presented and with no thought of exciting opposition or discussion.

The Chicago Woman's Club has a membership of about 800 women. In its personality it fairly represents the wealth and culture of the women of Chicago. Every applicant for membership is rigidly scrutinized and investigated to determine her mental and moral fitness for this exclusive fellowship. The club motto is *Humani Nihil Alienum Puto* ("Nothing Human is Foreign to Me"). The loyalty of the members of the Chicago Woman's Club to this motto had never been questioned before. When, however, this great club came to know the color of this new applicant, there was a startling cry that seemed to have no bounds. Scarcely has a question of such small significance in itself assumed such a national range of interest and controversy. There was scarcely a publication of any kind in the country that did not enter into a discussion of the rights and wrongs, the justice and the injustice, and the dangers real and imaginary over the simple question of admission to the club of a person who admittedly came within the meaning of the club's motto. The Women's Clubs everywhere took up the matter and discussed the question, had lectures upon it, wrote essays on it, and some of them went so far, by way of testing their own feelings, as to vote upon the question of admitting the Chicago colored applicant as an honorary member. The whole anti-slavery question was fought over again in the same spirit and with the same arguments. This simple question was the old bugbear of social equality.

After fourteen months' agitation and heart-aches and hysteria, the common sense of the members triumphed over their prejudices.

The colored applicant stood the test of the club's law of eligibility, which was declared to be "Character, intelligence and the reciprocal advantages to the club and the individual, without regard to race, color, religion or politics." The most gratifying thing about this long-drawn-out and exciting contest is that fully nine-tenths of the most influential publications in the United States, without regard to politics, were in favor of the colored applicant, and insisted upon high grounds in settling all similar controversies. Certain it is that no more interesting contribution to the literature of the color question in this country can be found than that growing out of this discussion.

It is also gratifying to note that none of the fears insisted upon by those opposed to the admission of the colored applicant have been realized, but on the contrary the club has steadily grown in interest, membership and influence.

THE RUFFIN INCIDENT.   The "Ruffin incident," as it has been aptly called, furnishes the second national controversy over the color question growing out of the attitude of the white women's club toward the colored woman as a club member. The meaning of the "Ruffin incident" is the refusal of the National Federation of Women's Clubs at their biennial meeting at Milwaukee, Wisconsin, to admit to its membership any club composed exclusively of colored women. This as an issue was brought out by Mrs. Ruffin's loyalty to the Woman's Era Club, of which she was president and from which she was sent with proper credentials as a delegate.

There is such a widespread misapprehension of the facts, and so little has been published that can be relied upon as authentic, that the following carefully prepared official statement of the entire controversy has been secured from the Woman's Era Club to be used in this chapter. We think it will be of historical value in the future discussion of this question.

OFFICIAL STATEMENT FROM THE WOMAN'S ERA CLUB OF BOSTON, MASSACHUSETTS. The following is a condensed statement of the *Woman's Era Club* (colored) of Boston, concerning the "Ruffin incident," referred to above: The Milwaukee episode has made the Era Club of Boston a target of criticism, friendly and unfriendly, of 2,500 women's clubs, and through them of 150,000 women. For this reason the club feels itself justified in making this general statement:

"It is urged by critics:

"*First.* The Massachusetts and the Woman's Era Club are to be condemned for attempting to force the color question upon the Biennial, when least prepared for it.

"*Second.* That the action of the President of the Federation, Mrs. [Rebecca D.] Lowe, in admitting the Woman's Era Club was not ratified by the Board, therefore the Board's action in excluding Mrs. Ruffin was perfectly legal.

"*Third.* That Mrs. Ruffin should have accepted a compromise—should have been willing to forego the privilege of representing the club of which she was president—and enter the convention as a delegate from Massachusetts, which privilege was offered her.

"*Fourth.* That colored women should confine themselves to their clubs and the large field of work open to them there.

We think it best to answer these points by a brief statement of the career of our club and the events immediately leading to its entrance into the general federation. * * * In allying itself with the general movement for women, the club has sought to elevate itself by taking advantage of every opportunity possible to help or to be helped. It sought to spread the club movement among colored women, and to that end, called together in Boston the first convention of colored women ever held in America, the convention which ultimately resulted in the National Federation of Colored Women's Clubs. * * *

"We became a member of the Massachusetts State Federation, and no club in that body had a deeper pride in it and the women it represents than we. Our association with Massachusetts club women had been such that the possibility of color discrimination had been lost sight of. Our delegates had been received at meetings, receptions, and conventions with that courtesy invariably extended by ladies toward all with whom they come in contact; nothing less was expected; certainly nothing less was received.

"With this explanation it can be readily understood that when invited to join the General Federation, the Woman's Era Club accepted the honor in all sincerity, as free from any thought of forcing an issue, as was doubtless the true-hearted

Mrs. Anna D. West, state chairman of correspondence for Massachusetts, who gave us the invitation.

"The club went through the prescribed form in making its application for membership in the General Federation. * * * A reply was immediately received from Mrs. Lowe, in which she said:—

ATLANTA, GA., April 30, 1900.

"'**Dear Madam President:** I hope you have by this time received your certificate of membership in the General Federation.

It is with great pride that I write to extend to your club my congratulations, and at the same time to assure them of my desire to be helpful to them in any way possible. * * * Extend to your club greetings from me, and tell them to call upon me for all that they need and to send me all they can spare for encouraging and strengthening the union of our work. Believe me,

Fraternally yours,
Rebecca D. Lowe.'

"The dues were forwarded, a receipt and certificate of membership were received, and a ratification of the action of the president, Mrs. Lowe, was received by Mrs. West, dated May 14, 1900, as follows:

"'It gives me great pleasure to inform you that the application of the Woman's Era Club for membership in the General Federation has been accepted by the Executive Committee. Congratulating you on the success of your work, I am

Sincerely yours,
Minnie M. Kendrick,
Corresponding Secretary, General Federation.'

"Acting upon this situation, the Woman's Era Club sent Mrs. Ruffin as its delegate to the biennial convention held at Milwaukee, Wisconsin. She was also elected a delegate by the Massachusetts State Federation, and also an alternate from the N.E.W. Press Association.

"Upon arriving at Milwaukee, Mrs. Ruffin was forced into a humiliating position for which she was wholly unprepared. The Massachusetts delegation was immediately notified that the Board had met and would not receive an application for membership of the Woman's Era Club. Mrs. Ruffin was informed that she could not enter the convention representing a 'colored club' but would be received as a delegate from a 'white club,' and to enforce this ruling an attempt was made to snatch from her breast the badge which had been handed her on the passing of her credentials.

"Mrs. Ruffin refused to enter the convention under the conditions offered her, that is, as a delegate from the Massachusetts State Federation, for which she was also a delegate. * * *

"The General Federation of Women's Clubs has no color line in its constitution; there is nothing in its constitution, in its oft-published statement of ideas and aims, in its supposed advanced position upon humanitarian questions to lead any club, with like aims and views, to imagine itself ineligible for membership.

"The Woman's Era Club having been regularly admitted, no legal or moral ground can possibly be found upon which it could be ruthlessly thrown out at the pleasure of a few individuals.

"As a member of the Massachusetts State Federation, the Woman's Era Club is still a member of the General Federation.

"The question before the Board and before the country is not whether colored clubs shall be admitted to the General Federation, but whether that unwarrantable action shall be sustained. Shall women, asking for suffrage and a large participation in public life, endorse a ruling which, as a specimen of bossism, could not be overmatched by the lowest political gathering in the country?

* * * * * *

"The Woman's Era Club believes it voices the sentiments of the colored women of the country when it says it is perfectly willing to abide the decision of the majority as to whether or not there shall be color discrimination in the General Federation. We, as members of the club, will, however, regret to see the standard lowered, the higher ideals repudiated, the power of the club work dismissed, by any declaration that it is the cause of white women for which it stands, and not the cause of womankind.

"Whatever may be the result of the deliberations of the General Federation upon the question of the color line, the decision should be explicit and final, so that in the future there may be no possibility of the trampling upon the feelings and aspirations of those they consider beneath them.

"The wearers of the despised 'color,' many millions strong, cannot annihilate or eliminate themselves; they are forced, in the passing of the years, to touch the larger life of the Nation at many points; but should this touch be deemed undesirable by those with the greater power, it is only human that the weaker side should be allowed to protect itself."

* * * * * *

The whole country was aroused over this Milwaukee incident. As in the case cited, the newspapers of the country made much of the case and were generally on the side of the strong and womanly stand taken by Mrs. Ruffin. The individual clubs composing the Federation have been preparing themselves to meet the issue at the next biennial meeting. The women composing the delegates to the Federation went home to their respective clubs with hearts burdened with this vexatious color-line question. In reporting to their clubs, there were embodied recommendations as to what should be the attitude of their clubs in the next biennial. As a result many of the clubs have already committed themselves as a protest against a fixed policy of narrowness and exclusion.

PROTEST OF WHITE CLUBS. Among the first clubs to take a decided stand against such injustice was the Catholic Woman's League of Chicago, which was the first to register a decided protest against the treatment of the Woman's Era Club. It is notable that the Catholic women's clubs throughout the country are uncompromising in their stand for an equality of opportunity.

The Chicago Women's Club again fought out this question against fierce opposition from some of its members, but under the leadership of its best women, including many cultured women of Southern birth and with the assistance of their one colored member, they once more triumphed over their prejudices.

These discussions in many clubs are creating much bitterness, and there are heard on every side threats of the withdrawal of Southern clubs, and some Northern clubs that sympathize with the Southern woman. It is also curious to observe how slight has been the advance in thought and argument over the same arguments of antebellum days. The women are still haunted by the old phantoms "Do you want your daughter to marry a Negro?" "Do you want social equality?" "White supremacy?" These are all used in the same manner and with the same assurances of effectiveness as they were fifty years ago against the abolitionists. It is the same old fight of light against darkness and progress against caste. Prejudice resists all that tends to soften the heart and enlighten the mind. It defies logic. It has no part with charity; humanity is not its shibboleth. It ever gropes in the dark and takes no pride in the onward sweep of the great forces of love and sympathy that inevitably blend into the controlling sentiment of the brotherhood of man. The colored women of the country have borne the burden of more misery than has ever been imposed upon womankind by a Christian nation. She knows herself and asks for the assistance and encouragement of those who are more or less responsible for this burden. Yet there are thousands of free strong women in this country who would refuse her appeal.

FRIENDS OF THE COLORED WOMAN. There is, however, a brighter side to this question. The women who are committed to a more liberal view on the admission of colored clubs to the National Federation are equally tenacious of their position. They insist the great Federation shall not commit itself to any policy of exclusion, by which the deserving woman of any race or color shall be kept from its benefits and inspirations.

There are thousands of such women, and they prefer that the Federation should go to pieces and cease to be rather than to make vital in their work the prejudices and principles of fifty years ago. They believe in Terrence's motto as above quoted. They believe that the white women of the country should not be unwilling to aid in every way colored women who are struggling to work out their own salvation. They are not disturbed by the cry of social equality. They stand for progress and for the broadest sympathy and for womankind. This seems to be the sentiment of the majority of the noble women in the country, and they have no doubt of saving the Federation from committing itself to the meaner policy of exclusion.

THE ATTITUDE OF COLORED WOMEN IN THE CONTROVERSY. The colored women have kept themselves serene while this color-line controversy has been raging around them. They have taken a keen and intelligent interest in all that has been said for and against them, but through it all they have lost neither their patience nor their hope in the ultimate triumph of right principles.

The Federation has never been troubled by many applicants from colored clubs. Some influential colored women even go so far as to believe that little is to be gained as to clubs, by exposing themselves to the humiliation of being rejected. Then again there is the serious danger of being misrepresented by some ambitious or self-seeking women who would bring discredit to the claims of colored women's clubs. The case of the Woman's Era Club is rather the exception. It sought membership in the Federation because that was the logical and proper thing for it to do. In the first place it is a New England club, composed in the main of superior women, who personally and through their club had affiliated with the best white clubs of New England. Its president, Mrs. Ruffin, is an honored member of many of the clubs composing the Federation. It was solely a question of loyalty to the larger interests of the federated club work in the country that induced the Era Club to lend its forces to strengthening and supporting the more inclusive work of the Federation. Then again by its very aims, purposes and doctrines as declared, the Federation extends an invitation to all qualified organizations of womankind, without hint as to color, race, or previous condition.

It is really surprising that more of the colored clubs have not sought the inspiration, instruction and help that are so freely offered by the Federation to all clubs. The fact that so few clubs have applied for admission shows how groundless are their fears that the Federation is in danger of being "Africanized."

As before stated, there are many clubs in Northern communities in which may be found colored members. Many prominent white clubs have extended cordial invitations to prominent colored women to address them on all questions of peculiar interest to women. In fact, as between individual clubs, there has been an increase of cordiality and reciprocal advantages in this interchange of service.

Many colored women have been trained and schooled for leadership among their own women by the experiences gained in well-organized white associations.

HOW THE COLOR-LINE CONTROVERSY HAS HELPED COLORED WOMEN. It can be said that colored women have gained more than they have lost by this widespread controversy as to their fitness for membership in white clubs. Through the justice of the press, the best things among colored women and the best women have been brought into public notice to an extent that never could have been gained by other means. Thousands of people have learned things that they never knew before, and have been converted to a respectful consideration of the claims of colored women as to their standing in a community.

The public is beginning to learn and to discriminate that colored women are not all alike, that there are social differences, mental differences and character differences. The public has learned how these dark-skinned women have literally redeemed themselves by the thousands. For the first time they have learned of their versatility, their culture, their charms, and their virtues. They have learned of many clever writers, many fluent speakers, many doctors, dentists, some lawyers, some linguists, some artists, some business women, and thousands of teachers. All these things have certainly added to the force of public sentiment that is growing stronger day by day in favor of equal justice to the colored race.

The agitation has also had the indirect effect of strengthening and improving the work of colored women themselves. Colored women have begun to learn that if they would give their clubs prestige and influence with the great association of white women, they must bring to the front and encourage their best women, that their representatives must be representative of the best they have.

It should also be noted that there has been a closer affiliation of white and colored clubs in the same communities. White women of influence have offered their services to colored women, and colored women of influence have found their way to the lecture platform, through which they have been able to reach the hearts of the people.

RECOGNITION OF THE CLUBS.   These women's clubs are coming more and more to be recognized as the center of the ethical activities and best influence of the community in which they live and work.

The churches, schools and other institutions have all learned to appeal to these clubs and to seek their co-operation in everything important. In other words, colored women's clubs have established for themselves a character. They have gained the prestige that comes from things done, and done for the benefit of the people. They are always accessible to the young and old, to those who need them, and to those who need them not. Their methods are democratic and open, and their aims and purposes are always changeable to meet the requirements of their communities. In some localities the crying need is instruction to mothers and sanitary decency; in others it is day nurseries and kindergartens; in others it is night schools for old and young, or employment agencies; protection for the young women of poor homes and no homes. In still others it is the fostering of a taste for art, for culture, for music. In other words, the colored women have, through their clubs, established for themselves a Woman's Tribune, where every question, every interest, every hope and every despair, and every need can be brought and are brought, and thus made the concern and anxiety of all.

SOME FRANK ADMISSIONS.   It is not claimed in all that has been said in behalf of colored women's clubs, either as a local or national organization, that it is entirely free from an admixture of some of the meannesses of our poor human nature. It is due to candor to admit that unworthy ambitions, jealousies, envies, spitefulness, piques, tale-bearing, suspicions, affectations and many of the other little sins peculiar to human nature generally, and to femininity in particular, have played their part in retarding the progress of the club movement.

The important thing, however, to be noted is that in spite of hindrances, the women have advanced their work, have sustained the integrity of the National Association, and can to-day claim to have the most spirited, thorough and well organized National Association among the colored people.

CLUB WORK CANNOT BE EXAGGERATED.   Is it possible to exaggerate the importance of this work of the colored women in the country? Scarcely so, when it is understood how great is the variety of regenerating agencies needed to bring the colored people up to the standard of qualified citizenship in this country.

THINGS TO BE OVERCOME.   In America the Negro has no history, no traditions, no race ideals, no inherited resources, either mental, social, or ethical, and no established race character. The race is coming into its own power of self respect, self help and self pride by the forces of the initiative, submission and assimilation. The term Negro excites only the emotion of pity or contempt or anxiety or, at best, hope.

The term colored woman has been more of a reproach in this country than anything else.

These are the conditions under which colored women have begun their work of social reform. Courage, patience, love, and the best qualities of the human heart are all needed for those who would assume this work hopefully and successfully.

Can they succeed in bringing to their race a better social status? Can they alone make for themselves a name that shall be respected, and remove from them the reproach of bonded conditions? Is the final work of making the Negro race worthy of its place in this country to be left to women? Scarcely so. The chief value of woman's work to-day as purposed and carried out in their club work is that of helping to educate the Negro race as to its fundamental needs. The club has helped to turn the searchlight of Negro intelligence upon the darkness of Negro ignorance, of the things that make a race strong and respected. The colored race is learning for the first time the social value of the many smaller activities that women everywhere are carrying on with more or less intelligence. The Negro race is learning that these things which the women are doing come first in the lessons of citizenship, that there will never be an unchallenged vote, or a

respected political power, or an unquestioned claim to positions of influence and importance, until the present social stigma is removed from the
home and the women of the race.

Women have suffered so much and have been so much humiliated by
our Christian civilization that their zeal for vindication of themselves and
their race is without bounds or possible abatement.

Like old Zarca in George Eliot's *Spanish Gypsy*,[25] they are ambitious

> To make their name, now but a badge of scorn,
> A glorious banner floating in their midst,
> Stirring the air they breathe with impulses
> Of generous pride, exalting fellowship,
> Until it soars to magnanimity.

No race can long remain mean and cheap with aspirations such as
these. Let the women be not discouraged. They are helping to make history for a race that has no history. They are furnishing material for the
first chapter which shall some day recite the discouragements endured, the
oppositions conquered, and the triumph of their faith in themselves.

FOUR

THE CLUB MOVEMENT AMONG THE COLORED WOMEN

The Club movement among the colored of the country is the one organized effort amongst us that apparently has suffered no abatement of the enthusiasm and sincerity of purpose that characterized its beginning. The idea that the colored of the country can organize and remain organized for practical usefulness in the social uplift of the Negro race, is still vital and promising beyond any movement that has claimed public interest.

Organization of Clubs and Leagues of our women is peculiarly a heart movement and has in it a large degree of sincerity and unselfishness among the rank and file of its members. The whole range of purposes to which these clubs are committed calls for work, sacrifice and consideration. The temptations of office, the chance for money making, the thirst for power and "influence," and the other baleful incidents of politics have played but a small part in this development of women's clubs. In saying all this I am not unmindful that these clubs do carry a certain burden of incompetency, petty ambition and unseemly vanity.

To be president of the National Federation [of Colored Women] is a worthy ambition, and it is perhaps too much to say that worthy methods have always been used by every candidate who has posed, and in devious ways, planned, for her own election. Indeed, it seems to be just now an open secret that slates are being made and broken, "promises" exchanged, and "trade" arranged to land some favorite daughter, mother, or sister in the presidential chair at the coming St. Louis Convention.

This biennial stirring of ambitions is so thoroughly human that it cannot be helped and for awhile at least can be openly deprecated. We have learned the lesson all too well from the masculine side of our humanity that if you want to fill an honorable office, you must not out go out to meet it, but must fight for it and be not over scrupulous as to weapons or methods.

The struggle for the presidency and other offices of the National Federation is one of the danger points in the developments of club work as a national movement. In its organizing work the Federation has before it the difficult task of creating ideals of administration in consonance with the spirit and purposes of the movement, and so must look to the methods of

"The Club Movement among the Colored Women," *Voice of the Negro* 1, no. 3 (1904): 99–102.

man made politics for suggestions to win places of power and trust in a purely non-political organization.

In further developing this noble movement of co-operative helpfulness among colored women there must be a determination to avoid the possibilities of the "boss" as that term is understood in political parties. The next thing in meanness, in the usurpation of other people's power, to the political "boss" would be a political "mistress" in a woman's organization. Such terms as the "big four," "secret caucus," "trading," "trimming" and "combining" should not be heard in a woman's organization, committed to the high tasks that the National Association stands for. Such terms suggest factions that are more or less hostile to the large ideas and purposes of the whole organization. Everything should be done to foster and promote the idea among the rank and file of the club members that they are sovereigns and the source of power and authority, that primarily the organization exists for them, and that the honors and responsibilities of office can be won by merit and not by any finesse of "boss" manipulations of delegates.[26]

The office of President of the National Federation of [Colored] Woman's Clubs should be made the most exalted position that any colored woman could hold in this country, and every member of a Club and every Club in this country should share in the privilege and honor of placing the most capable and deserving woman in that office.

What is here said is not so much a criticism as a warning of possible dangers to the future usefulness of the Association. Fortunately the Federation has a membership sufficiently intelligent to save it from too much politics and the petty envies and jealousies that are purely womanly peculiarities. Unless it can be animated and inspired by the largeness of its opportunity and the dignity of its calling to save itself from the above tendencies it will be in danger of losing the co-operation of the women who are capable of everything, except bickering and small personalities.

The Association is particularly fortunate in its present administration under the guidance of its high-minded and cultured president, Mrs. Silome Yates, and she has been ably assisted by the National Organizer, Mrs. L.A. Davis[27] and other officers in keeping in intimate touch with the individual clubs.

The policy of the present administration has given the National Association an integrity of character that will inevitably win the respect of the best colored women everywhere. The educated young woman fresh from college, the cultured woman in the home, the efficient woman in business, the colored teacher, and the women who are working for the protection of our young women from the dangers of city life and well dressed idleness should all find strength and inspiration in this great Federation of Colored Women.

To live up to its ideals, the clubs of the Association need at all times the best intelligence of our women. Every woman who can contribute anything of helpfulness should find hospitable welcome in the clubs of the

Association. Any woman whose heart has responded to the conscience call for Kindergartens, Nurseries, Reading Rooms, etc., for the children and the unfortunates everywhere, ought to be made to feel that this work call be better done through the agency of this great organization, than through any other means.

This much is said because there are so many excellent women who are not a part of this club movement. Why? The most general answer is that the clubs are impracticable: that not one club out of fifty lives up to its avowed purposes: that certain clubs, for example, that make a pretense of studying art, literature and music do nothing of the kind; that certain other clubs, that are pledged to the more practical work of carrying out certain reforms and establishing kindergartens, reading rooms and other specific charities, do the work spasmodically, just before the Biennial convention, and sometimes, not at all.

While much of this criticism is true, the women who note these defects and make no effort to remedy them are not wholly blameless.

I think the whole trouble lies in the fact that many of our clubs are imitative and not original, in their plans of work: I personally know of some colored women's clubs that have adapted as their own the Constitution, by-laws and entire programme of some white women's clubs. The absurdity of this is all too obvious. The club movement among colored women means something deeper than a mere imitation of the more favored class of whites, because it has grown out of the organized anxiety of women who have only recently become intelligent enough to recognize their own social condition and strong enough to initiate and apply the forces of reform. It is a movement that reaches down into the sub-social condition of an entire race and has become the responsibility and effort of a few competent in behalf of the many incompetent.

The fact is that the colored race is not yet sufficiently aroused to its own social perils. The evils that menace the integrity of the home, the small vices that are too often mistaken for legitimate pleasures, give us too little concern. The purpose of colored women's clubs is to cultivate among the people a finer sensitiveness as to the rights and wrongs, the proprieties and improprieties, that enter into—nay regulate the social status of the race.

To accomplish all this, the members of individual clubs must study the needs of the community in which they live; they must lay hold of the problems that lie nearest them and be honest enough to attempt only that which they know most about and which ought to be done in the interest of their own homes, their own families and the community in which they live. They will thus become the civic mothers of the race by establishing a sort of special relationship between those who help and those who need help.

The colored of the country have built up a splendid Association. The next anxiety should be to turn the Association to practical account. The organization, as such, is of little value unless it can and does actually do the things for which it was called into being.

By way of illustration let me simply refer to some of the activities that are actually being carried on by one of the white women's clubs of Chicago.[28] These accidentally realized some time ago, that there was in the city no hospital for crippled children. They immediately went to work making their appeal to the public conscience and never halting in their efforts until the Hospital became an established fact. This club also inaugurated a system of serving pure milk to children of the poor and unfortunate at a nominal price as well as providing ice during the debilitating heat of the summer months. They saw the need for vacation schools, public playgrounds, cleaner streets and better sanitation in store and factory and never desisted until the entire community was interested and joined with them in seeing that these needed reforms were carried out. There is scarcely a phase of our municipal life, that concerns and children and the home, that is not under the vigilant eye of some committee of this great body of workers toward definite ends, and its influence is felt throughout this city and the whole country.

It will not be a fitting comment to say that these women are wealthy, more intelligent and had superior advantages. The point to be emphasized is that they are not satisfied with an organization that merely pretends to do something for society. The principles and purposes of the organization are translated into work that aims to touch helpfully every phase of humanity about it.

Our clubs must realize that it simply amounts to good morals not to attempt to do that which we are not prepared by experience and training to do. Each club should strive to work out its own individuality, know its own needs, and find its own work. Unless many of our clubs can be reorganized on this common sense basis, the National Association will be in danger of losing its prestige for the large usefulness that it has so well earned.

Our National Conventions will cease to be interesting in any important sense if they become merely a parliament for clever essays, bright speeches and parliamentary tilts. What the country demands, and has a right to expect from these great National gatherings, is a report of progress on things practical. One Convention pledged itself to the work of Prison Reform, another to the establishing and fostering of Kindergarten Schools in the South. Have these pledges been kept? Our young women are largely out of employment and white women are developing an interest in Domestic Science to such an extent. that house work, cooking and kindred arts will soon be classed among the professions. Can the National Association of Colored Women take hold of this work in such a way as to bring the benefits of this new movement to our idle and unfortunate young women? I have a faith in the women of the Association and believe that they can create an interest in this, as well as other things, that will mean much to the saving of our young women.

The colored have done well in creating and developing this splendid Federation. They have abundantly demonstrated their ability, their cleverness, and their constancy of purpose, and the appeal to them now is to do better by making the Association more telling and positive in its efforts to educate the race as to its fundamental needs.

This is a grave responsibility because the Negro is learning that the things that our women are doing come first in the lessons of citizenship; that there will never be an unchallenged vote, a respected political power, or an unquestioned claim to position of influence and importance until the present stigma is removed from the home and the women of its race.

Whether the National Association shall live or not to carry out its pledges to itself and the people, the interest that it has awakened in the great problems which concern the social uplift of the race must remain a part of the anxieties and responsibilities of the men and who are striving in church and in school and other agencies of reform to give a standard of character to the Negro race.

FIVE

THE PROBLEM OF EMPLOYMENT FOR NEGRO WOMEN

It can be broadly said that colored women know how to work, and have done their full share of the paid and unpaid service rendered to the American people by the Negro race. This is a busy world; the world's work is large, complicated, and increasing. The demand for the competent in all kinds of work is never fully supplied. Woman is constantly receiving a larger share of the work to be done. The field for her skill, her endurance, her finer instincts and faithfulness is ever enlarging; and she has become impatient of limitations, except those imposed by her own physical condition. In this generalization, colored women, of course, are largely excepted. For reasons too well understood here to be repeated, ours is a narrow sphere. While the kinds and grades of occupation open to all women of white complexion are almost beyond enumeration, those open to our women are few in number and mostly menial in quality. The girl who is white and capable is in demand in a thousand places. The capable Negro girl is usually not in demand, This is one of the stubborn facts of today. Shall we waste our energy and soul in fretting over it, or shall we bravely say, "Well, what I would do, I cannot, so I will do that which I can in the best way I can." Thoreau said that "if people would spend half as much effort in trying to be happy with what they have, as they spend in wishing for what they haven't got, the world would be far happier."[29] It seems to me that this bit of philosophy aptly applies to our case in this matter of employment.

In the face of this condition, then, what can we do? To answer this question there is required large-heartedness and much wisdom. This answer must be worked out, not by our women alone, but by the co-operation of the best minds and best hearts of all the people. In considering the present-day opportunities and lack of opportunities for colored women I shall not consider the teachers nor the few women here and there who are in the professions. We need have no anxiety about the superior woman. She will make her way in the world in spite of restrictions. But it is with the average colored woman that we must reckon. We find her engaged in some one of the following occupations: domestic service, laundering, dressmaking, hair dressing, manicuring, and nursing. Here and there is a type-writer and

An address delivered at the Hampton Conference in July 1903 and found in its proceedings. See *Southern Workman* 32 (September): 432–37.

stenographer, a book-keeper, or a government employee. In Southern communities colored women as a rule are not employed in factories, nor do they form part of the great army of clerks of all kinds.

In the city of Chicago domestic service is the one occupation in which the demand for colored women exceeds the supply. In one employment office during the past year there were 1,500 applications for colored women and only 1,000 of this number were supplied. Girls of other nationalities do not seem to compete with colored women as domestics. It is probably safe to say that every colored woman who is in any way competent can find good employment. Her wages for general housework range from four to seven dollars per week, while a good cook receives from seven to ten dollars. Now what is the condition of this service? The two most important things are that the wages paid are higher than those given for the same grade of intelligence in any other calling, and that colored women can command almost a monopoly of this employment.

It might be safe to presume that since our women are so much in demand for this service they give perfect satisfaction. In considering this it is important to bear in mind that there are two kinds of colored women who perform domestic service. First, there are those who take to the work naturally and whose training and habits make them perfectly satisfied with it; and second, those who have had more or less education and who are ambitious to do something in the line of "polite occupations." The women of the latter class do not take to domestic service very kindly. They do not enter the service with any pride. They feel compelled to do this work because they can find nothing else to do. They are always sensitive as to how they may be regarded by their associates and friends and shrink from the term servant as something degrading "per se." There is a general complaint among housekeepers that the younger and more intelligent colored women are unreliable as domestics. They say that as soon as a young woman has earned enough money to buy a fine dress she leaves her place, that she demands a holiday every time there is a picnic or a funeral and wears herself out in social dissipations of all kinds. These are some of the complaints that may be heard concerning the present generation of young women who "work out." I am sorry to say that there is a great deal of truth in them. Women who take up any kind of work with a fixed dislike and shame for it are not apt to win the good will of their employers.

But of course there is another side to this story. It must be remembered that the ordinary mistress of a house is far from being an angel. Although I am a woman and a housekeeper, I must admit that the average housewife is apt to be a petty tyrant, and while she has smiles, graciousness, and gentleness for the parlor, [she is likely] to show all kinds of meanness and harshness in the kitchen. She seldom assumes that there is a higher nature in her helpers that might sometimes be appealed to. Many mistresses cannot rid themselves of the idea that the woman whom she employs to do housework is inferior and servile by nature, and must receive the treatment accorded to inferiors. The woman who understands this haughtiness of spirit and exaggerated superiority is always resentful and on the defensive. If it were possible to change the disposition and heart of the average American housewife, and so to elevate the service that the cook or housemaid would not be looked down upon because she is a servant and as such not supposed to possess womanly instincts and aspirations, a better grade of helpers would gladly enter this field of employment.

It is of course an easy thing to condemn our young women who have been fairly educated and have had good home training, because they prefer idleness to domestic service, but I am rather inclined to think that we must share in that condemnation. If our girls work for wages in a nice home, rather than in a factory or over a counter, they are ruthlessly scorned by their friends and acquaintances. Our young men, whose own occupations by the way will not always bear scrutiny, will also give her the cut direct, so that between the scorn of her associates and the petty tyranny of the housewife, the colored girl who enters domestic service is compelled to have more than ordinary strength of character.

But after all is said, I believe that it is largely in the power of the young woman herself to change and elevate the character of domestic service. She certainly cannot improve it by taking into it ignorance, contempt, and inefficiency. There is no reason why a woman of character, graciousness, and skill should not make her work as a domestic as respectable and as highly regarded as the work of the girl behind the department-store counter. For example, if, by special training in domestic service, a girl can cook so well and do everything about a house so deftly and thoroughly that she will be called a real home helper and an invaluable assistant, it is in her power, with her intelligent grasp upon the possibilities of her position, to change the whole current of public opinion in its estimate of domestic service. These young women, as a general thing, belong to families that are too poor to keep them well dressed if they are idle, yet colored girls on the streets of Chicago and other cities are often better dressed than the girls of any other race in like circumstances. There is a strong suspicion prevalent that this fine dressing is at a cost that demoralizes the social life of the colored people. This is the most serious consequence of our restricted employment. The girl who is barred from the occupation she would like to follow, and has no taste, talent, or desire for what she must do, is apt to become discouraged and indifferent. If she finds that society on all sides is hostile to her ambitions, she will become in turn hostile to society and contemptuous of its ethics and code of morals.

What, then, shall we do for the young colored woman with refined instincts and fair education? She is ambitious to choose and follow the occupation for which she is best fitted by talents and inclination, but she is shut out from most of the employments open to other women, and does not realize that her refinement and training are as much needed and as well paid for in domestic service as in other occupations. We are afraid of the word "servant." In England the terms master and servant are not hateful to the thousands of self-respecting Englishmen who bear them. If we could in some way create a sentiment that the girl who can carry as much intelligence and graciousness of manner into the kitchen will be as much respected and will get married just as soon as her sisters in other occupations, much of the present-day false notions about domestic service would be changed. A young woman of character and intelligence, who is competent to do domestic work, can never be a servant in an offensive sense and will not be so regarded. To bring about this change so as to enable our girls to enter upon this occupation without loss of self-respect and without the danger of ostracism by so-called society is a problem worthy of the best thought and devotion of our men and women.

What is called the servant-girl problem is one of the most vexatious of the many social questions of the hour. The work of housekeeping is neither a trade nor a profession; it is without discipline or organization and is largely irresponsible and uncertain. It is usually a case of a good mistress and a bad servant or a bad mistress and a good servant. Thousands of housekeepers attempt to manage their help who have never learned to manage themselves. The housekeeper's manner to the butcher, the baker, the milkman, the shoemaker, the dressmaker, and the milliner and to every other person upon whom she is more or less dependent, is often more respectful than it is to the woman upon whom she is dependent every hour of the day for case and comfort, health and happiness. Many of the leading women of the country have begun to study this problem for the purpose of elevating the service.[30] The first thing to be done is to bring it strongly to our consciousness that domestic service is not necessarily degrading. In the city of Chicago, schools of domestic science are as eagerly patronized as schools in which book-keeping and typewriting are taught. They are slowly teaching the all-important fact that the thing we call domestic service has in it the elements of high art and much science. It is an occupation that intelligence elevates, that character adorns and ennobles, and that even now brings a higher salary to women than almost any other kind of employment.

When domestic service becomes a profession, as it surely will, by the proper training of those who shall follow it, what will be the condition of colored girls who would participate in its benefits? It is now time to prepare ourselves to answer this question. In my opinion, the training for this new profession should be elevated to the dignity and importance of the training in mathematics and grammar and other academic studies. Our girls must be made to feel that there is no stepping down when they become professional housekeepers. The relative dignity, respectability, and honor of this profession should first be taught in our schools. As it is now, the young woman in school or college knows that if she enters domestic service, she loses the relationships that she has formed. But schools of domestic science cannot do it all. The every-day man and woman who make society must change their foolish notions as to what is the polite thing for a young woman to do. The kind of stupidity that calls industrial education drudgery is the same kind of stupidity that looks upon the kitchen as a place for drudges. We must learn that the girl who cooks our meals and keeps our houses sweet and beautiful deserves just as high a place in our social economy as the girl who makes our gowns and hats, or the one who teaches our children. In what I have said on this particular phase of our industrial life, I do not wish to be understood as advocating the restriction of colored girls to house service, even when that service is elevated to the rank of a profession. My only plea is that we shall protect and respect our girls who honestly and intelligently enter this service, either from preference or necessity.[31]

It seems to me that we lose a great opportunity if we fail to take hold of this problem in a thoroughly broad and philosophic way and work out its solution. If we wish to contribute something substantial to the social betterment of American living, we have the opportunity in helping to solve this servant-girl problem. Vexation of spirit, waste, indigestion, and general demoralization cry out from the American home for relief from its domestic miseries. We have it in our power to assist in answering this Macedonian cry. It would help to give our race a standing if we could count several of our men and women as the best thinkers and most effective workers in the solution of this problem. Shall we lead or shall we follow in this movement? Shall we, in this as in many other things, beg for an opportunity further on instead of helping to create opportunities now?

There is still another consideration which suggests the importance to the colored people of taking the lead in helping to improve and elevate this service. Race prejudice is kept up and increased in thousands of instances by the incompetent and characterless women who are engaged in this work. While there are thousands of worthy and really noble women in domestic service who enjoy the confidence and affection of their employers, there is a large percentage of colored women who, by their general unworthiness, help to give the Negro race a bad name. For white people North and South are very apt to estimate the entire race from the standpoint of their own servant girls. When intelligence takes the place of ignorance, and good manners, efficiency, and self-respect take the place of shiftlessness and irresponsibility in American homes, one of the chief causes of race prejudice will be removed.

It should also be borne in mind that the colored girl who is trained in the arts of housekeeping is better qualified for the high duties of wifehood and motherhood.

Let me say by way of summary that I have dwelt mostly upon the opportunities of domestic service for the following reasons:

1. It is the one field in which colored women meet with almost no opposition. It is ours almost by birthright.

2. The compensation for this service, in Northern communities at least, is higher than that paid for average clerkships in stores and offices.

3. The service is susceptible of almost unlimited improvement and elevation.

4. The nature of the work is largely what we make it.

5. White women of courage and large intelligence are lifting domestic service to a point where it will have the dignity of a profession, and colored women are in danger, through lack of foresight, of being relegated to the positions of scrub women and dishwashers.

6. The colored girl who has no taste or talent for school teaching, dressmaking, or manicuring is in danger of being wasted in idleness, unless we can make domestic service worthy of her ambition and pride.

7. There can be no feature of our race problem more important than the saving of our young women; we can, perhaps, excuse their vanities, but idleness is the mildew on the garment of character.

8. Education has no value to human society, unless it can add importance and respectability to the things we find to do.

9. Though all the factories and offices close their doors at our approach, this will be no calamity if we are strong enough to so transform the work that we must do that it shall become an object of envy and emulation to those who now deny us their industrial fellowship.

SIX

THE WOMAN'S PART IN A MAN'S BUSINESS

One of the speakers, at the last National Convention of the National Negro Business League,[32] was honest enough to make public confession that he owed his success as a business man to his wife, and I believe that if they were generous enough, the majority of the successful men could truthfully say that they too owe more to their wives than to any other one thing for their achievement as business men.

It is because of this unseen, and often unacknowledged, influence that makes for a man's success in the business world, that I wish to say a word in behalf of this silent partner, who concealed from the public eye often stands between the business man and bankruptcy.

Within the last few years, we have come to feel a new pride and a strong sense of confidence in the future of the Negro race, because of the fine courage and wonderful success our men are gaining everywhere as men of business integrity and influence. Indeed we have all been thrilled at times to hear that some of our business men relate how they have conquered prejudice and all kinds of adversity in their strivings to build up large enterprises. But a doubt is raised in some quarters as to whether they merit all of this unqualified praise. Are they not inclined to forget the brave little woman behind the scene whose whole life, through sacrifice, finer instinct and prayers have been as much a part of their business success as the more tangible things of bargain and sale? If these same business men were to take pencil in hand to make an inventory of their assets and all the factors that have entered into their successful business career and leave out the wife, daughter, or the girl book-keeper, they would be sadly lacking a true sense of real values.

Now if we attempt to answer the question, "What is a woman's part in a man's business," there is a sentimental as well as a practical answer that might be given, and one is quite as important as the other, because the intangible things of the spirit are sometimes more real than the things we perceive by the senses. For example, what is business? Is it merely the things that some one has and that some one else wants? Is it mere money, checks, accounts and exchange of commodities? It seems to me that it means something deeper and of more permanent value than all this. If be-

"The Woman's Part in a Man's Business," *Voice of the Negro* 1, no. 11 (1904): 543–47.

hind all this passion and strife to have and to hold or to buy and to sell, there is no finer motive than the mere piling up of profits—no love of wife, child, or home—no incentive to make those who are near and dear to them participate in their success, business would be a very cheap and vulgar thing indeed. A man either goes up or down according to the incentives that lie behind his ambitions and efforts. If it be his honorable ambition to be worthy of a worthy woman, to educate a promising son or daughter, and to establish a respected family name, all his energies and talents will be strained to the uttermost to battle against all possible failure or disappointments. It must appear then that these sentimental considerations are as much a part of a man's business career as fresh air, good sanitation and good government are the essential conditions of the physical world and the government under which he lives.

There is still another view concerning the importance of the colored woman's part in the business affairs of our men in the future. In the first place, we are living in what may be called a woman's age. The old notion that woman was intended by the Almighty to do only those things that men thought they ought to do is fast passing away. In our day, and in this country, a woman's sphere is just as large as she can make it and still be true to her finer qualities of soul. Her world is constantly becoming larger and fuller of the things that are spiritual and beautiful by virtue of her wider influence and larger participation in human affairs. Man is becoming less savage and woman more positive in raising the standards of human living. Sex lines in the professions and business are giving way to the increasing demands for more intelligence and conscience in human affairs. Of course a woman must always be a woman, but nature's laws, and not mere prejudices, must fix the boundary lines to her mind, ambitions and aspirations.

Looking at woman then from this view point of her larger vision and opportunities, what can we say of her possibilities in the business development of our race?

I do not think it too much to say that the American Negro woman is the most interesting woman in this country. I do not say this in any boastful spirit, but I simply mean that she is the only woman whose career lies wholly in front of her. She has no history, no traditions, no race ideals, no inherited resources and no established race character. She is the only woman in America who is almost unknown; the only woman for whom nothing is done; the only woman without sufficient defenders when assailed; the only woman who is still outside of that world of chivalry that in all the ages has apotheosized woman kind. Wars have been declared and fought for women; governments have been established and developed in the name of woman; art, literature and song have all conspired to make woman little less than angels, but they have all been white women. Colored women share in no practical way and indeed are not included in those ideals and creations, and since time began have been the inspirations and motives of man's supremest efforts and ambition.

Alas, what a cheap and common thing would this life be and how unspeakably insignificant would the status of womankind be to-day had not all the world of man made her the one object, nay the shrine of his most passionate devotion. Yet colored women must face an age in this part of the world that insists that they shall not be included in this world of exalted and protected womanhood.

We believe that it is to be the high privilege of the Negro business man to lift the colored woman up and out of her hateful obscurity until she shall be known, loved and exalted because she is a woman and not be despised and distrusted simply because she is a black woman.

As I understand the significance of the progress of the successful Negro business man, it is that in his increasing business relationship with the white race he is opening up a new and respected way of contact, a contact that will give us a kind and extended acquaintance with the white race that we have never before had. If our men can obtain and hold the acquaintance and confidence of the business world, they will be in a position to conquer more prejudices than we have yet been able to estimate. Colored women will never be properly known and the best of them appreciated, until colored men have become more important in those affairs of life where character and achievements count for more than prejudices and suspicions.

Every colored man who succeeds in business brings his wife and daughter a little nearer that sphere of chivalry and protection in which every white woman finds shelter and vindication against every hateful presumption.

Every Negro business man who takes his wife into his confidence, who respects her judgment when deserved, who does all he knows how to do to exalt and idealize her talents and virtues and that of her kind, until she shall become the all-sufficient motive for his further endeavors, is doing his part to make Negro womanhood a part of all that is best and most beautiful in the world's conception of an ideal woman.

A beautiful home built by a man is a tribute, not only to his own wife and family, but also a tribute to womankind everywhere. Every girl well educated is a tribute to womankind. Every school house or hall beautifully adorned and furnished, every artistic window placed in a church as a memorial to wife or daughter is a tribute to woman, and the men who have done these things, or can do them out of their well-earned success as business men, are doing their share to exalt Negro womanhood in America.

That colored women are becoming more and more worthy of this exaltation can be easily proven. She is making progress and year by year is contradicting the cruelly false things imputed to her. The colored girl, like the white girl, is pushing her way into every school whose doors are not closed to her complexion. She is learning book-keeping, stenography and business principles; her fingers are becoming deft in every trade and handicraft that is accessible to her; and above all she is diligently studying the smaller opportunities that escape the eye of the average young man, who is always looking for something large, and seldom finds it.

Let me illustrate what I mean by this statement. There is a woman in Chicago who knew that she knew how to do one thing well, and that was bread making. One of the largest stores in the city employed her by the week as a cook. She understood her business so well that her bread making increased the business of the store so much, that it became the foundation of a new and important department of the store, and to-day that colored woman directs the work only, while several white girls are employed and kept busy making and selling the goods made under this woman's directing skill.

Another colored women in Chicago began some years ago, on a small scale, to do hair work. From a small beginning, she now has a well established business that gives employment to several women. This woman began this business at a time when there were no examples of what was possible in this line of trade.

There are now many credible young women in our large cities who have stopped worrying over the fact that they cannot get employment as clerks in department stores and have made feminine sewing such a well paid profession that they make several times the salary paid to white clerks, and the moral and sanitary conditions of their environment are certainly much better.

As a further evidence of how our young women are training themselves for service in Negro business enterprises, it can be truthfully said that it is no longer necessary for a colored business man, in any kind of business, to employ white girls as accountants or clerks, as he can always secure a competent colored girl, if he so desire. It may also be added that wherever these colored girls are found alert and intelligent, the business man can feel quite sure that his interests are being protected and that a thirst for whisky, cigars or racing does not threaten his cash box.

I believe that the colored woman has as fine an aptitude for business as any other woman in the world, and making all due allowance for her limitations, she is engaged in as great a variety of occupations as any other class of women, which is another proof of her aptness and versatility.

The Negro woman is really *the new woman* [italics added] of the times, and in possibilities the most interesting woman in America. This is the woman who is destined to play an important part in the future business man's career. Indeed she is to be the conservative force in the business of many a man who is today prosperous and hopeful. Many a time he will turn to her in distress when, through over confidence or display, his credit is gone and bankruptcy is staring him in the face, to find his heart gladdened by the sight of many dollars, she has stealthily saved out of the surplus, he was trying to throw away.

There need be no fear that because of her larger participation in the business affairs of life, the colored woman will lose her power and influence as a wife and home maker. A woman has a large degree of adaptability and hence is capable of doing almost everything that a man can do besides doing what is strictly a woman's work.

The progress of the colored woman is normal. In our development as a race, the colored woman and the colored man started even. The man cannot say that he is better educated and has had a wider sphere, for they both began school at the same time. They have suffered the same misfortunes. The limitations put upon their ambitions have been identical. The colored man can scarcely say to his wife, "I am better and stronger than you are," and from the present outlook, I do not think there is any danger of the man getting very far ahead. It is because of this equality of condition and training that colored women are destined to share more intimately in the management of Negro business enterprises, than is true of any other class of women.

As a concession to any doubts that may arise as to this optimistic view of the value of colored women, I will admit that I have been talking only of that type of colored woman who represents the farthest reach of progress amongst us. Her heart is being purged from the dross of a hated bondage, her mind is alert, and she sees and feels, as no one else can, the whole range of baleful influences that shut her out of one half of the better world of love and beauty. Her deft fingers are on every pulsation of pain and progress of the narrow world in which she must live and work. She is the one woman in America who must find her enjoyment in contemplating the remote future and not by living in a joyous present. She must view the promised land of a better and juster age than ours and not aspire to enter it.

Yes she is a woman of love—a woman of honor, a woman whose vision of the true, beautiful and good lends enchantment to her being. With the interest of this kind of woman in a man's business he cannot fail, and without her he has already failed.

SEVEN

THE COLORED GIRL

What becomes of the colored girl? This is a question that cannot fail to be of interest to men and women everywhere, who have at heart the well-being of all the people.

That the term "colored girl" is almost a term of reproach in the social life of America is all too true; she is not known and hence not believed in; she belongs to a race that is best designated by the term "problem,"[33] and she lives beneath the shadow of that problem which envelopes and obscures her.

The colored girl may have character, beauty and charms ineffable, but she is not in vogue. The muses of song, poetry, and art do not woo and exalt her. She is not permitted or supposed to typify the higher ideals that make life something higher, sweeter and more spiritual than a mere existence. Man's instinctive homage at the shrine of womankind draws a line of color, which places her forever outside its mystic circle.

The white manhood of America sustains no kindly or respectful feeling for the colored girl; great nature has made her what she is, and the laws of men have made for her a class below the level of other women. The women of other races bask in the clear sunlight of man's chivalry, admiration, and even worship, while the colored woman abides in the shadow of his contempt, mistrust, or indifference.

How much easier it would be to be a good Christian and to be loyal to the better instincts of manhood, if these girls of color were not like other girls in heart, brain and soul. Yet her presence is inevitable. The character of American womanhood is, in spite of itself, affected by the presence of the colored girl. The current of her aspirations finds a subtle connection with the aspirations of the thousands who socially feel themselves to be beyond and above her. Nay, more; those who meanly malign and humiliate her are unconsciously sapping the sweetness and light ont of their own lives. The colored girl is a cause as well as an effect. We cannot comprehend the term American womanhood without including the colored girl. Thanks to the All-wise Creator of men and things, the law of life is infinitely deeper than the law of society. The ties of kinship and love continually cross and recross the color line of man-made prejudices. The woman beautiful, the woman courageous, the woman capable is neither white nor colored; she is bound to be loved and admired in spite of all the meannesses that are of human

"The Colored Girl," *Voice of the Negro* 2, no. 6 (1905): 400–3.

origin. For, after all, "color is only skin deep." Has the colored girl the heart, spirit and subtle tenderness of womanhood? Such a question would be impertinent in an age where human life meant something too sacred to be loved or scorned, according to color.

It is because of this tyranny of race prejudice that the colored girl is called upon to endure and overcome more difficulties than confront any other women in our country. In law, religion and ethics, she is entitled to everything, but in practice there are always forces at work that would deny her anything. But yet, as meanly as she is thought of, hindered as she is in all directions, she is always doing something of merit and credit that is not expected of her. She is irrepressible. She is insulted, but she holds up her head; she is scorned, but she proudly demands respect. Thus has it come to pass that the most interesting girl of this country is the colored girl. Upon her devolves the marvelous task of establishing the social status of the race. Black men may work and save and build, but all their labor and all their savings and creations will not make a strong foundation for the social life of the race without the pure heart, cultivated mind, and home-making spirit of the colored woman. It is a heart aching task, but the colored girl must and will accomplish it.

At this hour when a thousand social ills beset her, she is taking hold of life in a serious and helpful spirit. It is becoming more and more evident that she is not afraid of the age in which she lives nor its problems. She is a daughter of misfortune but she contributes her full share to the joys of the life about her. She is the very heart of the race problem. She is beginning to realize that the very character of our social fabric depends upon the quality of her womanliness.

It would seem trite to recount her services to the cause of education. Take the colored girl out of our schools and all progress would cease. As an educator she does more work with less compensation than any other teacher in the country. Follow her, if you will, into the remote corners of the schoolless South, and you will find material for such a story of gentle martyrdom as would forever put to shame those who hold our girls in light esteem. As a teacher and guide to thousands who have had no moral training in home and school, she has fully earned the right to be, at least, respected. No class of our people have so quickly caught and appropriated the self-sacrificing devotion of the pioneer New England teacher as the colored girl. She has shown in cases innumerable that she can abandon social pleasures, good salaries, ordinary comforts, and the flattery of men for the sacred cause of bringing light out of darkness to the masses. Would you know the real heroines of the colored race, do not look for them among the well dressed throngs that parade our streets and fill our churches, but look in obscure places like Mt. Meigs in Alabama, the settlement in Georgia under the benign direction of Miss Julia Jackson,[34] or in the alleys of South Washington, where Mrs. [Sarah Collins] Fernandez[35] works, prays and waits. Here you will find women of real consecration and the spirit of Jane Addams, working with as well as for the unfortunate all around them. This type of colored girl is increasing every day in numbers and influence. She will some day become the heart and the very life of everything that is best amongst us. This is a work that calls for courage, patience, love, and the best qualities of the human heart, because it must be wrought out in the midst of the very worst conditions and emphasized by example, as well as by teaching and precept.

Yet there are men and women who profess to be fair and just who still insist that the colored girl is without character. It is true that we have our trifling girls, and in this respect we are thoroughly human.

While we believe that the colored girl of character amongst us is a constantly increasing factor in our progress, she has but few ways of making herself known beyond her immediate environment. She has inspired no novels.[36] Those who write for the press and magazines seldom think of this dark-skinned girl who is persistently breaking through the petty tyrannies of cast into the light of recognition. She has enterprise and ambition that are always in advance of her opportunities. At this very moment she is knocking at every door through which other women, less equipped than she, have passed on from one achievement to another.

In Chicago, for example, where the color line is quite rigidly drawn against the colored girl in almost every direction, still it is possible to find her pluckily challenging this humiliating color line, and in many surprising instances with success. I know of more than a score of girls who are holding positions of high responsibility, which were at first denied to them as beyond their reach. These positions so won and held were never intended for them; to seek them was considered an impertinence, and to hope for them was an absurdity. Nothing daunted these young women, conscious of their own deserving, [who] would not admit or act upon the presumption that they were not as good and capable as other girls who were not really superior to them. It is certainly not too much to say that the colored girl is fast developing character and spirit sufficient to make her own way and win the respect and confidence of those who once refused even to consider her claims of character and fitness.

What the colored girl craves, above all things, is to be respected and believed in. This is more important than position and opportunities. In fact there can be for her no such thing as opportunity, unless she can win the respect of those who have it in their power to humiliate her. How can she win this respect? This question is addressed to colored men quite as much as to white men. I believe that as a general thing we hold our girls too cheaply. Too many colored men entertain very careless, if not contemptible, opinions of the colored girl. They are apt to look to other races for their types of beauty and character. For the most part the chivalry of colored men for colored women has in it but little heart and no strength of protection. They ought to appreciate that a colored girl of character and intelligence is a very precious asset in our social life, and they should act accordingly.

Among the Jewish people, for example, their women are safe-guarded and exalted in ways that make their character and womanhood sacred. The colored girl has already done enough for herself and her race to deserve at least the colored man's respect. We have all too many colored men who hold the degrading opinions of ignorant white men, that all colored girls are alike. They lose sight of the fact that colored girls like other girls are apt to be just as pure, noble, and sweet as the best of our men shall insist upon their being. How rare are the reported instances of colored men resenting any slur or insult upon their own women. Colored women can never be all that they would be until colored men shall begin to exalt their character and beauty and to throw about them the chivalry of love and protection which shall command the recognition and respect of all the world. There is something fundamentally wrong in our social instincts and sentiment, if we fail to recognize the ever enlarging difference between the pure and impure, the upright and degraded of colored women.

The colored girl of character and accomplishments is abroad in the land. She wants and deserves many things, but the greatest of her needs is the respect and confidence of those who should exalt and respect her. Is the colored man brave enough to stand out and say to all the world, "Thus far and no farther in your attempt to insult and degrade our women?"

It is not in any mere sentimental sense that this plea is made for a more generous respect for colored women by colored men. Our women have comparatively none of the social paraphernalia and settings that command general admiration. If they are to be respected and admired to their full deserving, it must be for what they are and not for what they have. In this respect they are unlike the women of other races. The very unpopularity of their complexion obscures their merits.

The colored man, as well as the white man, is more apt to be attracted by womanly appearance than by womanly merit. For example, there are at this hour thousands of superior young colored women in this country who are compelled to fill occupations far below their accomplishments and deservings. Are they respected and admired because of the courage of their determination not to be idle? Scarcely. Those who make up and are responsible for what is called the higher life amongst us are apt to scorn the colored girl who works with her hands. Only the parlor girl finds social favor. This sort of borrowed snobbishness is responsible for the going wrong of many of our girls.

What our girls and women have a right to demand from our best men is that they cease to initiate the artificial standards of other people and create a race standard of their own. In no other way can we make prominent and important the colored girl of character and intelligence. What the colored girl needs today is encouragement to do whatever her hands find to do, and be protected and honored for it. If the colored girl of character and intelligence must cook, who shall say that she is not as deserving of the honors of the best social life as the girl who plays the piano or manipulates the typewriter?

The way to exalt the colored girl is to place a higher premium on character than we do upon the quality of her occupation. A fine girl is the supreme thing. Let her be loved, admired, encouraged, and above all things heroically protected against the scorn and contempt of men, black as well as white.

EIGHT

COLORED WOMEN OF CHICAGO

What is the status and general improvement of the colored women of Chicago? Anything like statistics is out of the question. Whatever the general improvement of the condition of women in the city, it is shared alike by all women who are susceptible to progress.

To see colored women on the streets, in public assemblies, and in the everyday walks of life, they seem altogether prosperous and sufficient. If they feel the sting of race prejudice, they seem to be confident of their own worth and hopeful for better conditions.

One important evidence of progress is the enlargement and improvement of the home life of the Negro people. Ten or fifteen years ago they lived in districts of the city bordering on what may be called the "slums." Vices of all kinds menaced the morals and health conditions of their families. But it is now easy to discern a great improvement in this respect. Better economic conditions have enabled them to purchase and occupy residences on some of the finest avenues and boulevards of the city.

It scarcely need be stated that in reference to employment in the trades, shops, and stores, colored women are the least favored of any class of women in the city, yet it is impossible for them to be idle and respected. While only a few colored women are fortunate enough to gain positions in what are considered the higher callings, they are nevertheless industrious and increasingly willing to do whatever their hands find in order to earn a respectable living.

About fifty colored women have won positions as teachers in our mixed public schools. There is also a surprising number of young women holding good positions as clerks and stenographers. One young woman through civil service examination secured an important position with the Board of Education in Chicago, and is now private secretary to the assistant superintendent of schools.

Young colored women may also be found acting as assistants in dental offices, as court stenographers, as demonstrators of special goods in large department stores, as meat inspectors at the stockyards, a few in canning and hair factories, a few as clerks, and scores of them earn a comfortable living as manicurists, chiropodists, and hair culturists in private families.

Southern Workman 43 (October 1914): 564–66.

In addition to these there are a number of colored women who have their own millinery establishments, beauty shops, and dressmaking and costuming parlors that are elegantly appointed and up-to-date in every detail. There is also an increasing number of professional nurses, several of them holding positions as nurses in the public schools and members of the Visiting Nurses' Association. There are several colored women connected with the Juvenile Court acting as probation officers, and one adult probation officer. There are half a dozen colored women physicians, three dentists, and one practicing attorney. Eight or ten young colored women are employed in the Public Library. There is a large number of music teachers, both vocal and instrumental. As a further evidence of progress, young colored women are eagerly crowding the night schools of the city in order to equip themselves for business positions.

A class of women that cannot be ignored, in this story of the life of the colored women of Chicago, is the women who work with their hands in the humbler walks of life, as cooks, housecleaners, laundresses, caretakers, and domestics. One of the most interesting sights in our public streets in the early morning hours is the large army of colored women going in all directions to do their day's work. These women deserve great credit for their eager willingness to aid their husbands in helping to provide a living for themselves and their families.

Another phase of the life of these colored women is their passion for organization. There are clubs for the study of civics, social clubs to promote the refinements of life, clubs for the care and protection of dependent children, religious organizations in the interest of churches, and a number of social settlements and secret societies.

The most important undertaking among colored women is the establishment of the Phyllis Wheatley Home. It was organized and incorporated some years ago, for the purpose of giving shelter and protection to the young colored women who wander into Chicago unacquainted with the snares and pitfalls of a great city. The Home is a comfortable brick building, simply furnished, and offers a home for young women until they have secured employment, and one to which they can appeal and find a welcome at any time. Mrs. L.A. Davis[37] is the founder and promoter of this enterprise, and is president of a progressive club of colored women who look after and support this noble work.

A new and important responsibility has come to Chicago women in the franchise. It is believed that this power granted to the women of the state of Illinois is going to lift colored women to new importance as citizens. They appreciate what it means and are eagerly preparing themselves to do their whole duty. They believe that they now have an effective weapon with which to combat prejudice and discrimination of all kinds. There need be no anxiety as to the conduct of these newly made colored citizens. They have had a large and varied experience in organizations and we expect to see in them an exhibition of the best there is in the colored race.

This splendid extension of the Fourteenth and Fifteenth Amendments will make many things possible and open many avenues of progress that have heretofore been closed to colored women. It is the hope of the leaders of the race that these new citizens will cultivate whatever is best in heart and mind that will enable them to meet the common tasks of life, as well as the higher responsibilities, with confidence and hope.

Part Three

· AFRICAN AMERICANS ·

NINE

RELIGIOUS DUTY TO THE NEGRO

The strength and weakness of the Christian religion as believed, preached and practiced in the United States is aptly illustrated in its influence as a civilizing and educational force among the colored people of this country. The Negro[38] was brought to this country by Christians, for the use of Christians, and he has ever since been treated, estimated, and gauged by what are called Christian ideas of right and wrong.

The Negro has been in America so long and has been so completely isolated from everything that is foreign to American notions, as to what is compatible with Christianity, that he may be fittingly said to be entirely the product of Christian influences. The vices and virtues of the American Negro are the same in kind and degree as those of the men and women from whom he has been learning, by precept and example, all that he knows of God and of humanity. The fetiches and crudities of the dark continent have long since ceased to be a part of his life and character, he is by every mark, impulse and aspiration an American Christian, and to the American church belongs the credit and responsibility of all that he is and is to be as a man and citizen of this republic.

Religion, like every other force in America, was first used as an instrument and servant of slavery. All attempts to Christianize the Negro were limited by the important fact that he was property of a valuable and peculiar sort, and that the property value must not be disturbed, even if his soul were lost. If Christianity could make the Negro docile, domestic and less an independent and fighting savage, let it be preached to that extent and no further. Do not open the Bible too wide.

Such was the false, pernicious and demoralizing Gospel preached to the American slave for two hundred years. But, bad as this teaching was, it was scarcely so demoralizing as the Christian ideals held up for the Negro's emulation. When mothers saw their babes sold by Christians on the auction block in order to raise money to send missionaries to foreign lands; when black Christians saw white Christians openly do everything forbidden in the Decalogue; when, indeed, they saw, as no one else could see, hypocrisy in all things triumphant everywhere, is it not remarkable if such people have any religious sense of the purities of Christianity? People

"Religious Duty to the Negro," in *The World's Congress of Religion*, ed. J.W. Hanson (Chicago: W.B. Conkey, 1894), 893–97.

who are impatient of the moral progress of the colored people certainly are ignorant as to how far false teachings and vicious examples tended to dull the moral senses of the race.

As it is, there is much to be unlearned as well as to be learned. That there is something higher and better in the Christian religion than rewards and punishments is a new lesson to thousands of colored people who are still worshiping under the old dispensation of the slave Bible. But it is not an easy task to unlearn religious conceptions. "Servants, obey your masters," was preached and enforced by all the cruel instrumentalities of slavery, and by its influence the colored people were made the most valued slaves in the world. The people who in Africa resisted with terrible courage all invasions of the white races became through Christianity the most docile and defenseless of servants.

Knowing full well that the religion offered to the Negro was first stripped of moral instructions and suggestions, there are thousands of white church members even who charge, or are ready to believe, that the colored people are a race of moral reprobates. Fortunately the Negro's career in America is radiant with evidence showing that he has always known the difference between courage and lawlessness of all forms, and anarchy in this country is not of Negro origin nor a part of his history.

There was a notable period in the history of this country when the moral force of the Negro character was tested to an extraordinary extent and he was not found wanting. When the country was torn asunder by the passions of civil war, and everybody thirsted for blood and revenge in every violent form, when to ravage and kill was the all-controlling passion of the hour, the Negro's opportunity for retribution was ripe and at hand.

The men who degraded the race and were risking everything to continue that degradation left their widows, their daughters, their mothers, wealth, and all the precious interests of home in the keeping of a race who had received no lessons of moral restraint. It seems but tame to say that the Negro race was loyal to that trust and responsibility. Nowhere in Christendom has such nobleness of heart and moral fortitude been exampled among any people, and a recollection of the Negro's conduct under this extraordinary test should save the race from the charge of being lacking in moral instincts.

There is yet another notable example of the moral heroism of the colored American in spite of his lack of real religious instruction. The African Methodist Episcopal church, with its million members, vast property in churches, schools, academies, publications, and learned men and women, is an enduring monument to the righteous protest of Christians to establish the mean sentiment of caste in religion and degrade us to a footstool position at the shrine of Christian worship. The colored churches of all denominations in this country are not evidences of our unfitness for religious equality, but they are so many evidences of the Negro's religious heroism and self respect that would not brook the canting assertion of mastery and superiority of those who could see the Negro only as a slave, whether on earth or in heaven.

There is another and brighter side to the question as to how far the Christian religion has helped the colored people of America to realize their positions as citizens of this proud republic. Enough has already been said to show that the colored American, in spite of all the downward forces that have environed [sic] him, must have been susceptible to the higher influences of the false teachings thereof. Though the Bible was not an open book to the Negro before emancipation, thousands of the enslaved men and women of the Negro race learned more than was taught to them. Thousands of them realized the deeper meanings, the sweeter consolations and the spiritual awakenings that are a part of the religious experiences of all Christians. These thousands were the nucleus out of which was to grow the correct religious life of the millions.

In justification of the church it must be said that there has always been a goodly number of heroic men and saintly women who believed in the manhood and womanhood of the Negro race, and at all times gave the benefit of the best religious teachings of the times. The colored people gladly acknowledge that, since emancipation, the churches of the country have almost redeemed themselves from their former sin of complicity with slavery.

The churches saw these people come into the domain of citizenship stripped of all possessions, unfurnished with intelligence, untrained in the school of self-sacrifice and moral restraint, with no way out of the wilderness of their ignorance of all things, and no leadership. They saw these people with no homes or household organizations, no social order, no churches, no schools, and in the midst of people who, by training and instinct, could not recognize the manhood of the race. They saw the government give these people the certificate of freedom and citizenship without telling them what it meant. They saw politicians count these people as so many votes, and laughed at them when pleading for schools of learning for their children.

They saw all the great business and industrial organizations of the country ignoring these people as having any possible relationship to the producing and consuming forces of the nation. They saw the whole white population looking with distrust and contempt upon these men and women, new and untried in the responsibilities of civil life. While the colored people of America were thus friendless and without status of any kind, the Christian churches came instantly, heroically and powerfully to the rescue. They began at once not only to create a sentiment favorable to the uprising of these people, but began the all-important work of building schools and churches.

They aroused the philanthropic impulse of the American people to such a degree that millions [in] money and an army of men and women have covered the hills of the South with agencies of regeneration of the white and black slaves of the South. The churches have vied with each other in their zeal for good work in spreading the Gospel of intelligence. Going into states that knew nothing of public school systems they have created a passion for education among both races. States that have been hostile to the idea of universal intelligence and that at one time made it a criminal offense to teach black men and women to read and write, have, under the blessed influence of the missionary work of the churches, been wonderfully converted and are now making appropriations for the education of colored children and founding and maintaining institutions that rank as normal schools, colleges and industrial schools.

Whatever may be our just grievances in the southern states, it is fitting that we acknowledge that, considering their poverty and past relationship to the Negro race, they have done remarkably well for the cause of education among us. That the whole South should commit itself to the principle that the colored people have a right to be educated is an immense acquisition to the cause of popular education.

We are grateful to the American church for this significant change of sentiment, as we are grateful to it for making our cause and needs popular at the fireside of thousands of the best homes in the country. The moral force that vouched for the expenditure of nearly $40,000,000, voluntarily given for educational and church work in the South during the last twenty-five years, is splendid testimony of the interest felt by the American people in the cause of the intellectual and moral development of the Negro race. Bearing in mind all this good work done by the churches since emancipation, it is proper to ask, what can religion further do for the colored people? This question is itself significant of the important fact that colored people are beginning to think for themselves and to feel restive and conscious of every limitation to their development.

At the risk of underestimating church work in the South I must say that religion in its more blessed influences, in its wider and higher reaches of good in humanity, has made less progress in refining the life and character of the white and colored people of the South than the activity of the church interests of the South would warrant us in believing. That there is more profession than religion, more so-called church work than religious zeal, is characteristic of the American people generally, and of the southern people particularly.

More religion and less church may be accepted as a general answer to the question, "What can religion further do to advance the condition of the colored people of the South?" It is not difficult to specify wherein church interests have failed and wherein religion could have helped to improve these people. In the first place the churches have sent among us too many ministers who have had no sort of preparation and fitness for the work assigned them. With a due regard for the highly capable colored ministers of the country, I feel no hesitancy in saying that the advancement of our condition is more hindered by a large part of the ministry intrusted with leadership than by any other single cause.

Only men of moral and mental force, of a patriotic regard for the relationship of the two races, can be of real service as ministers in the South. Less theology and more of human brotherhood, less declamation and more common sense and love for truth, must be the qualifications of the new ministry that shall yet save the race from the evils of false teachings. With this new and better ministry will come the reign of that religion which ministers to the heart and gives to all our soul functions an impulse to righteousness. The tendency of creeds and doctrine to obscure religion, to make complex that which is elemental and simple, to suggest partisanship and doubt in that which is universal and certain has seriously hindered the moral progress of the colored people of this country.

The home and social life of these people is in urgent need of the purifying power of religion. We do not yet sufficiently appreciate the fact that the heart of every social evil and disorder among the colored people, especially of the rural South, is the lack of those inherent moral potencies of home and family that are the well-springs of all the good in human society.

In nothing was slavery so savage and so relentless as in its attempted destruction of the family instincts of the Negro race in America. Individuals, not families; shelters, not homes; herding, not marriages were the cardinal sins in that system of horrors. Who can ever express in song or story the pathetic history of this race of unfortunate people when freedom came, groping about for their scattered off-spring with only instinct to guide them, trying to knit together the broken ties of family kinship? It was right at this point of rehabilitation of the home life of these people that the philanthropic efforts of America should have begun. It was right here that religion in its humanitarian tendencies of love, in its moral direction and purifying force, was most needed, and still is most needed. Every preacher and every teacher in the South will tell us that preaching from the pulpit and teaching in the schoolhouse is but half done so long as the homes are uninstructed in that practical religion that can make pure and sacred every relationship it touches of man, woman and child.

Religion should not leave these people alone to learn from birds and beasts those blessed meanings of marriage, motherhood and family. Religion should not utter itself only once or twice a week through a minister from a pulpit, but should open every cabin door and get immediate contact with those who have not yet learned to translate into terms of conduct the promptings of religion.

TEN

INDUSTRIAL EDUCATION—
WILL IT SOLVE THE NEGRO PROBLEM?

Industrial Education is a much overworked term. Among the colored people, at least, it has caused no end of confusion of ideas and absurd conclusions as to what is the best kind of education for the masses of the people. Scarcely any subject, since emancipation, has been talked about and discussed as this one subject of Industrial Education. All sorts and conditions of people have their opinion as to the merits and demerits of this kind of education, and have been curiously eager to give expression to such opinions in the public press, in the pulpit, and on the rostrum. Among these thinkers, writers, and speakers there are many who know absolutely nothing about the question, and there are others whose academic training has given them a fixed bias against any sort of mental training which does not include as a *sine qua non* the "humanities." On the other hand, there are those among the advocates of Industrial Education who insist that nothing else will solve the race problem. So the discussion goes on from one extreme to the other, with more or less earnestness and noise, truth and falsehood, sense and nonsense.

With the exception of occasional personalities and vindictive misrepresentations, this widespread discussion of the principles of Industrial Education has added enormously to the general interest in the subject of education for the colored and white people of the South. More than any other man, Dr. Booker T. Washington has made the subject of education in the South one of paramount interest to all the people. The helpful agencies that have been created and developed by this new propaganda of the training of the brawn as well as the brain of the people are quite beyond calculation. Industrial Education has long since ceased to be a theory. The discussion as to whether or not this kind of education is best for the Negro race may go on indefinitely, but in the meantime, the industrial system of education has taken deep root in the needs of the people.

But what is this Industrial Education? The following are some of the answers given by persons who ought to know better: "to teach the Negro how to work hard"; "to teach the Negro how to be a good servant and

"Industrial Education—Will It Solve the Negro Problem?" *Colored American* (July 1904): 491–95.

forever hewers of wood and drawers of water"; "to teach the Negro how to undervalue his manhood rights."

It is scarcely necessary to say that Industrial Education is immeasurably more than anything contained in these definitions. In the term Industrial Education, the emphasis is always upon education. Mathematics, drawing, chemistry, history, psychology, and sociology go along with the deft handling of the carpenter's and engineer's tools, with the knowledge of farming, dairying, printing, and the whole range of the mechanical arts. To the students in the industrial or manual training schools, their education means more than the mere names of the various trades imply. The carpenter has been given the foundation training by which he may well aspire to become an architect, the printer a publisher, the engineer a manufacturer, and the trained farmer a prosperous land owner. It can be readily seen that, by this kind of training, occupations that were once considered mere drudgery have become enlarged and ennobled by the amount of intelligence put into them. It was once thought that no one outside of the professions and other well deserved occupations needed to be educated. The tradesman or mechanic was not expected to know anything beyond the more or less skillful handling of his cash book or tools. An educated mechanic was the exception. Farming without the knowledge of forestry, dairying and the many other things that enter into the farmer's life was regarded as drudgery.

What was true of masculine occupations was equally true of woman in the whole range of her special occupations and domestic concerns. It was thought that the only occupations for which women needed any sort of training were those which fitted her for the parlor and "society." Piano playing was an accomplishment: cooking and housekeeping, drudgery. A woman's apron was a badge of sexuality, and the kitchen a place not to be frequented by ladies. Poor woman! How narrow was her sphere! How wide the distance between the sphere of her every-day home usefulness and the accomplishments of the "lady!" How different since the newer education has enlarged our sense of values. A new dignity has been added to the occupations that concern our health, our homes, and our happiness. Through the influence of schools of domestic science, cooking has become a profession; the trained nurse divides honors with the physician; the dressmaker and the milliner, by proper training, have become artists. In fact, Industrial training has dignified everything it has touched. It is not only banishing drudgery from the workshop and the home, but is widening the opportunities for talents of all kinds. There can be no such thing as caste in the every day work of life, if that work is under the direction and control of trained intellects. Whether we do our share of the world's work with the pen or with the tool, in the office or in the shop, in the broad green acres on the hill slopes, or in the senate hall, the question is always the same—how much intelligence and character do you bring to your work. We believe that it is not too much to say that this is the spirit, the purpose, and the result of Industrial Education.

Yet there are those who oppose this kind of education, as if it meant exactly the opposite of all this. It must be said that in a good deal of this opposition there is a curious blending of ignorance, envy, and perversity. The best that can be said of those who think they are sincere is that they represent a belated conception of the higher and larger functions of education.

It should be stated in passing that nearly all of the most competent educators of the county, including presidents of the leading universities, believe in the Washington idea of Industrial Education, for white as well as colored people. That the idea has the encouragement and support of the best thought of the day is witnessed by the large number of industrial, polytechnical, and agricultural schools that have been built and developed in the Northern states during the past ten or twelve years. These schools are always overcrowded by white students. It is very difficult to keep a white boy in a high school long enough to enable him to graduate, but he will remain in a manual training school without persuasion. A leading professor in the Chicago University[39] recently stated to his class that Booker T. Washington must always be rewarded as the true leader of American education in its largest sense. The conception as to what is real and fundamental in education has become so broadened that even the great universities are enlarging their curriculum so as to include schools of technology. Such being the sphere and purpose and resulting possibilities of industrial education, can it be right or just to urge it as especially suited to the condition of the colored people?

It is claimed by the academician that the Negro is not essentially different from any other people, and, therefore, he should not be singled out for any special kind of education. We certainly all like to believe that the Negro is as good as anyone else, but the important fact remains that the Negro is essentially different from any other race amongst us in the conditions that beset him. Just what these conditions are every intelligent Negro knows and feels. Among these conditions are illiteracy and restricted opportunities for the exercise of his talents and tastes. To multitudes of colored people illiteracy is a continuous night without a single ray of light. Inability to read and write is the least of his deficiencies; the ignorance of what to do to help himself and his kind is the pitiful thing. Any system of education that does not, in its helpful effect, reach from the school house back to the cabin is of small value in solving the race problem. The crying need of the multitude is, "Can you show me how to live, how to raise more and better crops, how to hold and use the benefits of my labor, how to own and keep the land that I have earned over and over again by my labor, how to appreciate the value of the earth's bounties and turn them into the currents of commerce? Any system of education that cannot give direct and helpful answers to this wail of despair, to this confession of incompetency and helplessness, falls far short of effectiveness. Industrial education aims to reach these conditions. It first aims to bring the benighted masses into conscious relationship with their own environments. It comes to teach these despairing people how to work out their own salvation by the tools and instrumentalities that are indigenous to their habitations. If agriculture must, for a long time to come, be the chief occupation of our people, then let their education for a long time to come be inclusive of all that which makes for thrift and intelligence in husbandry. If engineers, carpenters, plumbers, printers, wagon-makers, brick-makers, electricians, and other artisans are needed to build up and develop the rich resources of the communities in which they must live, is it not wise to train our own people to do all of this work so masterfully as to give them a monopoly against all others? It has been predicted already that the colored people will some day own the South, but this ownership can be realized only by the exercise of thrift, character and practical intelligence that can be gained in the best of the industrial schools.

It is not the contention of this article that Industrial Education must be the limit of education for colored people. We believe with Dr. [Jeremiah Eames] Rankin,[40] of Howard University, that "any system of education for the Negro that does not open to him the golden gate of the highest culture will fail on the ethical and spiritual side." At the same time the creators of wealth—the great captains of industry, who are the real builders of communities—have been those who wrought intelligently with their hands. The demand for colored artisans of all kinds is always in excess of the supply. The supply of lawyers, doctors and ministers and other professions always exceeds the demand. The race is not only poor in the resources and means of wealth, but poor also in the practical intelligence that creates wealth.

It will prove an immeasurable blunder if we shall now lack the foresight to provide for our young men and women the kind of training that will enable them to do everything in the line of industries that will equip them to become the real builders of the future greatness of the South. If by our neglect the master mechanics and skilled laborers of other races must be called into the South to do this work the Negro will be relegated to a position of hopeless servitude.

The advocates of industrial education are laying the foundation broad and deep for the future as well as providing for the present. They are wisely seeking to widen the Negro's sphere of usefulness. They realize the danger of equipping young colored men and women for occupations from which they are excluded by an unyielding prejudice. They are aiming to teach our aspiring young people that the positions and occupations from which they are now barred are not more honorable or more remunerative than those which they are permitted to enter, if they but carry the proper training and intelligence into those occupations. It teaches that the prizes of life lie along every pathway in which intelligence and character walk arm in arm. A professional man is not better than a mechanic unless he has more intelligence. An intelligent blacksmith is worth more to a community than an incompetent doctor, a hungry lawyer or an immoral minister.

The time is coming, aye, is now here, when a colored graduate from a school of domestic science will be more honored and better paid than are many white women who now hold the positions colored women cannot enter. The time is coming when there will be no excuse for a colored young woman to remain in soul-destroying idleness because she cannot obtain a clerkship. She can be trained in an industrial school for positions that she can fill and still be socially eligible among those who make "society." An increasing respect is being shown to the young man or woman who is brave enough to learn a trade and follow it with pride and honor. The graduate from an industrial school finds a place awaiting him or her with a good salary. The graduates from Dr. Jones's Cooking School, in Richmond, Va., receive from $14 to $16 per week, while the untrained cook receives $5 per week. The graduates from Provident Hospital and Training School [for Nurses] receive from $15 to $25 per week for their services; the untrained nurse not more than $6 per week. These instances are fair examples of how direct and immediate is the value of industrial training added to individual worth. These schools are every day creating new opportunities for honorable and well paid employment. The graduates of schools of this kind are seldom mendicants for employment. They have won their independence, and their efficiency is a part of the good in every community in which they live and work.

The graduates of Hampton, Tuskegee, and other industrial schools are the advance guard of efficiency and conquest. They touch more sides of the life of a community than any other class of our educated people. Rich and poor, black and white, prejudiced and unprejudiced, those who dread "Negro domination" and those who expect it must all at one time or another ask for the service of the best trained artisan in the community. Along every pathway of material progress in that great undeveloped country south of the Ohio, we will soon begin to read all sorts of evidences of what industrial education has done for these black builders of a new empire of power.

The heroic efforts of Dr. Washington and others to furnish a system of education that shall be of the greatest good to the greatest number should not and does not discourage what is called the higher education. In their tastes and aptitudes our young men and women are like those of other races. The doors of the universities are always open to the few who have the gifts and tastes for scholarship. The passion for higher education has not seemed to diminish as a consequence of the development of industrial schools. Every year witnesses a large number of Negro graduates from the best universities of the country. Any of these college graduates find their way down to Tuskegee, proving that Dr. Washington insists upon giving his Tuskegee students the advantage of studying under the best educated Negroes in the country.

The colored people are entitled to the best possible education that this country can afford, but this education should fit them for the life they must live. It should give as much encouragement to the would-be mechanic and agriculturist as to the would-be teacher, the lawyer or other professions. It should be the special aim to reach helpfully the lives of the thousands who live under conditions peculiarly their own and different from that of any other people.

These schools should educate their graduates toward and not away from the people. The evidence of this kind of education should make itself felt in every honorable relationship that the Negro bears to his community and to his government. Such an education will make the Negro efficient, self-respecting, proud, brave, and proof against every prophecy of evil that would consign him to a destiny of "hopeless inferiority."

ELEVEN

DO WE NEED ANOTHER NAME?

The present-day problems that confront the colored people are so many, serious, and practical, that impractical questions and remote interests do not often intrude themselves into the stirring discussions of to-day. Yet there are quite a respectable few of our thoughtful men and women who are worrying a great deal about the name we shall be known by. They propose nothing less than a complete surrender of the old designations and the adoption of something entirely new and unrelated to past conditions.

Those who are studying and writing upon the question are mostly of the present generation of Negro scholars and writers. They have made the question serious, respectable, and interesting and have succeeded in making the people feel and believe that all the designations by which the American descendants of Africans are known and described are hopelessly and disproportionately associated with all the miseries of bondage and race prejudice; that the existing names are hindrances to progress and persistently suggest inferiority to the educated young men and women of the race. In other words there is now by grace of new laws and new conditions, a new Negro,[41] and in order to force this important fact upon the attention and conscience of the American people, there is needed a new name that shall be more in harmony with the new conditions.

It does seem to be a curious fact that the so-called Negro, or colored race, when considered in all its variety of shade, admixture, and lack of fundamental differences from other native-born Americans, has no exclusively appropriate name. Negro (vulgarized as "nigger"), "colored," and "Afro-American," are the various designations of the race of people once held in American slavery.

The chief objection urged against the term Negro is that it is not ethnically descriptive when applied to hundreds of thousands of people who have been so completely transformed as to leave no physical resemblance to any of the African races. A mulatto, a quadroon, an octoroon, or a creole, is not a Negro except by a false classification, based upon the common condition of an inferior status.

The milder term "colored" is the one name that is suggestive of progress toward respectful recognition. In the use of the terms "nigger"

"Do We Need Another Name?" *Southern Workman* 33 (January 1904): 33–36.

and "colored" there is generally all the difference of sentiment that there is between the terms hatred and kindness, contempt and respect.

As a race name, of course, the word "colored" is lacking in precision and ethnic meaning, and its application is certainly attended with much confusion and error. Yet the name is largely favored, because it has been, and still is, the first refuge of those whose feelings toward the Negro have been changed from hatred and mistrust into kindness and confidence. This indefinite name is in favor by reason of its lack of essential or deep significance. It is thought that as the race progresses more and more toward the full enjoyment of all the blessings of equality in American life, the significance of the term "colored" will gradually fade as a term of difference and will finally become a mere term of convenience, having no deeper sense than the name brunette. When it is remembered that the so-called Negro race, or colored race, is in language, religion, and instinct as thoroughly American as any of the other races who have come to America and lost their race identity, there is no reason why thousands of them should be known and designated as anything else than Americans.

Yet many of the best thinkers and writers in this discussion are fiercely opposed to the further use of the meaningless term "colored" people. To quote one of them:

> Just listen to the name colored! Apologetic, somewhat tasteless, and falsely euphemistic. Imagine succeeding under the discouragement of such a nickname! Cats may be colored, rainbows colored, rags may be colored, but men never!

The discussion has now narrowed down to the comparative merits of the old historic word Negro, and the somewhat new, hyphenated term Afro-American. What is being written in defense of these terms is something almost entirely new to American thought. The sciences—ethnology, geography, and sociology—have all been called in to do service in this novel battle for a name.

Professor DuBois[42] writes:

> Finally, then, what of the name Negro? Here is a term strong, definite, distinct, and great. There is no doubt whom the user means—that dark and harsh-haired people who from the world's dawn have dwelt within the bosom of the sun! How rich and pregnant with history and legend comes the name out of the dark past. It points to something more than a hero history; it points to a human history; to half-divine Negro melodies, to Negro slavery, and the bitter, withering sorrow; then, too, to the day of emancipation and the hard, dogged struggle in a smiling world—a creeping toward the truth which shall make us free. What word more clearly shows that this vast people is a human, living, growing, world-spirit, who must and will be free not only in body, but in mind. No pent-up Utica. I am a Negro and a Negro's son.

Dr. A. R. Abbott,[43] of Toronto, thus contends for the term Afro-American:

> A new and distinctive name is required. I know of no other so appropriate as
> Afro-American. It may appear stilted and classical, but it will serve the pur-
> pose until some better can be devised to take the place of the misnomers now
> in use. The Afro-American race has reached that stage when its achievements
> are forming an important factor in the development of the modern civiliza-
> tion, and it does not propose to have its achievements buried under a cloud
> of tradition, superstition, and ignorance. The Negro may have a history, but
> the less said about it the better. We are a new race and so distinctly differen-
> tiated as to possess all the elements of permanency and growth.

Both of these scholars seem to admit the difficulty of this problem.
There are so many Negroes who are not Negroes, so many colored people
who are not colored, and so many Afro-Americans who are not Africans
that it is simply impossible even to coin a term that will precisely designate
and connote all the people who are now included under any one of the
terms mentioned.

It seems reasonably certain that the persons in America to whom the
term Negro is applicable and ethnically descriptive will retain that name
and endeavor to make it something strong and proud among the race
names of the world. The people to whom this term is not properly applicable but who, nevertheless, under existing conditions are always included in
that name will come more and more to be exclusively designated by the
less definite and less distinctive term, colored.

It certainly does not seem sensible to change the name of a whole race
of people in order to forget, or in some way hide from, the misfortunes
suffered by the American branch of that race. History will take much better care of that misfortune and place the responsibility, therefore, more accurately than the race itself can do by giving up an established name. Then
again there is always something just a little sinister in the suggestion of a
changed name. All the enslaved races of the world have gained in glory by
struggling progressively upward with their names preserved and glorified
by achievement.

Let the race preserve the name by which it is known and fill it more and
more with the splendors of its self-emancipation from the miseries and de-
pendencies that have thus far made the name a term of reproach in a
Christian nation.

TWELVE

THE NEGRO AND PUBLIC OPINION

The American Negro is a great deal of a foreigner to the average white American. It is true that he has been in this country almost longer than any one else, except the Indian, but the conditions under which he came and has been permitted to remain and increase have given him a character and a status that separates him from intimate and equality relationships with the rest of the countrymen.

The average white American knows the Negro only as he sees him on the street or engaged in some employment that does not permit of association. As this average American sees but little of the Negro and knows but little of him, he is at liberty to form any kind of erroneous opinions concerning him.

It is not too much to say that public opinion concerning the Negro in this country is largely based on ignorance of nearly everything that is good and prophetic in the life of the race. The ever increasing exceptions to Negro ignorance, Negro poverty, and social disorder have not as yet made much of an impression on public opinion. The status of the race is fixed by impoverished condition of the majority and not by the noble achievements of the ever increasing few.

That intangible, but all-sovereign, thing called public opinion is a good deal of a despot when it comes to showing favors or doing justice to those who are weak but deserve justice. Although public opinion is as apt to be wrong as right, and perhaps is more often wrong than right, it can not be easily changed or placated, and it yields neither to argument or tears, but to the dissolving processes of time.

In one age it will sanction the burning of Christians, in another the burning of witches and in still another the marketing of human beings as chattels and so on.

In turning from its habit of tyranny to the better habit of peace and good will toward all mankind, it can never be hurried. In answer to every appeal from suffering humanity, it always asks for time and more time. The price of justice is more injustice, the price of love is more hatred, and the price of peace is more battle fields.

It may not be very consoling to the colored people of this country to look longingly into the face of public opinion and read in its stern countenance a fixed purpose to keep us waiting, and no hint of how long. Our

"The Negro and Public Opinion," *Voice of the Negro* 1, no. 1 (1904): 31–32.

only assurance is, that given time enough, public opinion will change and change for the better. Every generation asks for a change in the nature of a more enlightened public opinion, but the answer is usually made to the succeeding generation and seldom to the one asking it.

The history of our own progress aptly illustrates the truth of all this. But few of the old abolitionists lived to witness the answer to their prayers and fulfillment of their prophecies. Many others became gray and ready for their reward before emancipation became a great fact in our history.

The statesmen and philosophers who fifty years ago were absolutely sure that human slavery was a "divine institution" and that the Negro was and always would be less than a man were always supported by public opinion. These false prophets and the opinion that supported them have nearly all perished from the earth.

In these better days, though days still fraught with vexing problems concerning our destiny, the descendants of those who taught and preached this mischievous doctrine, that a more enlightened public opinion had condemned, are now heard to preach and prophecy a new doctrine of degradation. This new doctrine is to the effect that the Negro is so much of a man and has such manly aspirations that all our principles and maxims of government, our ethical notions of right and wrong in civil, political, and social life must be stifled in order to prevent "social equality" and "Negro domination."

Public opinion today seems to give sanction to these miserable fears of the proud and chivalrous Anglo-Saxon.

Our special reason for fear today is that the colored people have not as many friends to do their fighting as they had about fifty years ago. Then more than half the white people of this country were arrayed against public opinion that sanctioned human slavery. Then the whole nation was interested in emancipation, and now only a few men and women of the white race are interested in the question of our emancipation for equality of opportunity. We cannot look to the successors of [the abolitionists] the Garrisons, the Phillippses, the Sumners, the Stowes, and the Lincolns. If men and women of like courage and like insistence are needed today we must look to ourselves and not to the white race. The voice of public opinion today seems to say: [t]he white race quite exhausted itself in fighting for and winning emancipation and the amendments. Emancipation was the door of opportunity, it is for you to keep open this door for your progress.

This is your task and in this the strength of your race is to be tested as never before. To some of our people this sort of advice may not be at all comforting. Our race habit of looking up to somebody as superior to ourselves, of asking for everything and creating but little, of complaining more than trusting to our own individual efforts is a great handicap to the cultivation of manhood, courage and pride of race. If we are to change and win public opinion in behalf of our larger liberties we must become stronger in the virtue of patience, more efficient in good works, more deserving in our achievements, and more intelligent and co-operative in our contention for rights.

This is all very trite and has none of the stirrings of a "bugle blast," but this suggestion contains most of the requirements that make for power and must win respect.

As I before stated, public opinion is stubborn, stolid and self-sufficient. It will not be forced, it cannot be deceived and is without sympathy, but it can be taught, it can be convinced, and in time can be won by valiant men and noble women, helping us to deserve a place in the family of races.

THIRTEEN

THE SMALLER ECONOMIES

The art of living well without spending all our income is one of the most important problems of our every day life. Both the educated and the uneducated are alike, ignorant of perplexing problems of living to obtain the maximum of good out of the minimum expenditure of time, money and effort. The lessons that are needed to equip the ordinary woman for the high service of homemaking are scarcely ever suggested or taught in the public schools, the Sunday schools, the churches or the home. The great majority of women are wholly under the tyranny of her dressmaker, the milliner, the merchant and the grocer.

In our wearing apparel, for example, we are more or less at the mercy of the modiste and the milliner. We go to them with all our vanities, our social ambitions and our envies, but seldom with any independent judgment or individuality of taste as to our pocket book limitations or to what becomes us. The woman who cannot give any intelligent direction or suggestion to her dressmaker and milliner, except the generally impossible one, to make her "look pretty," is almost sure to be imposed upon and perhaps ridiculed.

Every woman has an inherent right to be well gowned, and since it is for some man, as well as for the other woman, that becoming dress is coveted, it is man's primal duty to make fitting acknowledgment of her success. But good taste cannot be bought, and economy cannot be practiced if we are ignorant of what is becoming, the cost of material, and the many unnecessary, little expenditures that enter into the creation of what we must wear.

What is true of our wearing apparel is equally true of the higher art of home making and housekeeping.

Do we carry any practical knowledge into this, our undisputed sphere? Here, where are centered all our joys and sorrows and the sweet and bitter revealings of all the secret springs of the inner life? Seventy-five per cent of us must make confession that we know little or nothing of the duties and privileges that by common consent is regarded as drudgery and degrading. We are accustomed to think of the distance between the kitchen and the piano as so great that the knowledge of one means our ignorance of the other. How costly is this sort of ignorance? What a miserable creature the woman to whom housekeeping and homemaking are drudgery! Think of the high uses and obligations that gather around the term home. The place for the preservation of health, the shrine of our best affections, the theatre of our surest loves and the ties innumerable. What confusion, waste and bitterness must always wait upon the woman who crosses the sacred threshold without preparation. In her home there can be no such thing as economy and a rainy day bank account. No extra dollar for a good book, a bright picture or legitimate and healthy-giving recreation. "She doesn't know how to save," is the worst indictment that can be brought against a self-respecting wife and mother. In any other calling in life she would not be tolerated a moment. "A saving wife," is a compliment that usually implies all the other virtues. Such a woman will be found exercising a discriminating knowledge of everything that enters into the domain of a homemaker. She is not a slave to her dressmaker, her milliner or her grocer. She has learned the value of the thousand and one things that cost either money, time, or thought. Such a woman, with a worthy husband, will soon be cashier, banker and conservator of all the precious interests that belong to the heart and head of the home.

The prosaic things of the pantry as well as the brighter things of the parlor have a correlation, and not a separation of values. Such a woman does not live by imitating others, nor does she waste her time in envying the prosperity of her neighbors. She knows how and when and what to buy, how to use and how to save.

All these observations may seem trite and unimportant, yet it is the foundation, nay more, the sum total of the whole range of household economics. I am afraid that more homes have been wrecked by lack of this kind of intelligence and knowledge than have been ennobled and sweetened by an excess of it.

Truly, life is more than a precept or passing show, and blessed be the woman who can bring to her own and exclusive sphere of home-making, the pride, the good taste, and practical intelligence that will tend to enlarge the value of her work and ennoble it so as to make blessed the things that ignorance has made drudgery.

The time is certainly coming when it will be discreditable, yes, a disgrace, to any woman who has had no training in household economics. The accomplished woman of the future must be the woman whose accomplishments will include the kitchen and pantry as well as the drawing-room and the piano. If women are to keep pace with men in expanding the fields of usefulness and honor, they must learn to give a new value to the fundamental things that are now considered degrading and unimportant.

FOURTEEN

AN EXTENSION OF THE CONFERENCE SPIRIT

During the month of April [the 30th, 1904] last, The Chicago Woman's Club inaugurated and successfully carried through, a three day's conference for the purpose of studying "Women in Modern Industrialism."

This comprehensive subject led out into so many different interests that touch the economic and social life of all people, and the high character of the men and women who participated in the discussion, as well as the advanced ideas formulated and the deep interest manifested by the people on all sides, have given the work of the conference more than a local interest and significance.

To anyone who has had the privilege of attending the annual conferences held at Tuskegee, Hampton, and the Atlanta University, this Chicago Woman's Conference seemed to be an extension of the same anxiety and sincere purpose to get at the heart of the ills and perplexities that constitute the social problems that enter into our national life.

Among the men and women who spoke and urged a more inclusive sympathy and a more courageous stand for what is just and true in economic affairs may be mentioned, Mrs. Charles [Ellen] Henrotin, a former president of the National Woman's Federation, and president of the Chicago Woman's Club, and the originator and leading spirit of the conference; Jane Addams, of Hull House; Graham Taylor, of the Chicago Commons; Miss Mary McDowell, of the University [of Chicago Social] Settlement; Mr. Cooley, Superintendent of the Chicago Public schools; Mrs. Celia Parker Woolley, the well-known author and club woman; and many others of national reputation. These people may be fairly regarded as experts in the various lines of endeavor to bring about a better relationship between the educated and the uneducated, the rich and the poor, the weak and the strong. They are not interested in one class of people as against another class, but every day of their lives is spent in behalf of all the people, including white and black, who through no fault of their own, are compelled to live short of their deserving in the struggle "for life, liberty, and the pursuit of happiness."

The programme of the conference embraced the following subjects:

"The Home as a Financial Institution."
"Special Modifications in Education Needed to Meet the Requirements of Good Housekeeping."

"An Extension of the Conference Spirit," *Voice of the Negro* 1, no. 7 (1904): 300–3.

"The Status of Women in Literary and Artistic Professions."

"What Can the Public Schools do to Meet the Needs of Women for Industrial Training?"

"The Family and Financial Burdens Borne by Women."

"The Health of Women as Affected by Industrialism."

"Future Offered to Women in the Arts and Crafts."

"Women in the Professions."

"Status of Women Employed in Manufacturing, as Employers and Employees, as Clerks and Government Employees."

"The Political and Legal Disabilities of Women in Industry and Women in Trades Unions."

It will be readily admitted that these are all vital questions and too broad to admit of any line of color or caste.

By way of better understanding the spirit as well as the utterances of the speakers in this conference, it might be well to quote some of the more salient things said.

One speaker decried the present discrimination against women in remunerative occupations, and said, "You cannot get the good work that woman is capable of doing unless you give her ample compensation." In speaking of the value of trades for young women, another speaker said, "No girl, no matter in what financial circumstances she may have been reared, ought to marry unless she has some trade or profession at her finger tips, lest the death of her husband bring her face to face with adversity."

In discussing the question of the rights of women to receive the same pay for the same work that men receive, the following objections were urged:

First, "that, as a general rule, women are not constructive in the larger enterprises of business."

Second, "Men do not like to be subordinate to women."

Third, "Until women prove that they can be constrictive, until they can compel men, by their superiority, to recognize them as efficient leaders in any line of work they undertake, they will certainly remain on the lowest round of the ladder."

Under the topic, "The Health of Women Effected by Industrialism," the discussion revealed the fact that when a woman is successful in a large undertaking, her work usually acts as a tonic, and the successful women are generally both healthy and happy. But when she attempts to do a man's work, at the office or shop, and a woman's work in the home, she fails miserably. The woman in industrialism does not spend enough time in recreation, in sleep, and is careless in the matter of her food.

The women generally agreed that no portion of the working class of women is so well off, as to health, as those engaged in domestic service.

In the discussion of this question of Domestic Service, the whole conference was aroused to a high pitch of interest. One of the speakers,[44] on this topic, was on the Hampton Conference program last summer [1903]. It was rather gratifying to see that the conclusions that were so heartily approved at Hampton were as cordially endorsed at this conference. The sentiment here adopted was to the effect "that there is no reason why a woman of character, graciousness and skill should not change the whole current of public opinion[45] in regard to the respectability of domestic service."

As a further evidence of the interest taken in this subject prominent sociologists throughout the country were asked to answer the following question: "How can the servant girl problem be solved?"[46] The following are some of the answers given:

> 1st. Recognize that they are working at a trade.
>
> 2nd. Pay experts by the hour.
>
> 3rd. Let them share the family life.
>
> 4th. Give her the very best labor-saving inventions.
>
> 5th. Clearly define their duties and don't order suppers after the hired girl has completed her day's work.
>
> 6th. Eliminate the talk about social superiority, and recognize a servant as a human being worthy of consideration.
>
> 7th. Teach ignorant mistresses that caprice is not popular with the women who sell their time for specific duties.

The subject, "Home and Society," brought out many wholesome and helpful suggestions. One great need was declared to be education in domestic economy and raising the ideals of the home.

One woman of extensive experience and knowledge said: "The large attendance at academies and industrial schools shows that one-half of the world is trying to gain in the ability to think, and the other half in the ability to do." There is urgent need for a direct study of the problem of home, so much so that the establishment of a State School of Home Economics,[47] where young women may be taught how to conduct a home, with social and financial economy, should be urged. "It is just as much a disgrace for a girl to marry who does not understand the economic management of a home, as it is for a man to marry who is unable to support a family."

Another speaker on the same subject fully echoed the philosophy of the Southern conferences, in the following words:

"The ideal of scholarly leisure and the life of the student recluse is very attractive, but in the days to come, the true education will not be that which is devoted to pure academic work, but rather that which prepares for service. The parents of a girl in college know that, even if they are not compelled to, their children should be able to take care of themselves, which shows, as fathers and mothers, that they have a high degree of intelligence."

The very interesting and involved discussion with reference to trades unions received a large and intelligent consideration by those competent to speak as experts. In this particular discussion, men and women of the highest intelligence in all the walks of American life participated, and there was revealed in it all such sincerity and generousness of interest, as to show a new consciousness of sympathy, in the every day life of the people.

Those of us of the colored race persuade ourselves, at times, that ours is the only and the greatest problem in our civilization. The fact is that the spirit of injustice that we contend against is the same spirit of injustice that millions of white men, women, and children are everywhere struggling against in the form of oppressive hours of labor, inadequate wages, unsanitary conditions of employment and the many inequalities that are crystallized into law and custom. The strong language used in this conference by those who are oppressed in various ways and compelled to live below their rights as citizens sounded at times like the lamentations we so often indulge in. The interest taken in these high and perplexing questions, by women of wealth and position, and the sympathy revealed for those who are without the power to protect themselves happily show that the forces that are to solve both the black and white problems are in course of preparation. The largeness of soul and breadth of conception that are now enlisted in these economic problems must certainly include within the range of their corrective influence the wrongs under which we smart and suffer and justly complain.

FIFTEEN

VACATION VALUES

The vanished summer of 1905 has been full of stirring events. From the world wide importance of the Peace Conference in New Hampshire to the least noticed of the many gatherings of the season, there has been much to keep our minds alert and our hearts full of wholesome enthusiasm. If the summer of 1905 has come and gone and we are none the better or wiser for it, the fault must be in ourselves or in some untoward forces that frustrate and defy human plans and purposes.

People by the thousands, white and black, joyously left their little "pent up Uticas" and sought the great highways and by-ways for refreshment, change, and heart-stirring excitement. Across the bar of human separation, stranger hands have clasped stronger hands in friendly greeting and cold hearts have been warmed and sought and found new and lasting fellowships.

The fund of human kindness has been increased and much new knowledge gained that shall in some degree help to clarify our conceptions of duty, justice and friendship.

From the standpoint of our own people, the season must have been one of great educational value. In spite of the indignities and humiliations of travel in certain parts of our country, our folks were extensively away from home. It is safe to say that more colored people have been traveling for recreation during the past summer than ever before.

To us the world has become larger than it was twenty years ago, and our ability to assimilate and feel ourselves a part of this larger world is as positive an indication of our progress as any other one item of our gains. As we become more interested in all that is human in the world about us, our importance as men and women of worth is wonderfully advanced. What we need as much as anything else is a cosmopolitan spirit, but that spirit cannot be cultivated by being in one place all of the time and knowing only one kind of people, and they the least progressive and the least interesting of any in the country. The distance from Boston to Atlanta, for instance, is great and it will never be less to the man in Boston, who hates Atlanta, or to the man in Atlanta, who hates Boston. Distance is as much a matter of spirit as of geography. The larger, freer and more hopeful life of the larger cities of the North can never be transplanted to the benighted spots of our land, except by those who travel, observe, and resolve that

"Vacation Values," *Voice of the Negro* 2 (12), 1905: 863–66.

what is best and most righteous in human fellowship shall at least prevail in our hearts and minds.

It is true that many people carry their prejudices, their provincialism and their resentments wherever they go, but there is always an opportunity for people to be changed by the better and stronger environment by which they are surrounded. So far as the Negro is concerned, he has few hatreds and prejudices to overcome, so travel or new experiences are important and of value as a part of his education.

We have got to learn by travel and new contact and the liberalizing influences of whatever is best and most compelling in American life that the lines of opportunity are extensive and that we are in some way related in possibility to all the great things of the age in which we live.

We have begun to know each other helpfully by the intermingling of the people of all sections, and our sense of self respect has been wonderfully enhanced by the larger social intercourse of the best elements amongst us. Are we improving in manners, appearance and the ability to do interesting and important things? We can find reassuring answers to this question wherever our people are seen and heard in the great centres of popular interest during the past summer season. It has been a common comment, "Why, I did not know that we had so many fine colored people!" One is fairly overwhelmed with the ever increasing evidences of culture and achievements of all kinds in the present generation of our people. We hear much about what the schools, the churches and the various organizations are doing, as evidence of our progress, but the best proof of all is the people themselves, not now and then, or here and there an individual of merit, but the increasing numbers to be seen in Conventions, Chautauquas,[48] Conferences and social gatherings. It is here that we see the picked men and women from all parts of the country. They represent the best examples of what has been wrought in school, college, shop and field. It is no slight thing that the public spirit of these best representatives of our progress should put themselves in evidence in every place and on every occasion when and where it is proper for an American gentleman and lady to be. In the presence of these evidences of what we are and of what we are striving to do and be, the unjust American who prates about our inferiority becomes himself an object of pity and contempt. It is not enough that our best people be talked about, but they must be seen and heard in public places and occasions where only the best are bidden. Those who will not read our books or sing our songs or see us in our homes must meet us in the highway or travel [to] the assembly places where the best minds meet to study and discuss high themes of public interest. In no better way, at present, can we impress American people that we are intellectually and spiritually alive to all the forces of advancement and that we insist upon being a real and active part in every movement made in the name of the American people.

The colored man or woman who travels from Texas to New York to attend a National Convention of Business Men, or from Georgia to Ashbury

Park to attend a National Convention of the country's educators represents that spirit of enterprise that makes for National unity amongst us. It is no small thing to be animated by the feeling that as citizens we are part of the universal harmonies and have a right and sacred duty to be interested in the big things and best things of our National life. We are not to be kept permanently within the bounds set for us by prejudice. Each summer our moving well dressed and well mannered multitude make many new friends. Through these best examples the world is getting to know that all colored people are not alike.

It may be in a World Congress in London, England, a Chatauqua in Iowa, or a National Assembly of Educators in New Jersey, or anywhere else where it is important and possible to be, there you will find us being represented, in most cases, by picked men and women capable of speaking the word or acting the part in a way that puts prejudice eternally to shame.

The hundreds of our teachers attending the Summer Schools in the North is interesting proof of our eagerness to obtain whatever is best and most up-to-date in pedagogy. The leading educators have come to respect these teacher-students from the South. There is not a great school in the North that offers a summer course for teachers that is not liberally patronized by our progressive young men and women teachers from the Southland. In this way they have come in touch and helpful association with thousands of the best teachers and educators of the other race. In no other way would the makers of public opinion have an opportunity to know and respect our educated classes. These enterprising teachers of ours are among our most effective missionaries. Their presence and work during the summer counteract many false impressions and estimates that would otherwise go unchallenged.

In still another way do these summer outings and gatherings help us. If our best people are strangers to the great majority of the white race, we are almost to as great an extent strangers to one another. We are all too wide apart in our understanding of our common problem. Most of the Northern people are ignorant of the true situation in the South and the marvelous achievements of our people south of the Ohio river. It is quite common to hear Northern colored people express their contempt for those who live South because the latter endure so much without a protest.

Those who have earnestly studied the situation cannot fail to see a marked change of feeling since the Northern portion of the race have had an opportunity to meet and know the hundreds of southern people who can be found in every important Northern community. We are each year coming into a more intimate association with each other. Mutual respect has succeeded mutual misunderstanding. The successful business man of the South has set a stimulating example that is being followed energetically in Chicago and other Northern centers of Negro population. These men of the South who come North with their families and other evidence of their prosperity furnish interesting proof that the real man or woman is in many cases stronger than the forces that are formed and fashioned to overthrow them.

This better knowledge of each other will eventually make for larger strength for race advancement and a more united contention for justice. It is becoming clearer to our consciences that nowhere are we securely free when anywhere liberty is denied. Prejudice is sectional, but freedom is National. In other words what has been going on during the past few years in bringing large bodies of our people together socially or for more serious ends has wonderfully strengthened the spirit of unity amongst us. There is beginning to be such a thing as pride of race, because it is possible for us to see and know much to be proud of. A race that has no pride of self is not fit for responsibilities. We are beginning to see through the eyes of our larger knowledge of each other that the time is coming when union for important purposes is going to mean something permanent. There is an increased assurance from year to year in the fact that our strong men and accomplished women everywhere are seeing and hearing of each other. In every important Negro gathering during the summer, there has been a note of increased confidence that what has been resolved can be executed. All of this has come about by the opportunities we have had of knowing what kind of people we are. This ever increasing opportunity for acquaintance and contact has brought to view a surprising variety of talents and accomplishments that we did not know existed a few years ago.

But there is a lighter and brighter side to this freer intermingling of our people from all parts of the country, and that is the purely social side. Society amongst us as seen in every important centre, during the summer, was a very different thing from what it was twenty years ago. We can discover the buildings of a real aristocracy based on culture and achievements. It was possible, in more than a dozen cities, to meet in well furnished parlors a company of ladies and gentlemen, every one of whom was a college graduate or a successful man or woman in business. Our whole social life has been sweetened and brightened by these evidences of our social advancement. Social standards are higher and our ideals have their roots in culture and character. Hospitality has been abundant and beautiful and the touch of love and friendship have established relationships that shall long survive the social delights of the summer of 1905.

Sixteen

Refining Influence of Art

How can we create a love of art among the people who live in places remote from art galleries? A group of women in the Chicago Woman's Club, assisted by the Central Art Association, have been attempting to answer this question and have met with gratifying results. These women have simply followed the plan of those who have developed the traveling library as a means of circulating good literature among the people, and as in the library circulation, this effort has been rewarded with expressions of gratitude and pleasure.[49] Copies of the splendid masterpieces of Italian, French and American art have created an appetite and appreciation of the beautiful in communities barren of every suggestion of what is artistic and with no conception of the refining influence of a beautiful picture.

Groups of pictures are sent to country schools for a certain length of time and circulated through the community to be returned and exchanged for others as is done with the traveling libraries.

The cost of this exhibit is merely nominal, but the educational value and influence is so considerable that what was started as an experiment is destined to become a permanent educational force among people who cannot afford to maintain art galleries.

It is to be hoped that a request for these picture loans will come from the pictureless homes and schools of the colored people.

It is because the world of art with all its joyousness and beauty is being more and more brought within the reach of every one who would appropriate its treasures that we are coming to believe that no woman sufficiently realizes the sacredness of her trust and privileges as a home-maker who is not ambitious to make her home bright, beautiful and refined, as well as comfortable and convenient. Indeed it seems that the entire art world, by the use of the decorator's skill, is assisting women to understand and appreciate the uses of art as seen in the simplest articles of home-furnishings.

There was a time when art was exclusive and had no interest in or sympathy with the common people. It then lent itself only to the decoration of palaces, churches and temples. The great masters felt that art was exalted only when the ceilings of some great cathedral or the walls of some kingly palace were enriched by their genius. Then it was that the faces only of saints, kings and the nobility were worthy [of] the inspiration of the por-

"Refining Influence of Art," *Voice of the Negro* 3, no. 3 (1906): 211–14.

trait artist. Then it was that art found more glory in portraying the triumphs of war than the laughing face of a winsome child. But thanks to the growth of liberality in all things and the humanizing influences of science and education, art is no longer the exclusive pleasure and luxury of the wealthy and the nobility.

Art now finds as much inspiration in the cottage as the palace, and is as much glorified in reproducing on canvas the face of a pure woman or an honest man, as the faces of sickly princes. In other words, art has become the ardent lover of humanity, seeking in every way possible to glorify and illumine our every day lives. If the great masters of art like Michael Angelo, Raphael and Leonardo [da Vinci], who exalted the church and Christianity by all that is classic in art, could have visited some of our recent exhibits, notably in Chicago and St. Louis, what a change in artistic sentiment would have greeted their astonished sight. Instead of saints, gods and angels, they would have beheld men, women and children, domestic scenes, flowers, and landscapes, rivers, mountains and birds affording themes for the modern artist. These old masters would have marveled at the skill that can awaken sympathy in the waif on the street, in the pathetic face of the desolate man or a widowed mother and can make the face of childhood gleam with the light of innocent laughter. They would have seen these 20th Century artists faithfully interpreting nature for us, suggesting a majesty in the mountain, a placidness of the brook, a loveliness in the skies and a fragrance of the field, to which most of us are insensible.

Among the prize pictures exhibited in recent expositions, representing the common incidents of every day life, might be mentioned the celebrated painting entitled "Breaking Home Ties."[50] The artist has seized upon one of the most pathetic incidents in family life. Those who have experienced the distress of heart in parting for the first time with some beloved member of the family hearthstone [are] drawn into full sympathy with the sufferers in this great painting. The artist has told here in a wonderfully impressive way the simple story of the power of a mother's love and the sacred influences of a good home.

Another small canvas dealing with an humble subject may be recalled in this connection, which bears the title "Rent Day." This picture represents the humble home of an old colored couple on the day when the dreaded landlord comes for his rent. The two old people are carefully counting out the small coin, representing many a hard day's toil. The expression on the faces of the couple and on that of the pompous landlord tells the whole story of the new relationship of landlord and tenant between the two races. The beauty and power of this picture is the success of the artist in expressing in the plain faces of these aged people the soul of honor and the spirit of industry which has enabled them to grope their way along from bondage to the responsibilities of freedom. As far as art could do it, this picture has interpreted for millions of people the best characteristics of the Negro peasant.

Paintings of this latter sort are so rare as to suggest a painful lack of interest in Negro themes that would tend to arouse and cultivate popular interest in the best things in our history and present status. In other words, American art, like American literature, is always doing the bidding of American prejudice. The beautiful faces of our women, the best types of our honest peasantry in the South, the intelligence, strength and responsibility of our cultured men and women and the scenes and incidents illustrative of our progress are seldom represented on canvas as a part of American life. What an inspiration to the soulful artist should be the desperate existence of the American Negro. What a wealth of romance, of tragedy, and poetic suggestion in the rapid and bloody transition of these people from bondage to freedom and from freedom to citizenship! Had there been some Harriet Beecher Stowe[51] in art, what a profound impression on the world of art and civilization would have been produced by the representation on canvas, by some master hand, the American Negro in what he was, is, and is to be. We have been so much caricatured by would-be artists that public opinion, even as to our features, has been almost hopelessly perverted. This refusal of brush and chisel to tell the truth concerning our progress seems to say that if the American Negro wants the helping agency of art it must produce its own artists.

The name of Jean Francois Millet[52] will always be called blessed among the benefactors of mankind for what he did by his brush for the French peasantry. While other artists became eminent by painting magnificent landscapes and startling scenes of war, the gentle heart of Millet went out in loving quest for his fellow-countrymen who were half slaves, friendless and weighted down with ceaseless toil in the rural provinces of France. Nothing in modern art is so heart-searching, so beautifully expressive of the dignity of human nature, so full of the religious spirit of fraternity as Millet's spiritually great paintings representing the peasant life of France.

What Millet did for France it is possible for some artist, with like power of love or kinship, to do for America and the American Negro.

But to bring the question of the refining influence of art into closer relationship to our home-life, we must learn to appreciate that the aim of true art is to drive out all impurities, to give color and warmth where the chill of loneliness might brood, and to suggest the refinements of beauty and taste that ever beckon us to be better than we are. Art inspires that subtle force that lifts women from drudgery to loveliness, that makes men more chivalrous and children more beautiful. Among the Greeks, there was in every home a household god, who was supposed to guide the destinies of the family. We might with profit borrow from this religious custom of the Greeks the suggestion that art in the form of sculpture, painting or etching may furnish to each household amongst us some hero, heroine or sentiment that shall be to us the saving influence of home blessedness. The Sistine Madonna with its historical and spiritual value understood would minister to the reign of love in every home. If we would teach our children to be gentle and humane, place on the wall for their admiration the kindly face of Rosa Bonheur[53] with her arm around the neck of a domestic animal. Let our daughters gather strength and inspiration from the pictured faces of women who have done much to glorify womankind. Let art give to the boys the inspiration and companionship of such [abolitionist] heroes as John Brown, [Abraham] Lincoln, [Frederick] Douglass, [William Lloyd] Garrison and other great men. Many of the world's greatest men found their inspiration in some great book. Art is capable of doing equally as much by bringing before us the faces of those who have achieved the best results in human history. Such faces silently stimulate the souls to high endeavor.

What portraits do for some, all forms of the beautiful and true in art may do for all of us. Many of us are never touched with the mystic beauty of a flower until art has interpreted it for us. A landscape with its enchanting vistas, its harmonious adjustment of sky, forest and river seldom fills us with appreciation of the ever revealing wonders of nature, until some great artist tells it all on canvas. It is said that the poet [Friedrich] Schiller[54] never saw the ocean and yet he described it with such power that old seamen saw more in Schiller's verse than they had ever thought of in the overwhelming presence of the ocean itself. So it is that art can draw us toward the very heart of nature and the artist become a teacher and preacher of true righteousness.

I sometimes feel a heartache for many of our young people because they have so few inspirations that lift them above the course and vulgar things of life. Their tastes are formed out of surroundings and experiences that do not make for morality and high living. They grow up into manhood and womanhood without the purifying suggestions and influences of those who live and breathe in an atmosphere of culture.

Recognizing the dismal fact that there are thousands of the race as yet hopelessly beyond the reach of the chastening touch of art gallery privileges, I still believe that many of us who can, sadly neglect the putting of ourselves under the influence of the galleries and art exhibits, which are freely open to us. And further it seems to me that the place of music in our schools and colleges has no greater claim or better right than the teaching of the true, beautiful and good as expressed in paintings and statuary. It should not be said of us we have but little taste for the things that minister to the higher senses.

Let our schools begin to pay some attention to the fine arts, and it will appear how practical such teaching may become in the measure of the refinements of life about us. There is an exaltation of soul in the study of art that makes one loathe the crooked, awkward and ugly things of life.

We can see more clearly the largeness, the glory and the brightness of the world, the beauty of women and the nobility of men when the love and knowledge of art enters more fully into our every day lives.

Part Four

· SOCIAL SETTLEMENTS ·

SEVENTEEN

THE NEED OF SOCIAL SETTLEMENT WORK
FOR THE CITY NEGRO

The most stirring social phenomenon of our day is the enormous interest we have begun to feel in human life.[55] Quoting from the subtle philosopher of Hull House, Miss Jane Addams, "We are learning that a standard of social ethics is not attained by traveling a sequestered pathway, but by mingling on the thronged and common road where all must turn out for one another, and at least see the size of one another's burdens."[56] Who is my neighbor? There is a more kindly anxiety in this question than there used to be. The difference between the answer given to this question to-day and that which would have been given one hundred years ago measures the whole range of man's progress in social consciousness.[57] Our anxieties have become less selfish, and we are gradually approaching that ideal state of which Emerson speaks when he says, "No one can be perfectly free until all are free; no one can be perfectly happy until all are happy."[58]

Meanwhile we are beginning to feel more and more distinctly that the man or woman who loves merely his or her own family and immediate associates does not express the highest type of the social virtues. In the realm of social ethics to-day the supremest virtue is that deeper and more spiritual impulse to helpfulness that will enable us to find delight in working with, rather than for, the unfortunate all about us.

"There goes an honest man." Why [do we say this]? Because he meets all his personal obligations. But does he as honestly meet all of his social obligations? He gives to the poor, but does he ever give himself in any personal service to the redemptive work of the social order? Questions and answers like these might be extended and would lead us into the wider and larger interest in human life out of which has grown the statement already made that "we have begun to feel an enormous interest in human life" [Addams 1902, 7].

A large American city of the commercial and manufacturing sort, like New York or Philadelphia or Chicago, is a tremendous aggregation of human problems. In such a community all the extremes meet in a more or less frantic struggle for adjustment. In the midst of enormous wealth there are thousands who are on the edge of starvation; with hospitals in large numbers, and a more or less perfect system of sanitation, thousands of infants

In *Southern Workman* 33 (September 1904): 501–6.

and adults are threatened every moment with disease and death. With hundreds of schools, colleges, and academies, thousands of children grow up in ignorance and viciousness. Though an army of police or guardians of peace and good order are to be found everywhere, yet defenseless men, women, and children are robbed, murdered, and defrauded nearly every hour of the day. When human life is so full of perils as well as opportunities, how great is the need for organized kindness to save men, women, and children from the effects of man's inhumanity to man! Those who are more or less responsible for the law, order, and decency in human life have begun to find out that a large proportion of the people who flock to our large cities are utterly incapable of adapting themselves to the complex conditions of city life. Fancy yourselves standing at the gateway of Chicago, through which a steady stream of colored people comes from the South, seeking freedom, liberty, opportunity, protection of the law, and education for their children. How various the throng of seekers for better conditions of life and living! How high their hopes and how ignorant they are of the disappointments that await them within the gates! They come for more liberty, and, alas, many of them find it all too soon and to their lasting sorrow. They come for better homes, only to find unsanitary tenements in the black belts of the city. Some of the more competent come with high hopes of easily securing employment in some of the higher class of occupations, but they find themselves shut out by a relentless prejudice, drifting at last into the easy path of immoral living. Hundreds of young women who have been trained for something better than menial service,[59] failing to find such employment, fall easy victims to the flattering inducements of a well-dressed idleness, the handmaids of shame.

This failure of thousands of our people to adjust themselves to the higher economic and industrial conditions of city life has given rise to a growing need for some form of organized kindness or effort to check the evil consequences of their failure. The colored people alone cannot adequately meet these requirements. Even the better part of our people are too poor in resources and experience to organize, sustain, and carry on the agencies needed to save those of their own kith and kin who cannot save themselves. Our churches, in many instances, have made some halting efforts to become centers of influence, but they have not been successful because they could not bring to the work an undivided and unselfish motive. A study of these conditions has led to a plan of relief that seems to reach the heart of all our social needs, and that plan is the social settlement.

I certainly need not, in this presence, take time to define what a social settlement is. To define the meaning and influence of Hull House, the Chicago Commons, and the University [of Chicago Social] Settlement in Chicago[60] would be to show how there is being worked out a friendlier adjustment of the relations between capital and labor, the rich and the poor, the fortunate and unfortunate everywhere. In these centers of kindly and helpful influences, the most important corrective forces of modern city life are being applied with an untrammeled sympathy and exactness of justice that can be found nowhere else. They are planted right in the midst of the people who are farthest removed from everything that is bright, beautiful, and uplifting. Where people are the poorest and most neglected, where the saloons are the thickest, sanitary conditions the meanest, and where there are the fewest churches, there you will find Hull House. I speak of Hull House in particular because it is regarded as the finest, the most typical, and the most complete example of socialized kindness to be found in the world. When you enter this homelike refuge from the open evidence of the degradation that environs it, you will be filled with an exalted sense of the beauty of human kindness. Here shines the gentle spirit of Jane Addams, that apostle of the newest gospel of "good deeds in a naughty world."[61] Serene, with philosophic penetration into the cause of our social disorders, beautifully sensitive to every form of human suffering about her, and always sisterly, motherly, or friendly as the case demands, Jane Addams has taught the world a new conception of the divine element in humanity, which neither rags, dirt, nor immorality can entirely obscure.

The number of activities and interests to be found in this ample enclosure create a feeling impossible to describe. There are reading rooms, a library, club rooms for girls and boys, club rooms for men and women, kindergartens, day nurseries, gymnasiums, theater, music rooms, facilities for the learning of every kind of trade and industry, provision for night schools, and in fact, every kind of agency to meet every sort of need of humanity.* * *[62]

Such being the spirit and practical helpfulness of settlement work, can it be made to serve the needs of colored people in our large cities? As a general rule these settlement institutions are located in districts where the foreign element predominates. Russians, Italians, Greeks, Jews, Hungarians, Poles and other nationalities constitute the strange admixture of life that surrounds these settlements. It is these people of foreign tongue and foreign customs who are seeking to adjust themselves to the freer and more responsible life of democracy in America that have the helpful agencies of Hull House and the Chicago Commons. What this class of newly-made citizens needs in the way of protection, guidance, and sympathy is needed even in a greater degree by the throngs of native-born colored people who are swarming into our larger cities. The possibilities of good from such work are quite beyond estimation.

But the poor colored people who come to these cities of the North are the only people for whom no directing agencies to save and protect have been arranged. Those who belong to the churches find their way to them, but the churches can do but little for them in the way of economic and industrial benefits. Those without such membership are more than apt to drift to the wide-open welcome of the saloon, the gambling table, and other forms of vice. The thousands of young and unmarried men who work for small wages and at night have no sort of home to go to are more than apt to be found in places whose business it is to make beasts of men. How different is the fortune of the white mechanic, laborer, or clerk for whom there is somewhere awaiting him a comfortable home, or a bright and warm reading room, a gymnasium, a place for innocent games, free lectures, soul-stirring music, or a rendezvous, at once delightful, refining, and educative. Thousands of noble white men and women continually pray and plan for the moral well-being of somebody's child who is being tempted to go astray in these big cities. Save our young men, protect our girls is the burdened heart cry of German, Jew, Greek, Swede, Hungarian, Russian, and American, but not so with us; the way to crime, to demoralization and ruin is easy and unobstructed, almost, by a single great effort in our large cities.

The young colored man, who is a waiter down in the heart of the city, has one hour of leisure in the afternoon. Where can he go for recreation, rest, and association? Home? He has none. To his room? That, such as it is, is from two to five miles away. Go to the Young Men's Christian Association? That exists only for the benefit of white young men. He very soon finds that he is not wanted there. He is not married because he cannot afford a wife, that is, a wife with the extravagant notions of dress and style that many of our colored girls have. The only place, then, where he really finds welcome to its warm enclosure in the winter and to its cooling cheer in the summer is the saloon, and here he easily finds his way or is piloted by some vigilant runner for the place. The all-important thing, my friends, is that society, in order to save the best of our generation to itself, is doing everything that heart and brain can devise to save white young men and white young women, while practically nothing is being done for the colored young men and women, except to prosecute and punish them for crimes for which society itself is largely responsible.

One of the most important needs of the hour in our large cities is a successful settlement institution located right in the midst of the blackest of the black belts of our city's population. The spirit of human fellowship once understood will carry us far across the bars that separate the strong and the good from the weak and the bad elements in our human society. In spite of the separating forces of race prejudice, there can be found a common ground where white and black can meet, plan, and work for those who so sadly need the service of the best. There are thousands of willing helpers in the white race, but thus far we have failed to use their power. The all-important thing is that they are waiting to respond to our call. These settlements for colored people must not be narrow, or merely a Negro charity clearinghouse—a place to encourage complaints, not a Negro settlement as such, but a settlement in which the best men and women of both races shall unite their strength to extend the law of brotherhood, helpfulness, and good will to the colored race as well as to the foreigners for whom so much is being done. It is not alone the race problem that is to be solved, "but the ever recurring human problem in which every class of suffering and ill-used humanity is concerned."[63]

Another effort to build a settlement on the broadest and kindest possible lines of helpfulness has just been started in Chicago. It is to be known as the "Frederick Douglass Center." This movement has grown out of that ever deepening social consciousness that is now fairly upon us. Some of the things for which it stands are as follows:

> To promote just and amicable relations between the white and colored people.
> To help to remove the difficulties from which the latter suffer in their civil, political, and industrial life.
> To encourage equal opportunity, irrespective of race, color, or other artificial distinctions.
> To establish a center of friendly helpfulness and influence in which to gather needful information and for mutual cooperation to the ends of right living and a higher citizenship.
> To inquire into the value of all legal and business disabilities from which men and women now suffer by reason of race or color.

This platform of principles and purposes is not to be interpreted in any narrow sense, such as protecting black people simply because they are black, but rather as an effort to discover individual worth and fitness, that shall apply to all classes of people, and to help in the creation of newer ideals[64] of citizenship.

The most encouraging thing about this proposed center is the number and character of the people who have become interested in it. Fully two hundred people have joined the association. In this list of membership may be found the names of the best representatives in almost every walk of Chicago life. Judges, educators, physicians, club women, business men, ministers, and the most exclusive society people—all giving their names and money with a spontaneous eagerness that is at once both surprising and delightful. Nothing has ever been attempted in Chicago, since my residence there, that has had back of it such splendid support as this effort to establish a black Hull House under the illustrious name of our great man—Frederick Douglass. The coming together in this center of the best white and colored people for carrying out the purposes outlined is both interesting and important in possible results.

Can the young colored man, well-equipped with trade or profession, obtain employment? Is there any way to check the increase of crime among the colored people in the cities? Is it possible to teach those who need teaching, how they can more effectively use the ballot? Can anything be done to make the city more interested in improving the sanitary condition of the districts where colored people segregate in their home life? Can we increase the interest of colored people in the means of education? Can the best that there is in the race be in some way enlarged upon and emphasized to the extent of arousing as much popular interest in the best of our people as there is now in our worst element? The settlement method of answering these questions is sure to be productive of far-reaching results. If the Chicago experiment succeeds, as I am sure it must, similar experiments will be made in every great center of Negro life. Outside of the educational enterprises, I believe this movement for social settlements for colored people gives promise of a wider range of social betterment than anything that has yet been attempted for the race.

By making this race problem a part of the human problem, in which all classes and races are vitally concerned; in trying to help the community by helping the Negro; in creating as much interest in the young colored man or woman, after they are educated and trained for life service, as before they were trained; in the broadening and deepening of human problems, this race question of ours can be lifted above the low plane of passion and partisanship, to the higher plane of human brotherhood.

EIGHTEEN

THE FREDERICK DOUGLASS CENTRE

A Question of Social Betterment and Not of Social Equality

It would seem that the surest way to injure a colored person as an individual, or to bring discredit, if not failure, to a Negro Institution or enterprise of any kind, is to raise against him, her or it, the malignant cry of "social equality."[65]

The truth of this was aptly illustrated in Chicago a few days ago, when one of the sensational dailies of this city, in a most startling manner and glaring headlines, "wrote up" one of the ordinary meetings of "The Frederick Douglass Centre," an organization recently launched in this city after the plan of Hull House, but wholly for the benefit of colored people who need it. Every feature of the affair was so exaggerated; what was actually said and done was so grossly misstated, in order to make it a "sensational scoop," that it went the rounds of the country as the most "astounding attempt to force social equality" that this country has ever witnessed.

The few Anglo-Saxon ladies who were guilty of this "social crime" of sitting in a parlor and interchanging views on the question of social betterment for the poor and needy, with a few colored women, and sipping tea together while they talked, were held up to the public as setting a "dangerous example" to the pure in heart.

The press East, West, North, and South took up, repeated, and passed along the "horrible" story of "The Black and White Tea," "White Women and Negresses," in the broad light of day in "a private residence, on a well-paved street, in view of innocent children going to school, and right in a neighborhood where there are churches, schools, policemen, drug stores, and other good things, sat together and planned together as to how they might together help to relieve social wretchedness in a big city and increase the effectiveness of human kindness and human love! Just think of it!

As if the horror of the thing was not sufficiently suggested by exaggerated type, the Kodak [camera] was used to heighten the contrast between the fair and plain faces of the company.

Was this misrepresentation of an innocent meeting among earnest, intelligent and love-giving American women justified? The newspaper that printed all of this hateful nonsense eagerly answers yes, and I suppose they

In *Voice of the Negro* 1, no. 12 (1904): 601–4.

were right from their standpoint, for the good women, Mrs. Celia Parker Woolley, Mrs. Magee, and Mrs. Dr. Shears, who were chiefly responsible for this "Black and White Tea," have been fairly overwhelmed with letters of indignant protest from men and women in all parts of the country. Some of the letters, especially from the South are too coarse for print. Now and then a letter of commendation was received, but most of them showed how ugly and intense is the spirit of caste in this country. Evidently the writers of these abusive letters addressed to their more humane sisters flattered themselves that they were administering a well-merited rebuke or punishment. Poor things! They little comprehended the mettle and character of the women who are the object of their abuse and vituperation. When certain of their more timid friends attempted to warn these Chicago women not to go too far in social matters, or to sympathize with them for being brought into such unenviable notoriety, all such advice, warnings and sympathy were immediately resented by them as cowardly. They are in earnest and not afraid of being misunderstood. They have a righteous purpose in hand and cannot and will not be hindered by the fears of those who are without purpose. They, as well as the competent colored women associated with them, are neither for or against social equality, but they are for what is right, what is just, and what is human and are willing to go, whenever and wherever, these promptings lead them.

In order to better understand the purpose and motive of the women who are responsible for this latest sensation over the "social equality" nonsense, it will be necessary to describe in full the plans, purposes and prospects of "The Frederick Douglass Centre." As already stated, this Association is in the nature of what is known as a Social Settlement, but it "stands for a new experiment in the work of social justice, though the deep moral necessity from which it springs forbids us to think of it as a mere "experiment." The city Negro has been the subject of much study by Sociologists in late years. There is no better place in the country than Chicago for this study. While the Negro population is increasing, the opportunities for their employment seem to be decreasing. It is also a fact that prejudice against the race seems to increase in the same ratio as its numbers increase. Many civil, social and political wrongs, and lessening of opportunities are plainly evident to people who have lived here long enough to know local conditions.

There is, however, in Chicago a goodly remnant of the old liberty loving spirit that is still responsive to the needs of those who are handicapped by reason of a dark complexion. Women like Jane Addams, Celia Parker Woolley, Mrs. Charles Henrotin, Miss Julia Lathrop, Mary McDowell and men like Jenkin Lloyd Jones, Judge Waterman, Rabbi [Emil] Hirsch and Dr. [Frank W.] Gunsaulus make it impossible for race hatred and prejudice to go unchallenged.[66] It is this valiant spirit that prevented the Chicago Woman's Club from barring its doors to the admission of colored women, that mingles the children of all races in the public schools, and that keeps open all public places for all the people. It is also this spirit that conceived the idea of a Frederick Douglass Centre, as a social settlement. I do not know of a similar Institution in this country. Certainly there is none whose purposes are so comprehensive, its plans so intelligently conceived and well defined.

In the Prospectus issued the objects are stated as follows:

(1) To promote a just and amicable relation between the white and colored people.

(2) To remove the disabilities from which the latter suffer in their civil, political and industrial life.

(3) To encourage equal opportunity, irrespective of race, color, or other arbitrary distinctions.

(4) To establish a centre of friendly helpfulness and influence, in which to gather needful information and for mutual co-operation to the end of right living and a higher citizenship.

As now organized, the work will be carried on by six committees, as follows:

(1) "Social Statics [*sic*]:"
To gather information about the colored people in Chicago and establish a scientific basis of inquiry and helpfulness.

(2) "Business Opportunities:"
To extend aid and counsel to worthy men and women seeking self-support and suffering from race prejudice.

[3] "Legal Advice and Redress:"
To inquire into cases of legal injustice fostered by race enmity and to uphold individual rights under the law.

[4] "Sanitation, Housing, etc.:"
To improve the condition of living among the colored population.

[5] "Club and Class Work:"
For intellectual culture.

[6] "Civics:"
For instruction in good citizenship.

At heads of these committees are some of the most prominent men and women in Chicago. I do not know of any organization in the country that has so quickly enlisted in its behalf such an array of high-grade citizens, who have eagerly volunteered their services for the work of Douglass Centre. In the list of over two hundred members of the Association you can easily select the names of prominent judges, lawyers, distinguished ministers, prominent men and women in other professions, business men and women, and these representing wealth and the highest culture.

Indeed one of the most hopeful things in the organization of this Centre is the eagerness with which the best people of both races responded to applications for membership.

If this movement does not succeed, its failure will not be due to lack of strong support by good people or for lack of a righteous purpose or an urgent need.

In the preliminary work of organizing the Centre, numerous meetings and conferences have been held in which white and black, rich and poor, prominent and ordinary folks have met together and frankly discussed the plans of the organization and work. Most of these meetings have been held in the residence of its gracious founder, Mrs. Woolley. With entire innocence of violating social proprieties, light refreshments have been provided and innocently partaken of, as a mere incident of the coming together for a high purpose.

The meeting that was made the subject of the sensational article already alluded to was a woman's meeting of the character just described. It was essentially a business meeting and not a social party. Such conferences, with the incident of tea drinking and its touch of social amenity, [are] of common occurrence in Chicago as elsewhere, and no one but a newspaper reporter with an inordinate greed for mischief making and its *"quid pro quo,"* would have found anything in it to write about.

The Frederick Douglass Centre has been incorporated and the Board of Directors is made up of men of both races.

The president, Mrs. Celia Parker Woolley, of this city, is not only the head of this great movement, but it is her conception. She is a fine type of progressive womanhood. She has culture, social standing, literary training and ability[; she is] a preacher, a club woman and a humanitarian in its broadest sense. She comes of Abolition stock and she has always kept alive in her breast the spirit that has given to us women like Miss [Susan B.] Anthony, Elizabeth Cady Stanton, Julia Ward Howe and their kind.[67]

We are fortunate beyond words in being able to claim as our friend, for this important work, a woman of such rare endowments and splendid consecration as Mrs. Celia Parker Woolley.

It is her hope, and of those who are associated with her, to make this Chicago movement so important in results that similar associations will be formed in other cities where the colored population is large. The possibilities of usefulness for the Douglass Centre are almost without limit. It is well that the colored people of the country should watch this movement and in every possible way encourage the brave men and women who have thrown aside social ease and social delights that they may be able to study and know what are our preventable distresses and hindrances and apply the remedy and the sure way of escape.

NINETEEN

SOCIAL BONDS IN THE "BLACK BELT" OF CHICAGO

Negro Organizations and the New Spirit Pervading Them

The last federal census [1900] showed the Negro population of Chicago to be about 35,000. The present population is estimated to be over 50,000, an increase of about forty per cent in five years. The colored people who are thus crowding into Chicago come mostly from the states of Kentucky, Tennessee, Alabama, Mississippi, Louisiana, Arkansas and Missouri.

The underlying causes are easily traceable and are mainly as follows:

1. Primarily to escape laws of race discrimination that have steadily increased during the last few years.
2. To obtain better school privileges.
3. On account of the good news circulated by the hundreds of young colored men and women who have been educated in the Chicago and Northwestern Universities and the professional schools, that Chicago offers the largest liberty to citizens of all colors and languages of all communities in the North.
4. Because of the many industrial strikes which in the last ten years have brought thousands of colored people to Chicago, either for immediate work as strike breakers, or with the prospect of employment through the opportunities for both skilled and unskilled workers [Herbst 1971/1932]. Whatever the cause, the fact remains that thousand of Negro men and women are now employed in the stockyards and other large industrial plants, where ten years ago this would not have been thought of.

This increase of Negro population has brought with it problems that directly affect the social and economic life of the newcomers. Prevented from mingling easily and generally with the rest of the city's population, according to their needs and deservings, but with no preparation made for segregation, their life in a great city has been irregular and shifting, with the result that they have been subject to more social ills than any other nationality amongst us. Notwithstanding the disadvantages suggested, the colored people of Chicago have shown in their efforts for self-help and self-advancement a determination that is altogether creditable.[68] While it is true that they contribute almost more than their share of the sins of the

"Social Bonds in the 'Black Belt' of Chicago," *Charities* 15 (7 October 1905): 40–44.

community, what they contribute in the way of restraining and correcting influences over their own lives, is much more important.

The real problem of the social life of the colored people in Chicago, as in all northern cities, lies in the fact of their segregation. While they do not occupy all the worst streets and live in all the unsanitary houses in Chicago, what is known as the "Black Belt" is altogether forbidding and demoralizing. The huddling together of the good and the bad, compelling the decent element of the colored people to witness the brazen display of vice of all kinds in front of their homes and in the faces of their children, are trying conditions under which to remain socially clean and respectable. There are some who are all the time breaking away from these surroundings and by purchase or otherwise are securing good homes on desirable streets. But the old and unsanitary shacks from which the good and the thrifty escape are immediately occupied by others less fortunate. For there are always too few houses to meet the demands of the newcomers.

The Organizing Faculty a Racial Passion

As already suggested the colored people themselves are not indifferent to the demoralizing conditions of their environments. The organizations created and maintained by them in Chicago are numerous and touch almost every phase of our social life.

Is this passion for organization peculiar to Negro people? Whether this be answered in the affirmative or not, it is a fact that the Negro individual does not like to be alone in good works. His bent for organization is a sort of racial passion. Suggest to the average man something that ought to be, and he immediately proposes an organization. There is scarcely a thing in religion, in politics, in business, in pleasure, in education, in fighting race prejudice, or anything else desirable that is not the object of organization. A catalogue of the organizations created by colored people in this country would make a very large book, and would contain an interesting story of the many ways by which the Negro seeks to improve his condition. It is a common complaint that the Negroes will not support and protect each other in any united effort, but this is clearly not so. It is true that more of these organizations fail than succeed, but the failing is not due to a lack of the co-operative spirit, which is the most helpful thing, in our race character. The failures are mostly due to a lack of comprehension and intelligence in working out the details. The weak point is administration. It is a common thing for men of no training and no experience to start an organization that requires the highest order of executive ability to carry out. They will take as a model the constitution and by-laws of some well-established white organization that is prominently successful. Officers, directors and committees will be made up exactly as in the organization which is its model—this, with the utmost enthusiasm and good faith that their success is assured. The colored man who ventures to suggest to them that they cannot succeed, for various and obvious reasons, is at once branded as a "traitor to his race." The enterprise may be fore-doomed, but the result will be charged up to the failure of the people to support and sustain it.

The pathway of our progress is thickly strewn with such failures, but they do not discourage other and similar attempts. A colored man who has joined and pinned his faith to an organization that has failed will join another society of the same kind tomorrow. It is at once pathetic and splendid to note how persistent is this faith that emancipation from the ills of poverty and ignorance and race prejudice is through co-operation. Indeed, no race of men and women feel more strongly than we do the force of that maxim that "in union there is strength."

The Negro Church

First in importance is the Negro church. There are 25 regularly organized colored churches. This number includes 9 Methodist, 8 Baptist, 1 Catholic, 1 Episcopal, 1 Christian and 1 Presbyterian. In addition to these there are numerous missions in various parts of the "Black Belt." These churches are for the most part housed in large and modern stone and brick edifices that cost from $7,000 to $40,000 each, and have a seating capacity of from 300 to 2,000 people. Most of these churches are burdened with oppressive indebtedness, and because of this their usefulness as agents of moral up-lift is seriously handicapped. For example, the members of one of the largest have raised and paid in over $60,000 during the last five years, but the church still carries an indebtedness of over $24,000.

Despite this serious handicap of a slowly diminishing debt, the colored church is the center of the social life and efforts of the people. What the church sanctions and supports is of the first importance and what it fails to support and sanction is more than apt to fail. The Negro church historically, as to numbers and reach of influence and dominion, is the strongest factor in the community life of the colored people. Aside from the ordinary functions of preaching, prayer, class meeting, and Sunday-school, the church is regarded by the masses as a sort of tribune of all of their civic and social interests. Thousands of Negroes know and care for no other entertainment than that furnished by the church. Theatres, concert halls, and art galleries mean nothing. What they fail to learn of these things in the churches remains unlearned. Nearly every night the church building is open, either for worship or for concerts, lectures, and entertainments of all kinds. Even political meetings of the most partisan sort are not barred. The party leaders find it to their advantage, if they want to secure a large audience of colored people, to hold their meetings in the colored church. In a purely social way, the church leads in setting standards of social conduct. Weddings and receptions of all kinds, except those including dancing, are held within its walls and in this respect the church has become progressively liberal. Among other nationalities, there are Young Men's Christian Associations, Young Women's Christian Associations, social clubs, gymnasiums, reading-rooms, university extension lecture courses, etc. The colored people, generally speaking, have none of these liberalizing and elevating influences, except as they are supplied by this single institution.

Within the last six years, the colored churches of Chicago have begun to recognize the larger social needs of the people, and as much as their intense denominationalism will permit, they are endeavoring to enlarge their influence as a factor for betterment. One of the large churches has carried on such activities as a kindergarten, a day nursery, a boys' club and reading-room, a penny savings-bank, gymnasium, a kitchen garden, mothers' club, and sewing school.

Nearly all of the large churches have literary clubs, which have become attractive to hundreds of young colored men of intelligence. The effect has been a wider and more intelligent interest in things that concern the progressive life of the people.

In fine the colored churches must be reckoned with in every movement of a social character that aims to reach and influence life. They might do more and be more to the ever increasing number who need guidance, social ideals, and higher moral standards, if they were less burdened with debts and an unyielding orthodoxy. The important thing, however, is that the Negro church in Chicago is becoming more and more liberal and intelligently interested and earnest in its endeavors to meet the peculiar requirements of the city Negro.

The Secret Orders

Next to the Negro church in importance, as affecting the social life of the people, are the secret orders, embracing such organizations as the Masons, Odd Fellows, Knights of Pythias, True Reformers, the United Brotherhood (a fraternal insurance association), the Ancient Order of Foresters, and the Elks. Nearly all of these secret orders have auxiliary associations composed of women. The Masons and Odd Fellows are strongest in point of numbers and influence. There are about fourteen lodges of Odd Fellows and about as many of Masons. Their estimated membership is respectively 2,000 and 1,600.

The colored people believe in secret societies. I believe it is safe to say that fifty per cent of the better class of Negro men are enrolled in some secret order. These affect every phase of their social life and represent the best achievements of the race in the matter of organization. In no other way is the organized Negro so reliably responsive to the requirements of his social obligations. In no other form of organization do the terms brotherhood and mutual obligations mean so much.

Thousands of dollars are paid into the treasuries of these societies every month, and it is very rare that we hear of any charge of dishonest dealings in money matters. They take care of the sick and provide for the dead with a promptness, fidelity and abundance of sympathy that is not to be found in any other form of society amongst us. The lessons of right living, of charity and truthfulness are enforced in these societies more rigidly even than in the churches.

Most of the colored men belong to more than one secret order and many belong to as many as four or five at a time and live up to their obligations in all of them. In nothing does the colored man live such a strenuous life as he does as a lodge man. The lodge, more than any other merely social organization, is a permanent and ever increasing force.

Other Organized Activities

There are other social organizations among the colored people of Chicago that are indicative of a desire for progress and improvement. For example, there is one organization that supports an institution known as the "Old Folks' Home," in which some twenty-five old colored men and women are comfortably cared for and saved from eking out their existence in the dreaded almshouse.

There is a Choral Study Club composed of about one hundred young men and women under competent leadership and devoted to the study of music. A business league, composed of colored business men and women, is a part of the National Business League of which Booker T. Washington is founder and president. A physicians' club has undertaken a campaign of education as to the cause of tuberculosis and methods of prevention, together with lessons on domestic sanitation and kindred subjects.

And there are, of course, numbers of purely pleasure clubs. Love of pleasure is in good part a hopeful characteristic of the Negro people. Painfully conscious as we all are of our present position, which tends to exclude us from things that are most prized in human relationships, there is an ill-pervading lightheartedness which saves us from the pessimism that must inevitably banish from the soul all hope and joy. Young men's social clubs, young women's social clubs, fellowship clubs, whist clubs, and social charity clubs fill nights and holidays with laughter, song and dance.

The Negro in His Relations to the Dominant Race

From what has been said in describing Negro organizations it might be inferred that the colored people are quite capable of taking care of themselves and of advancing their own condition in every direction. Let us be undeceived in this. In every community the Negro is practically dependent, for nearly everything of importance, upon the dominant race. He must live in places set apart for him, and that often in the worst portions of the city. He must find work below his capabilities and training. He must live on the outer rim of life's advantages and pleasures. His merit, whatever it may be, is more apt to be discredited than recognized. Even though he be educated, public opinion still persists in rating him as ignorant, and treating him as such. His virtues are generally overlooked or reluctantly believed in. He is the victim of more injustice than is meted out to any other class of people. In the matter of employment, the colored people of Chicago have lost in the last ten years nearly every occupation of which there once was almost a monopoly. There is now scarcely a Negro barber left in the business distinct. Nearly all the janitor work in the large buildings has been taken away from them by the Swedes. White men and women as waiters have supplanted colored men in nearly all the first-class hotels and restaurants. Practically all the shoe polishing is now done by Greeks. Negro coachmen and expressmen and teamsters are seldom seen in the business districts. It scarcely need be stated that colored young men and women are almost never employed as clerks and bookkeepers in business establishments. A race that can be systematically deprived of one occupation after another becomes an easy victim to all kinds of injustice. When they can be reduced to a position to be pitied, they will cease to be respected. It is not surprising then that there has been a marked lowering of that public sentiment that formerly was liberal and more tolerant of the Negro's presence and efforts to rise.

The increase of the Negro population in Chicago, already referred to, has not tended to liberalize public sentiment; in fact, hostile sentiment has been considerably intensified by the importation from time to time of colored men as strike-breakers. Then again a marked increase of crime among the Negro population has been noted in recent years. All these things have tended to put us in a bad light, resulting in an appreciable loss of friends and well-wishers.

The Frederick Douglass Center

Out of these seemingly hopeless conditions a new movement has grown that is destined to have an important bearing on the status of the Chicago Negro. The organization of the Frederick Douglass Center and the Trinity Mission Settlement are in response to these needs of the hour. The Frederick Douglass Center is unlike anything of the kind in the country. It is the outgrowth of a comprehensive study of the situation by some of the best people of the city of both races. The head and soul of the movement, Mrs. Celia Parker Woolley, is a woman who has given up social pleasures and the pursuits of culture in behalf of a people and of a problem to grapple with which requires more than ordinary patience and intelligence.

The Frederick Douglass Center is intended primarily as a center of influence for the better relationship of the white and colored races along the higher levels of mutual dependence and helpfulness. The society is incorporated under the laws of the state of Illinois. Its by-laws recite its purposes as follows:

1. To promote a just and amicable relationship between the white and colored people.

2. To remove the disabilities from which the latter suffer in their civil, political, and industrial life.

3. To encourage equal opportunity irrespective of race, color, or other arbitrary distinctions.

4. To establish a center of friendly helpfulness and influence in which to gather needful information and for mutual co-operation to the end of right living and higher citizenship.

In order to properly house the movement there has been purchased, at a cost of $5,500 a large three-story, gray-stone house on Wabash Avenue, near Thirty-first street. The location is adjacent to the "Black Belt" in the rear, and the white belt of aristocracy and wealth on Michigan avenue in the front. This new home for social improvement is fitted up with an attractive assembly room for meetings, a club-room and workshop for boys, a reading-room and offices and living-rooms for the head resident. Arrangements are being made for mothers' meetings in the interest of the home, men's meetings, classes in manual training, cooking and dress making, club work for intellectual and moral culture, and domestic employment. Lectures are also being provided for under the departments of sanitation, neighborhood improvement and civics.

Mrs. Woolley has succeeded in interesting in this new work many of the well-known people of Chicago, judges, lawyers, professors, business men and women of wealth and culture. Along with these she has the co-operation of nearly every colored man and woman of standing.

The Trinity Mission

Another effort toward social betterment is the Trinity Mission. This is the beginning of a more distinct social settlement. It is located in the very heart of the "Black Belt" on Eighteenth street between State and Clark streets, a neighborhood properly called "Darkest Africa." Here there is scarcely a single ray of the light of decency. Neither church nor school, nor anything else of a helpful character can be found. The head of this enterprise is a young man, Richard R. Wright, [Jr.] son of President [R.R.] Wright, [Sr.] of the State Industrial School, at College, Georgia. A creche, a reading-room and a home for working girls are being carried on and substantial encouragement has come from people who are in sympathy with the principle of settlement work.

One of the results of these new organizations is the serious view the more intelligent colored people are beginning to take of the responsibilities of city life among their people. The Negro's worth as a citizen is to be tested in the great cities of the North as nowhere else in the world—the use he makes of his opportunities here, and his strength of character in resisting the malign influences of city politics.

To summarize:

1. The colored people themselves have begun to develop a sort of civic consciousness as manifested in the tendency of the Negro church and the Negro lodge to participate more largely in efforts to improve the social condition of their people.

2. The men and women who have organized in various ways to bring about a better Chicago, as well as a larger Chicago, have begun to recognize that if the ever-increasing, Negro population is treated and regarded as a reprobate race, the result will be an increase of crime and disorders of all kinds that will grow more and more difficult to handle and regulate.

3. Recent organizations with the settlement spirit are preparing to do many things in a rational way that have never before been attempted, and to make answer to many false and harmful things that now go unchallenged. In other words, by these new movements the Negro is to be generously included in all efforts to promote civic righteousness among all the people.

TWENTY

THE FREDERICK DOUGLASS CENTER

[The Institutional Foundation]

Interest in the race problem as it exists in the large cities of the Northern states is finely exemplified in the first year's achievements of a Chicago social settlement known as "The Frederick Douglass Center." In less than a year this institution has demonstrated many new and helpful ways of improving relations between the two races.

The Frederick Douglass Center is not an experiment or merely the projection of an eager philanthropy; on the contrary, it is one of the most seriously considered efforts ever made to do something large, thorough, and constructive in behalf of a proscribed people. It is an undertaking conceived, worked out in detail, and bravely established by a white woman of broad culture and achievement in letters, of high social standing, and of a chivalrous spirit—Mrs. Celia Parker Woolley. Her heart has always been in the right place on this question and she has brought to its study years of thought and constant, growing effort.

The Douglass Center is a settlement plus something else. It is not organized to do slum work in what may be called the black belt of Chicago, but to be a center of wholesome influences to the end that well-disposed white people may learn to know and respect the ever increasing number of colored people who have earned the right to be believed in and respected. To quote from the charter of this new organization: "The Frederick Douglass Center is organized to promote just and amicable relations between the white and colored people; to remove the disabilities from which the latter suffer in their civil, political, and industrial life; to encourage equal opportunity, irrespective of race, color, or other arbitrary distinctions; to establish a center of friendly helpfulness and influence in which to gather useful information and for mutual cooperation in attaining to right living and a higher citizenship."

Those who know the general low estimate in which colored people are held in these cities can readily appreciate the urgent need of such an influence as the Douglass Center aims to create and extend. The well-known scholar and editor, Mr. Edwin Mead[69] of Boston, in a recent letter to the (Boston) *Transcript* refers to Mrs. Woolley's undertaking as "the bravest

---

"The Frederick Douglass Center," *The Southern Workman* 35 (June 1906): 334–36.

and most devoted work known to me tending towards true neighborhood relations." Such endorsement is none too strong. Whatever can be done in a sane, rational, and just manner to check the conditions that make for a wider separation of the races in their non-social relations will be courteously attempted by this settlement center.

What are some of the tangible and intangible results of this new center of good influences at the end of its first year's existence? The Frederick Douglass Center is an incorporated institution. Its business activities are under the direction of a board of directors composed of three white and four colored persons. The present directors are Mrs. Celia Parker Woolley, Mrs. E[lizabeth] L. Davis, Dr. C[harles] E. Bentley, Mr. S. Laing Williams, Mr. John O'Connor, and Mr. F[erdinand] L. Barnett. The membership of the association numbers something over three hundred men and women, about equally divided between the two races. It is safe to say that in the membership of no other organization in this country can be found such an interesting admixture of people of varying stations, achievements, and accomplishments. It is a most encouraging indication of how many good and great people there are who are willing to stand up and be counted as ready to lend a helping hand to the cause of Negro betterment. In the roll of members may be found several judges and ex-judges, prominent members of the bar, well-known physicians, eminent educators, both of the city schools and the Chicago University, business men, philanthropists, prominent clergymen of both races, and well-known women like Miss Jane Addams, Miss [Sophonisba] Breckinridge of Kentucky, and others representing the best social life of Chicago. The names of Dr. Booker T. Washington and Dr. [W.E.B.] DuBois are enrolled as honorary members. Let it be understood that these names are not mere ornaments. For many weeks before the center was organized Mrs. Woolley had numerous conferences with many of the prominent men and women and frankly discussed her plans and purposes and in every instance she was assured of their hearty cooperation. In other words it can be said that the Frederick Douglass Center is endorsed and supported by many of the best people in Chicago from all the higher walks of life.

The Center has a home of its own, which is not yet fully paid for. It consists of a three-story, white stone house of twelve rooms, situated on Wabash Avenue, on the eastern edge of what is known as the black belt. A beautiful assembly room filled with books, appropriate pictures, and inspiring mottoes, apartments for the head resident, a club room for boys, and a culinary department are a part of the outfit.

Its work has thus far been largely educational, not in a schoolroom sense, but in ways that tend to realize its declared purpose "to promote a just and amicable relationship between the white and colored people." Among the activities already developed and being successfully carried on are a department of civics, a Woman's Club, a club for the study of sociology, a kindergarten, an arts and crafts club for boys, a sewing class for girls, a fiction class in literature, now studying George Eliot, a forum for the discussion of live questions, and a bureau of information. These are not paper clubs; they represent a real, earnest, and growing interest in the things we all need for the enlargement of mind and heart.

These opportunities for study and discussion have brought together an interesting group of young and old people. One may feel perfectly safe in going to the Douglass Center on any night. One evening you may hear the head of the Civil Service Commission urging young, colored men and women to make themselves proficient for public service—telling them how it can be done, and assuring them that these opportunities have an open door for them also. Again, you may chance to hear Mr. Wentworth, a prominent real estate man, discussing in an illuminating manner some of the live questions in civics, emphasizing the important difference between good citizenship and mere politics. Another night you may hear an explanation by an eminent lawyer of the benefits to each citizen resulting from the new city charter, a chance talk by Jenkin Lloyd Jones, or a delightful interpretative reading by Mrs. Woolley.

In the matter of neighborhood improvement, the Center is endeavoring to create a feeling of civic pride in maintaining clean streets, clean alleys, and wholesome sanitary conditions. It has also taken up the subject of vacation schools, one of the new needs of children with scant home training and influence, with the hope of establishing one in that district, where the colored children are largely in the majority. These studies and new interests have brought the colored people into new relationships with the people who are responsible for everything that makes for the better and higher life of the city and its citizens. Already, through the good influences of this active center, the colored people are learning that the only way they can have a conscious share in the common life of the community is to contribute their proportion of interest and duty to the common good. Another interesting feature of the Frederick Douglass Center is the Sunday afternoon meetings in the assembly room. These services are of a religious ethical character, and are addressed by the best men and women of both races. Special music is furnished. These meetings are very popular and severely test the seating and standing capacity of the hall.

In still another way the Center is sustaining its mission of helpfulness and that is in bringing together for harmonious action the various elements among the colored people of the city. The tendency to divide into factions, more or less unfriendly, seems to characterize Negro life in a great city. The Douglass Center has offered a common ground for common aspirations and common action. In this new institution our people have shown a spirit of cooperation more generous than any other influence has been able to effect for a long time. They have by united effort contributed over one thousand dollars to the building fund of the institution. A softening of differences, mutual trustfulness, and a more kindly interest in one another are among the beneficent results of this center of good works.

TWENTY-ONE

A NEW METHOD OF DEALING WITH THE RACE PROBLEM

An event of widespread interest was the first annual meeting of The Frederick Douglass Center of Chicago, Ill., held at the Center house on Wabash Avenue, on the eighth day of May last.

When this Institution was organized, incorporated, and established one year ago, it was regarded as altogether a new departure in methods of dealing with the so-called race problem. It will be remembered, perhaps, that the Frederick Douglass Center was created out of a deep anxiety on the part of many prominent and large-souled white women and men, not only to help worthy colored people to realize all their citizenship rights and privileges, but also to save white people from the soul-belittling effect of inherited and cultivated prejudices. It will also be remembered that this new association is not a "settlement" and does not aim, primarily, to do Settlement work. "Center" is the vital term in its declaration of purposes and principles—a place or Institution from which shall generate influences helpful to a more cordial relationship between white and black people. These purposes or objects are best stated as follows:

> "To promote a just and amicable relation between the white and colored people.
>
> To remove the disabilities from which the latter suffer in their civil, political and industrial life.
>
> To encourage equal opportunity irrespective of race, color, or other arbitrary distinctions.
>
> To establish a center of friendly helpfulness and influence in which to gather useful information and for mutual cooperation to the ends of right living and a higher citizenship."

What has been accomplished in the first experimental year?

The detailed report of the many intellectual and ethical activities of this first year gives abundant and encouraging answers. However, the best results can scarcely be shown in facts and figures. The movement has been mostly ethical and spiritual, but there are some figures that are significant of the generous interest shown in the work of this new Center of beneficent in-

"A New Method of Dealing with the Race Problem," *Voice of the Negro* 3, no. 7 (1906): 502–5

fluences. The movement was started a little over a year ago without money or habitation. At the end of the year it occupies its own home, consisting of a three-story white stone building purchased at a cost of $5,500. During this year the members of the Association and friends of the Center have paid $4,000 on the property. The significant thing about this good showing is that the colored people themselves have paid quite half of this sum. In addition to this amount paid on the building, the current expenses of furnishings and equipment have all been paid. To accomplish these results, white and colored people have worked together in a spirit of comradeship and good fellowship, each experiencing a spirit of uplift both helpful and inspiring.

The roll of membership comprising the Association is perhaps the most interesting to be found connected with any institution in the country. There are between three and four hundred members, men and women, white and black. The names of prominent white persons in every walk of life are to be found in line with colored men and women representing the best life of the race. The high character of the membership of the Frederick Douglass Center is sufficiently indicated when the names of Jane Adams of Hull House, Mary McDowell of the University [of Chicago Social] Settlement, Celia Parker Woolley, Graham Taylor of Chicago Commons, and several judges of the courts are to be found on its roll of membership. Prominent people also in Boston, New York, Philadelphia, Washington, Atlanta, and other places have indicated their interest in the Center by becoming members.

During the year it has been the center of the best social and intellectual life of the city. Among the distinguished visitors of the year have been Booker T. Washington, President Merrill of Fisk University, Prof. H.T. Kealing of Philadelphia, Editor J. Max Barber[70] of *The Voice of The Negro*, President R.R. Wright, [Sr.][71] of Georgia State College, L[ewis] G[arnett] Jordan,[72] and W.G. Stewart of Louisville, Ky.

During this first experimental year, the Center has become one of the most interesting places in the city. Nearly every afternoon and evening something is going on of interest to many. Among the more practical things are a Kindergarten and Sewing school. In another part of the building a Gymnasium and Boys Club are in progress. There is also a Girls' Club. The fact that the Center can attract and hold together such a large number of young people, of both sexes, ranging from 15 to 18 years of age, is one of the best evidences of its usefulness. The influences surrounding them here are thoroughly wholesome, interesting and uplifting. They engage themselves in a great variety of studies, health-giving exercises and innocent amusements. This is about the only place in the city where the "younger set" of the young people can find intellectual and physical recreation similar in kind to that afforded to the young people of other races.

In this opportunity provided for the young people, there has developed in them a sense of gratitude and a desire to reciprocate in every way possible. Indeed they have done almost as much as the older people to make the

Center interesting and important. Along with the other uses of the Center as a rallying place for study, exercise and recreation, they have instituted among themselves an organized interest in neighborhood decency and cleanliness. For example, they have formed themselves into squadrons to keep the streets, for a radius of about six blocks around the Center, clear of paper and other rubbish. Not only so, but they gather the papers and rubbish from unsightly vacant lots, sewing grass seed instead to make green and beautiful to the eye these neglected plague spots. Anyone familiar with the slovenly appearance of some of our streets and city lots can appreciate what it means for these school boys to voluntarily organize themselves into bands to make clean and cheerful these waste places. The enthusiasm of these boys and the effect of their work have raised the tone of respectability for the entire neighborhood, while the boys who engage in this kind of service are learning their first and most important lessons of good citizenship.

The co-operative spirit of the Center is aptly illustrated by the Woman's Club connected with the Center. This club has a membership of about seventy women, a third of whom are white. Most of the officers however are colored women. The character of the membership is high, and the women of both races are among the most representative of the city in all things that make for the higher life of the community. This Club affords a fine example of how genuine can be the comradeship of kindred spirits when class and race distinctions are minimized or held to the vanishing point. The work is keyed up to subjects and interests that profoundly effect the social life of the community. The Club is divided into departments representing the following activities:

> The Home Department.
> Educational Department.
> Philanthropic Department.
> Domestic Science Department.

With the amount of intelligence and experience to be found in this club, these Departments have meant something more than mere names on which to hang pretenses of "work along higher lines." Take for example the Education Department. As is well known, education in a big city like Chicago is a tremendous responsibility. There is needed all the time not only the official staff of teachers, superintendents and officers, but the active, diligent and continuous co-operation of parents and citizens. Hence this Department of Education under the aggressive leadership of women who are in touch with the whole range of religious, ethical and social problems has been wonderfully active. It can be stated generally that during the past year more has been done to arouse parental interest in the public schools where colored children are largely represented than ever before.

As an example of how practical has been the work of the Center Woman's Club, we need only call attention to what has been accomplished in securing for the first time a "Vacation School" in a District where its benefits will include colored children, almost entirely. The Vacation schools are, as the term implies, open during the Vacation months. They are in no sense compulsory and are not wholly supported by the Public School fund. The Course of study is quite different from the regular Curriculum, but is in the form of nature studies, modeling, light manual training, games and plays properly conducted, free excursions into the country once or twice a week, and instructions in many things that have proved both a delight and benefit to thousands of children in our hot and congested districts. These Vacation Schools are immensely popular, and eager applicants always exceed the accommodations, as they are not yet a part of the Public School system.

In neighborhoods where there are no play grounds,[73] and limited house yards, the children of poor people suffer many deprivations. To such these schools are a veritable boon. Now if the residents of a certain neighborhood want one of these Vacation schools, they cannot obtain it by merely asking for it. The community and their friends must pay a certain amount for teachers' service and equipment. The people in colored neighborhoods have never been able to raise the required amount of money. Under the leadership of the Frederick Douglass Center forces were organized to raise the required amount that has brought joy to the parents and children of the Black Belt.

The kind of energy, intelligence and cooperative enthusiasm that characterized the work and success of the Committee on Education has been significant of the work of the other Departments as well.

Perhaps the most distinctive work of the Center during the first year of its life has been to cultivate a more active and intelligent interest in Civic affairs. There is a tendency even among our most intelligent men and women to be self-centered in their interests. The corporate life of the community with its multitudinous interests and responsibilities, we seem to have but little interest in. We vote, pay taxes, pay licenses, send our children to school, drink the city water, use the city's light and pay for it, comply as best we can with the sanitary laws, etc., but there is no ambition amongst us to share in the making and creating of these activities. The colored people in these great centers of human life and action act as if they had no right to participate in the thought or discussion of the questions that concern the life and well-being of all the people. For example, when a new Charter is to be planned for and worked out into practicalities, when civil service is to be the law of appointments, when new schools and new courses of study are to be considered, colored people act as if they were not expected to be interested in these things. In other words, the colored people of this and other cities are the only race of people who take no part in the initiative of great civic movements.

To the credit of the Frederick Douglass Center this indifference to our civic responsibilities and opportunities has been recognized and one of the most interesting features of its program of activities has been the addresses by the head of the Civil Service Commission, prominent members of the teachers fraternity, one of the experts in the movement for a new Charter, and an address by the President of the Woman's Club on the value of Vacation Schools.

Although the Civil Service has long been a force in Chicago and also Cook county, this is the first time that its importance has been brought directly to the notice of our young men and women. In other words, if the proper interest had been urged upon our people years ago, many of our men and women would have been in the public service and by this time advanced by merit to positions of trust and responsibility. The Civil Service law is liberal, fair and just. The variety of talents and accomplishments required to run a government like Chicago is large enough to afford everybody a chance. A great number of our people could qualify for the public service if they would but make the effort, and thus far ignorance of these possibilities has restrained them from making the effort. What is true of the Civil Service is equally true of the proposed new Charter for our city government. In this revolution of the methods of government our competent men and women should be able to find many new opportunities for honorable employment. Yet the matter has not been brought pointedly to our attention, either by the press or other agencies. It is the purpose of the Douglass Center to make as much as possible of this effort to arouse a new interest among the colored people of the city to get in at the beginning and as far as possible be a part of the working force in the formation of these new conditions in our civil life.

Perhaps enough has been said to show that what one year ago was an interesting experiment, with no precedent to follow, has within twelve months become more than a realization. Those who saw here only another attempt to force "social equality" have lived to see that the Center is working out something better than social equality. The Center has reached hundreds of important white people and made those interested in our problems, who were heretofore ignorant of or indifferent to our progress or status. The Center is the only agency in the city that is easily and effectively responsive to every wrong, near or remote, that threatens to belittle the life of the colored people. It has won the respect and confidence of both races and in one year it has succeeded in making its mission felt as important and increasingly necessary.

Part Five

· EULOGIES ·

TWENTY-TWO

[IN MEMORY OF PHILIP D. ARMOUR]

The following letter comes to us from the pen of Fannie Barrier Williams of Chicago, Ill. We are glad to call the attention of our readers to Mr. Armour's largeness of heart and broad-minded philanthropy.

The death of P.D. Armour, the millionaire packer and philanthropist, has deprived the colored people of a friend who did more than is generally recognized for their advancement. Mr. Armour's helpfulness was of a practical kind and went to the heart of our difficulties—the lack of opportunities to earn a living in the great hives of industry built up by American capital and genius.

The colored people have a just complaint against nearly all the great employers of skilled and unskilled labor in the North in that they are meanly indifferent and even contemptuous to the demands of colored men and women for a chance to earn a livelihood. To such men the Negro is a hopeless problem, and they have no time for problems outside of their dividend-making enterprises. The fact that there is a prejudice against the Negro and that some white workmen refuse to work with or near him is excuse enough to make most employers shun the Negro except as an object for their "charity list."

Not so with Mr. Armour. His heart was large enough to recognize the demands and needs of these newly made citizens, and in the building up of his great industries he favored the Negro workman to an extent scarcely equalled by any other business man in the North.

His instructions were that "all must be treated alike." The Armour Packing House of Chicago alone employs about one thousand colored men and women in nearly every department and no complaint is ever heard of discrimination of any kind. Mr. Armour's confidence in the colored man as a worker has been justified in the fact that the number of colored employees has increased from year to year. Other packers in Chicago have not been slow to act, and as a consequence, there are perhaps more colored people, skilled and unskilled men and women, in all the great packing houses in Chicago than in any other single industry in the Northern states. But for this opportunity afforded to thousands of colored people, those who are

"Philip D. Armour," *Southern Workman* 30 (May 1901): 24–25.

constantly coming from the South seeking a larger freedom to earn a living would find the problem of obtaining employment a serious one.

Mr. Armour also showed his friendly interest in the race in other ways as well. In innumerable cases he has aided individual young men and women of the colored race in their struggles to obtain an education. I know personally of several young men and women whose education has been due solely to Mr. Armour's kindness of heart. All of these acts of public and private kindness were done by this great-hearted man as if they afforded him real pleasure. Few people outside of his beneficiaries knew anything about these outlets to Mr. Armour's Christian spirit. As absorbed as Mr. Armour was in his mighty affairs of business, the sick and poor and helpless of the race found in him a ready sympathizer who made a quick response to their needs, if they were worthy, and deserving.

The most enduring monument to Mr. Armour's great-heartedness is the Provident Hospital and Training School for Nurses in Chicago. It is doubtful if this splendid school and hospital with its present equipment for usefulness could have been realized, but for Mr. Armour's generous donations. He not only showed his interest by furnishing means for its upbuilding but he further interested himself by visiting the institution nearly every Sunday when he was well and in the city. The officers and nurses of the school loved Mr. Armour for his genial spirit and encouragement as much as for the money which accompanied them. His presence and encouragement were always an inspiration and a help. It is doubtful if the death of any other business man in the West could bring to the hearts of the Negro race more sincere sorrow than that felt for the loss of Mr. Armour. He was to thousands of colored men and women, as well as to their homes, something more than a dispenser of charity. He was felt, somehow, to be the one man who had given them an opportunity, and such a man is a real benefactor to a race whose opportunities are everywhere restricted by an unreasonable and unchristian race prejudice.

TWENTY-THREE

[EULOGY OF SUSAN B. ANTHONY]

[Ida Husted Harper's (1969/1922, 203) introduction to the eulogy went as follows: "Mrs. Fannie Barrier Williams of Chicago paid touching tribute in behalf of the colored people."]

My presence on this platform shows that the gracious spirit of Miss Anthony still survives in her followers. . . . When Miss Anthony took up the cause of women she did not know them by their color, nationality, creed, or birth; she stood only for the emancipation of women from the thraldom of sex. She became an invincible champion of anti-slavery. In the half century of her unremitting struggle for liberty, more liberty, and complete liberty for negro men and women in chains and for white women in their helpless subjection to man's laws, she never wavered, never doubted, never compromised. She held it to be mockery to ask man or woman to be happy or contented if not free. She saw no substitute for liberty. When slavery was overthrown and the work of reconstruction began she was still unwearied and watchful. She had an intimate acquaintance with the leading statesmen of the times. Her judgment and advice were respected and heard in much of the legislation that gave a status of citizenship to the millions of slaves set free.

The History of Woman Suffrage, vol. 5, 1900–1920, ed. Ida Husted Harper (1922; reprint, New York: Arno Press, 1969).

TWENTY-FOUR

REPORT OF MEMORIAL SERVICE FOR
REV. CELIA PARKER WOOLLEY, APRIL 7, 1918,
AT THE ABRAHAM LINCOLN CENTRE, CHICAGO

Mrs. Woolley belonged to that choice group of men and women who could not be happy so long as unrighteousness had sway over this country.

She conceived it to be a part of her mission in life to help to correct public opinion that is now either indifferent to or actively hostile against the present generation of colored people.

She also believed that the relationship between the two races could be adjusted in a way that would satisfy the demands of ethics, religion and the highest equity, for she felt that the spirit of human fellowship once understood would carry us across the superficial barriers of race lines and color lines that separate the stronger and weaker elements of human society.

But today looking back on the splendid possibilities of this noble life we cannot but ask ourselves: Were there not other fields to tempt the poetry of this ardent soul? Were there not other paths, where no shadow of sorrow sat, by which to travel towards the fullness of life? But it is right at this point where the power of choice comes to great souls, and Mrs. Woolley did not hesitate to choose between present good for self and the larger good of humanity. She knew she would be misunderstood, criticized, and even maligned, for prejudice and injustice are elements hard to combat. She established the Frederick Douglass Center and we all know how devotedly she served this cause. Her idea was always for justice and more justice. She went everywhere, prodding the American conscience to be just to the Negro and to enlarge the term citizenship so as to include all men.

Recalling these characteristics of Mrs. Woolley, it seems to me that she preeminently stood the supreme test of love to God in that she loved her neighbor as herself, without exceptions based on the mere circumstance of complexion.

Another beautiful thing to remember about Mrs. Woolley's efforts in our behalf is that she made everything she possessed, whether of culture, associates or friends, serve the cause she had espoused. She always placed

"Report of Memorial Service for Rev. Celia Parker Woolley, April 7, 1918, at the Abraham Lincoln Centre, Chicago," *Unity* 81 (18 April 1918): 116–17.

above everything else her duty to that race which her own race had outraged for over two centuries.

We shall also always lovingly recall that she never faltered in her devotion or lost her sympathy and respect for this ransomed race. She had an
abiding faith in the capacity of these people to rise above their limitations
and prejudicial hindrances. So that after all as a race, in the midst of the
degrading forces that have oppressed us, we have been wonderfully fortunate in our friends, and there is also this strange anomaly in our history
that the men and women who have done most for the Negro in his evolu-
tion from slavery to freedom and from freedom to citizenship are the men
and women who have been most exalted in this republic—and in this royal
company of great souls; with [the abolitionists William Lloyd] Garrison,
[Wendell] Phillips, Harriet Beecher Stowe, John Brown, and Lincoln, Mrs.
Woolley has taken her place and received her reward.

But I cannot refrain from voicing a sense of personal bereavement in the
death of Mrs. Woolley for she was my personal friend, but there is no con-
ceit in this, for she loved us all and permitted us to read her heart. There
are few in this city who could have left behind so many who could say,
"She was my personal friend." She could always be seen and heard by any
one of us and her wholesome advice, her inspiring optimism, and her generous spirit of comradeship will make her name and memory a sacred heritage. As the years go on, we will again and again invoke her benignant
spirit in our efforts to help ourselves and those who need our help. We shall
dedicate ourselves anew to the high task of helping to give character and
beauty to the Negro race. We should be able to see in Mrs. Woolley's death
the transfiguration of all our bitterness and despair into courage and hope,
for she taught more by the life she lived and the death she died than is given
even to those who have most enriched the annals of human greatness.

NOTES

1. This was a series of three articles in the *Independent*. See unsigned articles by a Southern Colored Woman, a Southern White Woman, and a Northern Woman, all published in the 17 March 1904 issue of the *Independent*. The editors erroneously assumed only white women lived in the North.

2. This is a confusing reference since Williams was born in 1855, before the war. Perhaps she changed the date for anonymity or vanity.

3. Williams is referring here to the idea of a color line in the same way that DuBois (1903a) used it.

4. Williams is referring here to "the Negro problem" in the same way that DuBois (1903a) used it.

5. Ralph Waldo Emerson (1803–1882) was the premier transcendentalist for many Unitarians in Chicago. See Emerson (1985) and Miller (1950; reprint, 1978), especially pp. 494–502. See also West (1989) on Emerson and the pragmatist tradition.

6. These women's groups had a religious basis for providing philanthropic or charitable services.

7. President Jeremiah Eames Rankin (1854–1904) of Howard University served from 1889–1903. He frequently wrote on religious subjects. See "Rankin," 1943.

8. Williams was responding here to slurs against African American women. See also her two essays on the club movement below.

9. Crispus Attucks (ca. 1723–1770) escaped from slavery and became a sailor. He was a hero killed by British soldiers during the Boston Massacre while leading a crowd of protesters, an event many consider the first step leading to the Revolutionary War (Adams 1969).

10. Entries on Coppin (Perkins 1993), Harper (Foster 1993), Early (Johnson 1993), Shadd [Cary] (Calloway-Thomas 1993), Grimke (Sumler-Edmond 1993), Sarah S.T. Garnet (Cash 1993), and Richards (Reid 1993) are available in *Black Women in America* (1993), a work that dramatically increased our knowledge of African American women. An entry on Brooks is available in *Noted Negro Women* (1893, 30–32).

11. I believe Williams is referring to Alice Ruth Moore Dunbar-Nelson (1875–1935) here (Hull 1993).

12. There were two eminent Howard sisters: Imogene and Adeline (see entry on Imogene in *Noted Negro Women*, 289–98, with a mention of Adeline, 289). I could not locate a reference to the Reasons. There were three eminent Ray sisters: Charlotte (1850–1911; see D. Thomas 1993, 965–66); Florence (*Noted Negro Women*, 179–80); and a third sister, with perhaps the initials H.C.

13. Addams was close to the kindergarten movement, especially through the work of John Dewey and George H. Mead at the University of Chicago. See Deegan (1999).

14. See Giddings (1984), Salem (1993), and Wesley (1984) for a discussion of the NACW.

15. Cook is noted in Williams (1900, 387).

16. I believe Ella D. Barrier was the sister of Fannie Barrier Williams. See "Negro Leader Dies at Local Residence," obituary posted by the Rochester, New York, Regional Library Council.

17. Accounts of the League are scattered in writings on Cooper (e.g., Lemert 1998). The women listed here were not included in *Black Women in America* or *Noted Negro Women*.

18. See Elizabeth Fortson Arroyo (1993).

19. James W. Jacks, president of the Missouri Press Association, published a newspaper article attacking African American women, after they announced their intent to form a national club. Jacks wrote that black women were "wholly devoid of morality and....were prostitutes, thieves, and liars." Jacks sent a copy of his article to Florence Belgarnie, secretary of the Antislavery Society of England. Belgarnie was shocked by his writings. She described them to the editors of Boston's *New Era,* and they published this information in June 1895 (Wesley 1984, 28–29).

20. See Dorothy Porter Wesley (1993).

21. See Kathleen Thompson (1993).

22. See entries on Washington and Ridley by Thompson (1993).

23. A list of the clubs that were members of the NACW follows in the original work (pp. 210–14) but is deleted here; a similar list is also found in Williams 1900.

24. See discussion of Williams's admission to the CWC in my introduction above.

25. I could not find these lines in George Eliot's work. Her book-length *Spanish Gypsy,* dating from 1868, is the tragic tale of a beautiful young woman about to marry her Spanish lover—a royal prince—when she discovers that her birth father, Zarca, is a gypsy king, and she must take up the leadership of her people upon her father's death. Although the gypsies are a despised minority in Spain, her group loyalty supercedes any individual wishes. This story line is echoed in the happier tale of requited love in Williams's (1902) fiction, "After Many Days: A Christmas Story."

26. Mildred I. Thompson (1990, 76–77) writes that Mary Church Terrell did not satisfy some of the political ambitions of Williams and Ruffin.

27. Williams referred to the name "Lisabeth" Davis, not the more recent spelling of "Elizabeth."

28. Probably a reference to the CWC, of which Williams was a member.

29. Henry D. Thoreau (1817–1862), a transcendentalist who advocated civil disobedience, individuality, and ecological responsibility, was a close friend of Emerson (393–415). See selections in Miller (324–30; 396–401). Thoreau also influenced the thought of Martin Luther King, Jr., and his practice of social protest.

30. The home economics movement, especially as it evolved in the Department of Household Administration, was organized under the auspices of the Department of Sociology at the University of Chicago. Led by the sociologist Marion Talbot (1936) and her able assistant Sophonisba Breckinridge, who resided at Hull-House in the summers between 1908 and 1920, it attempted to redefine the home as an institution equal to other institutions—such as the hospital and the paid workplace. Charlotte Perkins Gilman (see Deegan 1997), also associated with Hull-House, was interested in elevating women's occupations. See the work of for-

mer Hull-House resident Isabel Eaton in her section on domestic labor in *The Philadelphia Negro* (W.E.B. DuBois 1899, 425–509). Addams had recently completed *Democracy and Social Ethics* (1902) with a chapter on "Household Adjustment" (pp. 102–36).

31. This argument on industrial education differs greatly from resigned endorsement of lower-skilled employment; the latter position was advocated publicly (but perhaps modified privately) by Booker T. Washington.

32. This group aligned with Booker T. Washington.

33. During this era social scientists used the term "Negro problem" to define the field of study sociologists now call race relations.

34. There is an unsigned article, "Social Settlement Work Among the Colored People" (1904), following the article written by Williams on urban social settlements (see her essay "The Need of Social Settlement Work for the City Negro" below, and n. 65). This unsigned article was probably influenced by Williams, if not written by her. It contains information on Julia Jackson's work (pp. 137–38), including the founding of a social settlement and woman's club in Athens, Georgia. The article provides unique information on African American social settlements in 1904 and it establishes a format similar to that of Robert A. Woods and Albert J. Kennedy (1911) in their influential *Handbook of Settlements*.

35. Ibid. This unsigned article contains information on the work of Sarah Collins Fernandis [*sic*] (p. 137), including the founding of a social settlement and kindergarten in Washington, D.C.

36. Williams anticipates the power of novels, and such works are now available, written by influential authors like Alice Walker and Toni Morrison.

37. Davis is discussed in my introduction to this volume.

38. See DuBois (1899, n. 3), on the reason for capitalizing "Negro." Williams did not capitalize the word here although she usually did.

39. Williams is referring to the University of Chicago here. "Chicago University" was the name of a smaller, more religiously oriented institution that was replaced in 1892 by the more secular one known as the University of Chicago. John Dewey and George Herbert Mead were both teaching on vocational education at the latter institution when this essay was written (see Mead 1999, 2001). Williams is presenting an argument similar to theirs here and connecting it with the ideas of Washington.

40. See n. 34 above.

41. Williams is referring to the idea of a "new Negro" appropriate to her era and not to the use of this term in the Harlem Renaissance.

42. *The Souls of Black Folk* (Chicago: A.C. McClurg, 1903a).

43. See n. 28.

44. Williams spoke at the Hampton Conference on this topic (see chapter 5 here). I believe she was reporting on her speech and that she had been well received by her audience at Hampton. It was more modest to report "anonymously," while making sure that her race was identified and that a determined reader could find her paper in the proceedings of the Hampton Conference for 1903. See the *Southern Workman* 32 (September):432–37.

45. For Williams's analysis of the significance of public opinion see her essay on same below.

46. It would be interesting to know whom Williams contacted for the answers to her brief inquiry. This professional and collegial exchange documents her

knowledge of the names of the sociologists and their replies to her questions. Addams was probably consulted because of her writings on domestic relations and her friendship with Williams.

47. Departments of Home Economics were just starting in 1904. Marion Talbot and Sophonisba Breckinridge studied the home in 1904, but disliked the way home economics developed later. Williams probably supported their definition of home economics as concerned with social and cultural issues, concepts reflected in the conference Williams is discussing here. Williams was also familiar with the Armour Institute, which emphasized the social definition of Home Economics. See also n. 30 above.

48. Chautauquas were centers for adult learning that were often associated with recreation and leisure time. For their connections to Addams and male sociologists in Chicago, see Deegan (1988a, 92–98).

49. The creation of a lending library of art was unique to Chicago women and developed first at Hull-House. The idea was adopted nationally by women's clubs, the CWC being one of the first. Williams may have played a role in the program's development there. See Starr (In press).

50. This was a painting by Thomas Hovenden (1849–1895), an Irish immigrant to the United States. His picture was voted most popular at the Chicago World's Columbian Exposition. See "Hovenden" 1996.

51. Stowe's *Uncle Tom's Cabin* (1852) was instrumental in turning popular sentiment in the North against slavery. No comparable figural artist displayed the oppression of slavery.

52. See n. 30 of the introduction.

53. Rosa Bonheur (1822–1899), also known as Marie-Rosalie, was a painter and sculptor famous for her realistic depictions of animals. She wore trousers, smoked cigarettes, and kept a lioness.

54. Schiller was a German dramatist, poet, and literary theorist, whose most popular play was *William Tell* (1803).

55. An earlier version of Williams's article with the same title is found in *Proceedings of the Hampton Negro Conference* 7 (July 1904): 126–33. It is followed by "Social Settlement Work Among the Colored People" (pp. 133–44), which has no identifiable author. Perhaps Williams wrote it, perhaps it was a committee report, or perhaps it was written by someone else. It is a useful national survey (omitting the work in Illinois discussed by Williams) that summarizes the work of social settlements in the African American community.

56. Williams was paraphrasing this passage: "There are many indications that this conception of Democracy is growing among us. We have come to have an enormous interest in human life as such, accompanied by confidence in its essential soundness" (Addams 1902, 7). Addams used such phrases to convey an idea. She then applied the concept to the study of educational methods and the need for all people to be educated (Ibid., 178–220).

57. "Social consciousness" was an important sociological concept at this time (e.g., Mead, 2001).

58. I have not found this passage in the work of Emerson. Addams, however, expressed a similar sentiment in the passage: "We are bound to move forward or retrograde together. None of us can stand aside; our feet are mired in the same soil, and our lungs breathe the same air" (Addams 1902, 256).

59. Williams recognizes here the limitations of domestic service and other

forms of "women's work" with low wages and limited careers. She did not advocate acceptance, but human endurance, of such restricted opportunities.

60. These Chicago social settlements were headed respectively by three applied sociologists: Jane Addams, Graham Taylor, and Mary McDowell.

61. Addams tried to remove religious language from her discussion of ethics. Her "new gospel" criticizing old charity as based in class relations is found in *Democracy and Social Ethics* (1902, 13–70).

62. Asterisks are added to the text here for some reason. Perhaps the following report was discussed here or part of the speech was deleted.

63. This too may be a quotation from Addams, for Williams was clearly citing some passage.

64. Addams wrote of "newer ideals" in a number of works, particularly in *Newer Ideals of Peace* (1907), published shortly after this article.

65. Photographs of Elizabeth L. Davis, Celia Parker Woolley, and Fannie Barrier Williams accompanied this article in the original publication. Williams was described under her photograph as follows: "She is one of the leading colored women of Chicago, who was at the meeting of the Centre when a social tea was served" (p. 604).

66. The women were all active at Hull-House, and except for Henrotin, they were sociologists. The men were liberal, progressive, religious, or civic leaders. Jones and Hirsch were also active later in the NAACP.

67. These women were suffragists and abolitionists, some of whom found Anthony and Stanton questionable as allies to women of color. See Wells-Barnett (1970), for example, on Anthony, and the antithetical position held by Williams as expressed in her eulogy of Anthony below.

68. The Negroes of Chicago support some twenty lawyers, as many physicians, about a dozen dentists, about twenty School teachers in the public schools, and an ever-increasing number of them are carrying on successfully many small business enterprises that give employment to scores of educated young colored men and women. [As noted by Williams in footnote one in her article.]

69. Edwin Doak Mead (1840–1937) was an author, editor, popular lecturer, and Unitarian pacifist. See "Mead, Edwin Doak" 1940.

70. Barber supported Williams and the FDC by publishing her writings, three on the FDC specifically.

71. He was the father of Richard R. Wright, Jr., who headed Trinity Mission in Chicago, discussed in "Social Bonds" below. For more information, see "Wright" 1927.

72. Lewis Garnett Jordan (1838–19??) was a clergyman who actively supported prohibition. See "Jordan" 1927.

73. Jane Addams and the pragmatist George Herbert Mead were important figures in the playground movement. See Deegan (1999).

References

Primary Sources

Archives

Bentley Historical Library, the University of Michigan, Ann Arbor, Michigan
S. Laing Williams. "Necrology."
Cushwa-Leighton Library, College Archives, Saint Mary's College, Notre Dame, Indiana
Catherine Michele Adams. 1994. "Eliza Ann Starr." Unpublished manuscript.

Reference Works

Black Women In America. 2 vols. 1993. Edited by Darlene Clark Hine, with Elsa
   Barkley Brown and Rosalyn Terborg-Penn. Brooklyn, N. Y.: Carlson.
Notable American Women: 1607–1950. 3 vols. 1971. Edited by Edward T. James.
   [1980. *The Modern Period*. Edited by Barbara Sicherman and Carol Hurd
   Green. Cambridge, Mass: Belknap Press, Harvard University.]
Noted Negro Women: Their Triumphs and Activities. 1893. Monroe A. Majors.
   Chicago: Donohue & Henneberry.
Who Was Who in America, 1897–1942. Vol. 1. 1943. Chicago: A.N. Marquis.

Serials

Publications of the American Sociological Society, 1906–1921. Chicago: University
   of Chicago Press.
Southern Workman, 1899–1920.
Voice of the Negro, 1904–1907.
Colored American.

Works by Fannie Barrier Williams

1894a. "The Intellectual Progress and Present Status of the Colored Women of the
   United States Since the Emancipation Proclamation." Pp. 696–711 in *The
   World's Congress of Representative Women*, vol. 2, edited by May Wright
   Sewell. Chicago: Rand, McNally.
1894b. "Religious Duty to the Negro." Pp. 893–97 in *The World's Congress of Re-
   ligions*, edited by J.W. Hanson. Chicago: W.B. Conkey.
1895. "Opportunities and Responsibilities of Colored Women." Pp. 146–61 in
   Afro-American Encyclopedia, edited by John T. Haley. Nashville, Tenn.:
   Haley & Florida.
1900. "The Club Movement among Colored Women of America." Pp. 379–428 in
   A New Negro for a New Century, edited by Booker T. Washington. Chicago:
   American Publishing House.

1901. "Philip D. Armour." *Southern Workman* 30 (May): 24–25.

1902a. "Club Movement Among Colored Women." Pp. 197–231 in *Progress of A Race: The Remarkable Advancement of the American Negro,* edited by J.W. Gibson and W.H. Crogman. 1902. Reprint, Naperville, Ill.: J.L. Nichols, 1912.

1902b. "After Many Days: A Christmas Story." Pp. 31–45 in *Centers of the Self,* edited by Judith A. Hamer and Martin J. Hamer. New York: Hill and Wang, 1994.

1903. "The Problem of Employment for Negro Women." Pp. 40–47 in *Proceedings of the Hampton Negro Conference,* No. 7 (July). Hampton, Va.: Hampton Institute Press. (Reprinted in *Southern Workman* 32 [September]: 432–37.)

1904a. "Industrial Education—Will It Solve the Negro Problem?" *Colored American* (July): 491–95.

1904b. "A Northern Negro's Autobiography." *Independent* 57 (14 July): 91–96.

1904c. "The Need of Social Settlement Work for the City Negro." Pp. 126–33 in *Proceedings of the Hampton Negro Conference,* No. 8 (July). Hampton, Va.: Hampton Institute Press. (Reprinted in *Southern Workman* 33 [September]: 501–6.)

1904d. "Do We Need Another Name?" *Southern Workman* 33 (January): 33–36.

1904e. "The Negro and Public Opinion." *Voice of the Negro* 1 (1): 31–32.

1904f. "The Club Movement among the Colored Women." *Voice of the Negro* 1 (3): 99–102.

1904g. "The Smaller Economies." *Voice of the Negro* 1 (5): 184–85.

1904h. "An Extension of the Conference Spirit." *Voice of the Negro* 1 (7): 300–303.

1904i. "The Woman's Part in a Man's Business." *Voice of the Negro* 1 (11): 543–47.

1904j. "The Frederick Douglass Centre: A Question of Social Betterment and Not of Social Equality." *Voice of the Negro* 1 (12): 601–4.

1905a. "Social Bonds in the 'Black Belt' of Chicago." *Charities* 15 (7 October): 40–44.

1905b. "The Colored Girl." *Voice of the Negro* 2 (6): 400–403.

1905c. "Vacation Values." *Voice of the Negro* 2 (12): 863–66.

1906a. "Refining Influence of Art." *Voice of the Negro* 3 (3): 211–14.

1906b. "The Frederick Douglass Center." *Southern Workman* 35 (June): 334–36.

1906c. "A New Method of Dealing with the Race Problem." *Voice of the Negro* 3 (7): 502–5.

1907. "Eulogy of Susan B. Anthony." P. 203 in *The History of Woman Suffrage,* edited by Ida Husted Harper. Reprint, New York: Arno Press, 1969.

1914. "Colored Women of Chicago." *Southern Workman* 43 (October): 564–66.

[Mrs. S. Laing Williams]. 1918. "Report of Memorial Service for Rev. Celia Parker Woolley, April 7, 1918, at the Abraham Lincoln Centre, Chicago." *Unity* 81 (18 April): 116–17.

Obituary Notices

Chicago Tribune (8 March 1944): 22, col. 5.
New York Times (8 March 1944): 19, col. 1.
Chicago Defender (11 March 1944).

Published Correspondence

Washington, Booker T. 1972–1989. *The Booker T. Washington Papers.* 14 vols. Edited by Louis Harlan. Urbana, Ill.: University of Illinois Press.

Secondary Sources

Adams, Russell L. 1969. *Great Negroes, Past and Present.* Chicago: Afro-Am Publishing.

Addams, Jane. 1902. *Democracy and Social Ethics.* New York: Macmillan.

———. 1907. *Newer Ideals of Peace.* New York: Macmillan.

———. 1910. *Twenty Years at Hull-House.* New York: Macmillan.

———. 1918. "Memorial to Jenkin Lloyd Jones." *Unity* 82 (28 November): 148–49.

———. 1930. *The Second Twenty Years at Hull-House.* New York: Macmillan.

———. 1932. *The Excellent Becomes the Permanent.* New York: Macmillan.

Andrews, William L., ed. 1994. *Classic Fiction of the Harlem Renaissance.* New York: Oxford University Press.

Aptheker, Bettina. 1982. *Women's Legacy: Essays on Race, Sex, and Class in American History.* Amherst: University of Massachusetts Press.

Arroyo, Elizabeth Fortson. 1993. "Ruffin, Josephine St. Pierre (1842–1924)." Pp. 994–97 in *Black Women In America,* vol. 2, edited by Darlene Clark Hine, with Elsa Barkley Brown and Rosalyn Terborg-Penn. Brooklyn: Carlson.

Blackwell, James E., and Morris Janowitz, eds. 1974. *Black Sociologists: Historical and Contemporary Perspectives.* Chicago: University of Chicago Press.

"Brilliant Jurist Gets Final Call to High Bar." 1921. *Chicago Defender* (31 December): 4, col. 6.

Broschart, Kay. 1991. "Ida B. Wells-Barnett." Pp. 432–39 in *Women in Sociology,* edited by Mary Jo Deegan. Westport, Conn: Greenwood Press.

Brown, Hallie Q. 1892. Letter. Pp. 69–70 in "The Reasons Why the Colored American is Not in the World's Columbian Exposition." Chicago: Privately Printed, 1893.

———. 1894. "Discussion of the Same Subject [The Organized Work of the Colored Women of the South to Improve Their Condition]." Pp. 724–29 in *The World's Congress of Representative Women,* edited by May Wright Sewell. Chicago: Rand, McNally.

Calloway-Thomas, Catherine. 1993. "Cary Shadd, Mary Ann (1823–1893)." Pp. 224–26 in *Black Women In America,* vol. 1, edited by Darlene Clark Hine, with Elsa Barkley Brown and Rosalyn Terborg-Penn. Brooklyn: Carlson.

Campbell, James. 1992. *The Community Reconstructs: The Meaning of Pragmatic Social Thought.* Urbana, Ill.: University of Illinois Press.

Carby, Hazel V. 1986. "On the Threshold of Woman's Era." Pp. 301–16 in *"Race," Writing, and Difference,* edited by Henry Louis Gates, Jr. Chicago: University of Chicago Press.

Cash, Floris Barnett. 1993. "Garnet, Sarah S.T. (c. 1831–1911)." in *Black Women In America,* vol. 1, edited by Darlene Clark Hine, with Elsa Barkley Brown and Rosalyn Terborg-Penn. Brooklyn: Carlson.

"The Color-Line Exit." 1901. *Colored American* (2 February): 1, col. 1.

Collins, Patricia Hill. 1990. *Black Feminist Thought: Knowledge, Consciousness, and the Politics of Empowerment.* New York: Routledge.

Cooper, Anna Julia. 1892. *A Voice from the South*. Xenia, Ohio: Aldine Printing House.

———. 1894. "Discussion of the Same Subject [The Intellectual Progress and Present Status of the Colored Women of the United States since the Emancipation Proclamation]." Pp. 711–15 in *The World's Congress of Representative Women*, edited by May Wright Sewell. Chicago: Rand, McNally.

———. 1998. *The Voice of Anna Julia Cooper: Including "A Voice from the South" and Other Important Essays, Papers, and Letters*, edited by Charles Lemert and Esme Bahn, with an introduction by Charles Lemert. Lanham, Md.: Rowman and Littlefield.

Coppin, Fannie Jackson. 1894. "Discussion Continued [The Intellectual Progress and Present Status of the Colored Women of the United States since the Emancipation Proclamation]." Pp. 715–17 in *The World's Congress of Representative Women*, edited by May Wright Sewell. Chicago: Rand, McNally.

Davis, Elizabeth Lindsay, and George C. Hall. 1918. "Report of Memorial Service for Rev. Celia Parker Woolley, April 7, 1918, at the Abraham Lincoln Centre, Chicago." *Unity* 81 (18 April): 120.

———. 1922. *The Story of the Illinois Federation of Women's Clubs*. Chicago: Privately printed.

Deegan, Mary Jo. 1978. "Women in Sociology, 1890–1930." *Journal of the History of Sociology* 1 (Fall): 11–34.

———. 1981. "Early Women Sociologists and the American Sociological Society: Patterns of Inclusion and Exclusion." *American Sociologist* 16 (February): 14–24.

———. 1987. "An American Dream: The Historical Connections Between Women, Humanism, and Sociology, 1890–1920." *Humanity and Society* 11 (August): 353–65.

———. 1988a. *Jane Addams and the Men of the Chicago School, 1892–1918*. New Brunswick, N.J.: Transaction Books.

———. 1988b. "W.E.B. DuBois and the Women of Hull-House." *American Sociologist* 19 (Winter): 301–11.

———. 1989. *American Ritual Dramas: Social Rules and Cultural Meanings*. Westport, Conn: Greenwood Press.

———, ed. 1991. *Women in Sociology: A Bio-Bibliographical Sourcebook*, introduction by Mary Jo Deegan. New York: Greenwood Press.

———. 1995. "The Second Sex and the Chicago School, Women's Accounts, Knowledge, and Work, 1945–1960." Pp. 322–64 in *A Second Chicago School? The Development of Postwar American Sociology*, edited by Gary A. Fine. Chicago: University of Chicago Press.

———. 1996a. "'Dear Love, Dear Love': Feminist Pragmatism and the Chicago Female World of Love and Ritual." *Gender and Society* 10 (October): 590–607.

———. 1996b. "A Very Different Vision of Jane Addams and Emily Greene Balch." *Journal of Women's History* 8 (Summer): 121–25.

———. 1997. "Gilman's Sociological Journey from *Herland* to *Ourland*." Pp. 1–57 in *With Her in Ourland: Sequel to Herland* by Charlotte Perkins Gilman, edited by Mary Jo Deegan and Michael R. Hill. Westport, Conn.: Greenwood Press.

———. 1999. "Play from the Perspective of George Herbert Mead." Pp. xix–cxii in *Play, School, and Society*, edited and with an introduction by Mary Jo Deegan. New York: Peter Lang Press.

———. 2000. "Oliver C. Cox and the Chicago School of Race Relations, 1892–1940." Pp. 271–88 in *The Sociology of Oliver C. Cox: New Perspectives*, edited by Herbert Hunter. Greenwich, Conn.: JAI Press.

———. 2002. *Race, Hull-House, and the University of Chicago: A New Conscience Against Ancient Evils*. Westport, Conn.: Greenwood Press.

———, and Michael R. Hill. 1991. "Doctoral Dissertations as Liminal Journeys of the Self." *Teaching Sociology* 19 (July): 322–32.

———, and Linda Rynbrandt. 2000. "For God and Community." Pp. 1–25 in *Advances in Gender Research*, vol. 5, edited by Vasilikie Demos and Marcia Texler Segal. Greenwich, Conn.: JAI Press.

Douglass, Frederick. 1893. "Introduction." Pp. 2–12 in "The Reasons Why the Colored American is Not in the World's Columbian Exposition." Chicago: Privately Printed.

———. 1894. "Spontaneous Remarks to 'The Intellectual Progress and Present Status of the Colored Women of the United States since the Emancipation Proclamation.'" Pp. 717–18 in *The World's Congress of Representative Women*, edited by May Wright Sewell. Chicago: Rand, McNally.

Drake, St. Clair. 1983. "The Tuskegee Connection: Booker T. Washington and Robert E. Park." *Society* 20 (May/June): 82–92.

———, and Horace Cayton. 1945. *Black Metropolis: A Study of Negro Life in a Northern City*. New York: Harcourt, Brace.

DuBois, W.E.B. 1899. *The Philadelphia Negro: A Social Study. Together with a Special Report on Domestic Service by Isabel Eaton*. Introduction by E. Digby Baltzell. Reprint, New York: Schocken, 1967.

———. 1903a. *The Souls of Black Folk*. Chicago: A.C. McClurg.

———. 1903b. "The Talented Tenth." Pp. 33–75 in *The Negro Problem*, edited by Booker T. Washington et al. Reprint, New York: Arno Press and the New York Times, 1969.

———. 1904. "Industrial Education—Will It Solve the Negro Problem?" *Colored American* (May): 333–39.

———. 1940. *Dusk of Dawn: An Essay Toward an Autobiography of a Race Concept*. Introduction by Irene Diggs. Reprint, New York: Transaction Press, 1984.

Early, Sarah Jane. 1894a. "The Organized Efforts of the Colored Women of the South to Improve Their Condition." Pp. 718–24 in *The World's Congress of Representative Women*, edited by May Wright Sewell. Chicago: Rand, McNally.

———. 1894b. "The Relation of the Home and Christian Temperance" [as part of the African Methodist Episcopal Congress]. P. 1120 in *The World's Congress of Religions*, edited by J.W. Hanson. Chicago: W.B. Conkey.

Eliot, George. 1868. *Spanish Gypsy*. Vol. 18, *The Writings of George Eliot*. Boston: Houghton Mifflin, 1908.

Emerson, Ralph Waldo. 1985. *Selected Essays*, edited and with introduction by Larry Ziff. New York: Penguin Classics.

"Fannie Barrier Williams." 1894. *Cleveland Gazette* 12 (17 November): 2.

Faris, Robert E.L. 1967. *Chicago Sociology: 1920–1932*. Chicago: University of Chicago Press.

Feffer, Andrew. 1993. *The Chicago Pragmatists and American Progressivism*. Ithaca: Cornell University Press.

Fishel, Leslie H., Jr. 1971. "Fannie Barrier Williams." Pp. 620–22 in *Notable American Women,* vol. 3, edited by Edward T. James. Cambridge, Mass.: Belknap Press, Harvard University.

Fisher, Vivian Nyeri. 1993. "Brown, Hallie Quinn." Pp. 176–78 in *Black Women In America,* vol. 1, edited by Darlene Clark Hine, with Elsa Barkley Brown and Rosalyn Terborg-Penn. Brooklyn: Carlson.

Fortune, T. Thomas. 1904. "Industrial Education—Will It Solve the Negro Problem?" *Colored American* (January): 13–17.

Foster, Frances Smith. 1993. "Harper, Frances Ellen Watkins (1825–1911)." Pp. 532–36 in *Black Women In America,* vol. 1, edited by Darlene Clark Hine, with Elsa Barkley Brown and Rosalyn Terborg-Penn. Brooklyn: Carlson.

Fox, Stephen R. 1970. *The Guardian of Boston: William Monroe Trotter.* New York: Athenaeum.

Frank, Henriette Greenbaum, and Amalie Hofer Jerome. 1916. *Annals of the Chicago Woman's Club for the First Forty Years of Its Organization, 1876–1916.* Chicago: Chicago Woman's Club.

Garrison, William Lloyd. 1904. "Industrial Education—Will It Solve the Negro Problem?" *Colored American* (April): 247–48.

Gibson, J.W., and W.H. Crogman, eds. 1902. *Progress os a Race; or The Remarkable Advancement of the American Negro . . .* Harrisburg, Pa.: Minter.

Giddings, Paula. 1984. *When and Where I Enter: The Impact of Black Women on Race and Sex in America.* New York: Bantam Books.

———. 1988. *In Search of Sisterhood: Delta Sigma Theta and the Challenge of the Black Sorority Movement.* New York: William Morrow.

Gilman, Charlotte Perkins. 1898. *Women and Economics.* Boston: Small, Maynard.

———. 1935. *The Living of Charlotte Perkins Gilman: An Autobiography.* Foreword by Zona Gale. New York: D. Appleton-Century.

———. 1997. *With Her in Ourland: Sequel to Herland,* edited by Mary Jo Deegan and Michael R. Hill. Westport, Conn.: Greenwood Press.

Hall, George C. 1918. "Report of Memorial Service for Rev. Celia Parker Woolley, April 7, 1918, at the Abraham Lincoln Centre, Chicago." *Unity* 81 (18 April): 118.

Harper, Ida Husted, ed. 1922. *The History of Woman Suffrage,* vol. 5, 1900–1920. Reprint, New York: Arno Press, 1969.

Hendriks, Wanda. 1993. "Fannie Barrier Williams." Pp. 1259–61 in *Black Women In America,* vol. 2, edited by Darlene Clark Hine, with Elsa Barkley Brown and Rosalyn Terborg-Penn. Brooklyn: Carlson.

Herbst, Alma. 1932. *The Negro in the Slaughtering and Meat-Packing Industry in Chicago.* Reprint, New York: Arno, 1971.

"Hovenden, Thomas." 1996. *Dictionary of Art,* vol. 14, edited by Jane Turner. New York: Grove.

Hull, Gloria T. 1993. "Alice Ruth Moore Dunbar-Nelson (1875–1935)." Pp. 259–63 in *Black Women In America,* vol. 1, edited by Darlene Clark Hine, with Elsa Barkley Brown and Rosalyn Terborg-Penn. Brooklyn: Carlson.

Jackson, Philip. 1986. "Fannie Barrier Williams." Pp. 771–74 in *Biographical Dictionary of Social Welfare in America,* edited by Walter I. Trattner. New York: Greenwood Press.

Johnson, Catherine. 1993. "Sarah Jane Woodson Early (1825–1907)." P. 557 in *Black Women In America,* vol. 1, edited by Darlene Clark Hine, with Elsa Barkley Brown and Rosalyn Terborg-Penn. Brooklyn: Carlson.

Johnson, Charles S. 1934. *In the Shadow of the Plantation*. Introduction by Robert E. Park. Chicago: University of Chicago Press.

Jones, Jenkin Lloyd. 1904. "The Frederick Douglass Center." *Unity* 54: 148–49.

———. 1905. "The Frederick Douglass Center." *Unity* 55: 164–65.

"Jordan, Lewis Garnett" 1927. Pp. 113–14 in *Who's Who in Colored America, 1927*, edited by Joseph J. Boris. New York: Who's Who in Colored America.

King, Martin Luther, Jr. 1986. *A Testament of Hope: The Essential Writings of Martin Luther King, Jr.*, edited by James Melvin Washington. San Francisco, Calif: Harper & Row.

Klotter, James C. 1981. *The Breckinridges of Kentucky: 1760–1981*. Lexington: University of Kentucky Press.

Knupfer, Anne Meis. 1995. "Toward a Tenderer Humanity and a Nobler Womanhood." *Journal of Women's History* 7 (Fall): 58–76.

———. 1996. *Toward a Tenderer Humanity and a Nobler Womanhood: African American Women's Clubs in Turn-of-the-Century Chicago*. New York: New York University Press.

———. 1998. "For Home, Family, and Equality: African American Women's Clubs." *Chicago History* 27 (Summer): 4–25.

Kurtz, Lester R. 1984. *Evaluating Chicago Sociology: A Guide to the Literature, with an Annotated Bibliography*. Chicago: University of Chicago Press.

Ladner, Joyce A. 1973. *The Death of White Sociology*. New York: Random House, Vintage Books.

Lamping, Marilyn. 1982. "Fannie Barrier Williams." Pp. 432–33 in *American Women Writers*, edited by Lina Mainiero. New York: Frederick Ungar Publishing.

Leach, William. 1989. *True Love and Perfect Union: The Feminist Reform of Sex and Society*. Middletown, Conn.: Wesleyan University Press.

Lemert, Charles. 1998. "Anna Julia Cooper: The Colored Woman's Office." Pp. 1–43 in *The Voice of Anna Julia Cooper*, edited by Charles Lemert and Esme Bahn, with an introduction by Charles Lemert. Boston: Rowman and Littlefield.

Lengermann, Patricia, and Jill Niebrugge-Brantley. 1998. *The Women Founders: Sociology and Social Theory, 1830–1930*. Boston: McGraw-Hill.

Locke, Alain. 1925. "Enter the New Negro." *Survey Graphic* 53 (1 March): 631–34.

Logan, Rayford W. 1982. "Fannie Barrier Williams." Pp. 656–57 in *Dictionary of American Negro Biography*, edited by Rayford W. Logan and Michael R. Winston. New York: W.W. Norton.

McCulloch, James E. 1913. *The South Mobilizing for Social Service*. Nashville, Tenn.: Southern Sociological Congress.

McFeely, William S. 1991. *Frederick Douglass*. New York: W.W. Norton.

McMurry, Linda O. 1991. *Recorder of the Black Experience: A Biography of Monroe Nathan Work*. Baton Rouge: Louisiana State University Press.

———. 1998. *To Keep the Waters Troubled: The Life of Ida B. Wells*. New York: Oxford University Press.

Massa, Ann. 1974. "Black Women in the 'White City.'" *Journal of American Studies* 8 (December): 319–37.

"Mead, Edwin Doak." 1940. Pp. 429–30 in *The National Cyclopaedia of American Biography*, vol. 23. New York: James T. White & Company.

Mead, George Herbert. 1934. *Mind, Self and Society from the Standpoint of a Social Behaviorist*, edited and with introduction by Charles Morris. Chicago: University of Chicago Press.

———. 1999. *Play, School, and Society,* edited and with an introduction by Mary Jo Deegan. New York: Peter Lang Press.

———. 2001. *Essays on Social Psychology: George Herbert Mead's First Book,* edited and with an introduction by Mary Jo Deegan. New Brunswick, N.J.: Transaction Publishers.

Miller, Donald L. 1996. *City of the Century: The Epic of Chicago and the Making of America.* New York: Simon and Schuster.

Miller, Kelly. 1904. "Industrial Education—Will It Solve the Negro Problem?" *Colored American* (March): 185–87.

Miller, Perry, ed. 1950. *The Transcendentalists.* Reprint, New York: MJF Books, 1978.

Morris, Aldon D. 1984. *The Origins of the Civil Rights Movement: Black Communities Organizing for Change.* New York: Free Press.

Neverdon-Morton, Cynthia. 1989. *Afro-American Women of the South and the Advancement of the Race, 1895–1925.* Knoxville: University of Tennessee Press.

Northern White Woman, A. 1904. "Experiences of The Race Problem." *Independent* 56 (17 March): 594–99.

Peebles-Wilkins, Wilma, and E. Aracelis Francis. 1990. "Two Outstanding Women in Social Welfare History: Mary Church Terrell and Ida B. Wells-Barnett." *Affilia* 5, no.4: 87–91.

Perkins, Linda K. 1993. "Fannie Jackson Coppin (1837–1913)." Pp. 281–84 in *Black Women In America,* vol. 1, edited by Darlene Clark Hine, with Elsa Barkley Brown and Rosalyn Terborg-Penn. Brooklyn: Carlson.

Publications of the American Sociological Society, vol. 6, 12. Chicago: University of Chicago Press, 1912, 1918.

"Rankin, Jeremiah Eames" 1943. *Who Was Who in America,* v. 1. P. 1010.

Reed, Christopher Robert. 1997. *The Chicago NAACP and the Rise of Black Professional Leadership, 1910–1966.* Bloomington: University of Indiana Press.

Reid, John. 1993. "Fannie M. Richards (1841–1922)." P. 979 in *Black Women In America,* vol. 2, edited by Darlene Clark Hine, with Elsa Barkley Brown and Rosalyn Terborg-Penn. Brooklyn: Carlson.

Riggs, Marcia Y. 1993. "Fannie [Barrier] Williams." Pp. 556–58 in *African American Women: A Biographical Dictionary,* edited by Dorothy C. Salem. New York: Garland.

Rynbrandt, Linda. 1999. *Caroline Bartlett Crane and Progressive Reform: Social Housekeeping as Sociology.* New York: Garland Publishing.

Salem, Dorothy. 1990. *To Better Our World: Black Women in Organized Reform, 1890–1920.* Brooklyn, Carlson.

———. 1993. "National Association of Colored Women." Pp. 842–51 in *Black Women In America,* vol. 2, edited by Darlene Clark Hine, with Elsa Barkley Brown and Rosalyn Terborg-Penn. Brooklyn: Carlson.

Schutz, Alfred. 1962. *Collected Papers.* Vol. 1, *The Problem of Social Reality,* edited and with an introduction by M. Natanson. The Hague: Martinus Nijhoff.

———. 1967. *The Phenomenology of the Social World,* translated by G. Walsh and F. Lehnert, with an introduction by George Walsh. Evanston, Ill.: Northwestern University Press.

———. 1970. *Reflections on the Problems of Relevance,* Edited and with an introduction by Richard M. Zaner. New Haven, Conn.: Yale University Press.

Seigfried, Charlene Haddock. 1991. "Where are All the Feminist Pragmatists?" *Hypatia* 6 (Summer): 1–19.

———. 1996. *Pragmatism and Feminism: Reweaving the Social Fabric.* Chicago: University of Chicago Press.

Shields, John C. 1993. "Phillis (Peters) Wheatley (c. 1753–1784)." Pp. 2251–55 in *Black Women In America,* vol. 2, edited by Darlene Clark Hine, with Elsa Barkley Brown and Rosalyn Terborg-Penn. Brooklyn: Carlson.

Smith, Jessie Cary. 1992. "Fannie B. Williams (1855–1944)." Pp. 1251–54 in *Notable Black American Women,* edited by Jessie Cary Smith. Detroit: Gale Research.

Smith-Rosenberg, Carroll. 1985. *Disorderly Conduct: Visions of Gender in Victorian America.* New York: Oxford University Press.

"Social Settlement Work Among the Colored People." 1904. Pp. 133–44 in *Proceedings of the Hampton Negro Conference,* No. 8 (July). Hampton, Va.: Hampton Institute Press.

Southern Colored Woman, A. 1904. "The Race Problem—An Autobiography." *Independent* 56 (17 March): 586–89.

Southern White Woman, A. 1904. "Experiences of The Race Problem." *Independent* 56 (17 March): 590–94.

Spear, Allan H. 1967. *Black Chicago: The Making of a Negro Ghetto, 1890–1920.* Chicago: University of Chicago Press.

———. 1973. "Fannie Barrier Williams." Pp. 827–28 in *Dictionary of American Biography,* edited by Edward T. James et al. New York: Charles Scribner's Sons.

Stanfield, John. 1985. *Philanthropy and Jim Crow in American Social Science.* Westport, Conn.: Greenwood Press.

———. 1993. *A History of Race Relations Research: First Generation Recollections.* Newbury Park, Calif.: Sage.

Starr, Ellen Gates. In press. *On Art, Labor, and Religion,* edited and with an introduction by Mary Jo Deegan and Ana Maria Wahl. New Brunswick, N.J.: Transaction Books.

Stowe, Harriet Beecher. 1852. *Uncle Tom's Cabin.* With 27 Illustrations on Wood by George Cruikshank. London: J. Cassell.

Sumler-Edmond, Janice. 1993. "Charlotte L. Forten Grimke (1837-1913)." Pp. 505–7 in *Black Women In America,* vol. 1, by Darlene Clark Hine, with Elsa Barkley Brown and Rosalyn Terborg-Penn. Brooklyn: Carlson.

Talbot, Marion. 1936. *More Than Lore: Reminiscences of Marion Talbot . . .* Chicago: University of Chicago Press.

Terrell, Mary Church. 1940. *A Colored Woman in a White World.* Washington, D.C.: Ransdell.

Thomas, Dorothy. 1993. "Charlotte E. Ray (1850–1911)." Pp. 965–66 in *Black Women In America,* vol. 2, by Darlene Clark Hine, with Elsa Barkley Brown and Rosalyn Terborg-Penn. Brooklyn: Carlson.

Thompson, Kathleen. 1993. "Florida Ruffin Ridley (1861–1943)." P. 982 in *Black Women In America,* vol. 2, by Darlene Clark Hine, with Elsa Barkley Brown and Rosalyn Terborg-Penn. Brooklyn: Carlson.

———. 1993. "Margaret Murray Washington (c. 1865–1925)." Pp. 1233–35 in *Black Women In America,* vol. 2, by Darlene Clark Hine, with Elsa Barkley Brown and Rosalyn Terborg-Penn. Brooklyn: Carlson.

Thompson, Mildred I. 1990. *Ida B. Wells-Barnett: An Exploratory Study of An American Black Woman, 1893–1930.* Brooklyn: Carlson Publishing.

University of Chicago Settlement. 1901. Chicago: Privately printed pamphlet.

Washington, Booker T., ed. 1900. *A New Negro for a New Century.* Chicago: Amer-
    ican Publishing House. [Reprint, Miami, Fla.: Mnemosyne Publishing, 1969.]
———. 1904. "Industrial Education—Will It Solve the Negro Problem?" *Colored
    American* (February): 87–92.
———. 1907. *Frederick Douglass.* Philadelphia: G.W. Jacobs.
———. 1972–1989. *The Booker T. Washington Papers,* 14 vols, edited by Louis
    Harlan. Urbana, Ill.: University of Illinois Press.
Weimann, Jeanne Madeline. 1981. *The Fair Women: The Story of the Woman's
    Building, World's Columbian Exposition, Chicago, 1893.* Chicago: Academy
    Publishers.
Wells (-Barnett), Ida B. 1892. *Southern Horrors: Lynch Law in All Its Phases.* New
    York: New York Age Print. Reprint, *On Lynching.* Salem, N.H.: Ayer, 1990.
———, ed. 1893. "The Reasons Why the Colored American is Not in the World's
    Columbian Exposition." Chicago: Privately printed.
———. 1904. "Booker T. Washington and His Critics." *The World Today* 6 (April
    1904): 518–21.
———. 1970. *Crusade for Justice: The Autobiography of Ida B. Wells,* edited by Al-
    freda M. Duster. Chicago: University of Chicago Press.
Wesley, Charles Harris. 1984. *The History of the National Association of Colored
    Women's Clubs: A Legacy of Service.* Washington, D.C.: National Associa-
    tion of Colored Women's Clubs.
Wesley, Dorothy Porter. 1993. "Maria Louise Baldwin (1856–1922)." Pp. 79–80 in
    Black Women in America, vol. 1, edited by Darlene Clark Hine, with Elsa
    Barkley Brown and Rosalyn Terborg-Penn. Brooklyn: Carlson.
West, Cornel. 1989. *The American Evasion of Philosophy: A Genealogy of Prag-
    matism.* Madison, Wis.: University of Wisconsin Press.
Williams, S. Laing. 1906. "Frederick Douglass at Springfield, Mo." *A.M.E. Church
    Review* 23 (July): 7–14.
Woods, Robert A., and Albert J. Kennedy. 1911. *Handbook of Settlements.* New
    York: Charities Publication Committee.
Woolley, Celia Parker. 1887. *Love and Theology.* Boston: Ticknor.
———. 1889. *A Girl Graduate.* Boston: Houghton Mifflin.
———. 1892. *Roger Hunt.* Boston: Houghton Mifflin.
———. 1894. "Synopsis of Lecture on Margaret Fuller." P. 763 in *The World's
    Congress of Religions,* edited by J.W. Hanson. Chicago: W.B. Conkey.
———. 1903. *The Western Slope.* Evanston, Ill.: William S. Lord.
———. 1904. "The Frederick Douglass Center." *The Commons* 9 (July): 328–29.
"Wright, Richard R., Sr." 1927. Pp. 230–31 in *Who's Who in Colored America,
    1927,* edited by Joseph J. Boris. New York: Who's Who in Colored America.

INDEX